DOCUMENTS IN BRITISH HISTORY

VOLUME I
EARLY TIMES TO 1714

DOCUMENTS IN BRITISH HISTORY

VOLUME I
EARLY TIMES TO 1714

SECOND EDITION

Brian L. Blakeley
Jacquelin Collins

Department of History
Texas Tech University

McGraw-Hill, Inc.
New York St. Louis San Francisco Auckland Bogotá
Caracas Lisbon London Madrid Mexico City Milan
Montreal New Delhi San Juan Singapore
Sydney Tokyo Toronto

This book was set in Times Roman by The Clarinda Company.
The editors were Pamela Gordon and Niels Aaboe;
the production supervisor was Louise Karam.
The cover was designed by Carla Bauer.
Project supervision was done by The Wheetley Company, Inc.
R. R. Donnelley & Sons Company was printer and binder.

Cover painting credit:
Queen Elizabeth I, coronation portrait, artist unknown.
National Portrait Gallery, London.

This book is printed on acid-free paper.

DOCUMENTS IN BRITISH HISTORY

Volume I: Early Times to 1714

6 7 8 9 0 DOC DOC 9 0 9

ISBN 0-07-005701-X

Library of Congress Cataloging-in-Publication Data

Documents in British history / [compiled by] Brian L. Blakeley,
Jacquelin Collins. —2nd ed.
p. cm.
Rev. ed. of: Documents in English history, 1974, c1975.
Contents: v. 1. Early times to 1714 — v. 2. 1688 to the present.
ISBN 0-07-005702-8 (vol. 2)
1. Great Britain—History—Sources. I. Blakeley, Brian L.
II. Collins, Jacquelin (date). III. Blakeley, Brian, L., comp.
Documents in English history.
DA26.D58 1993
942—dc20 92-31437

ABOUT THE AUTHORS

BRIAN L. BLAKELEY is a professor of history at Texas Tech University. He has taught at Texas Tech since 1970. He received his M.A. and Ph.D. from Duke University in 1964 and 1966. He has published *The Colonial Office, 1868–1892* and several articles. His primary interests are in the history of modern Britain and of the British Empire.

JACQUELIN COLLINS is an associate professor of history and Associate Dean for Undergraduate Affairs in the College of Arts and Sciences at Texas Tech University. He received a B.A. and M.A. from Rice University in 1956 and 1959. He received a Ph.D. from the University of Illinois, Urbana-Champaign, in 1964 and a J.D. from Texas Tech University School of Law in 1984. His primary interests are in Tudor-Stuart England, constitutional and legal development, and Scotland.

CONTENTS

PREFACE

Welcome to the study of British history. Having spent our adult lives teaching the history of the several peoples making up the British Isles—the English, the Scots, the Irish, and the Welsh—we are naturally impressed with the contributions they have collectively made to the development of European and world civilization. In constitutional usage, economic innovation, and literary, scientific, and artistic achievement, few, if any, peoples have equaled the British. These accomplishments were probably, in part, due to the melting-pot nature of the British Isles. The kingdom of England, an amalgam of Celtic, Anglo-Saxon, Danish, and Norman peoples and cultures, eventually combined with the Scots, Irish, and Welsh to create the United Kingdom. In more modern times, the British Empire aided in the spread of British institutions, language, and ideas around the world. In addition, British history has a value independent of its world impact. Filled with heroic achievements and epic failures, admirable heroes and despicable scoundrels, and profound ideas and transient fads, the history of the British Isles is a mirror of our own hopes and fears. We understand ourselves and our history only if we appreciate others and their experiences.

In attempting to understand the past, beginning students frequently assume that history, in this case British history, is a compilation of facts, the mere learning of which imparts knowledge. With experience, however, they will come to the realization that written history is essentially the answers to questions that various historians have arrived at and recorded for others. These conclusions vary according to the questions posed and the beliefs and prejudices of the historians who have asked the questions and searched for evidence to answer their queries. It is not surprising, therefore, that each generation must write its history anew—not only contemporary history but also that of earlier items. Definitive history is possible only for historians who have abandoned the arduous task of seeking new answers to questions both old and new.

There is, nevertheless, a constant factor in history, a factor essential if historians are not to wander off into the wilderness of their own imaginations. This ingredient is the evidence used in answering the questions they have raised. A historian's evidence is also a means by which other historians can judge the extent of the research and the validity of the answers presented. This evidence is often referred to as "documents." Originally, when the descipline of history was less sophisticated, it was assumed that documents were written and that only written records could reveal the secrets of the past. Without these written documents there was only "prehistory," a shadowy and mysterious age visited by lesser beings such as archeologists and anthropologists. More recently, historians have come to understand that evidence is where you find it and worth whatever you make of it. Written records remain valuable, but a discerning historian may be able to answer some questions by a careful examination of other evidence—the workmanship of Anglo-Saxon artisans, the layout of a medieval manor as revealed by a World War II aerial photograph, or the coins of Tudor England. In using such evidence, the historian may have to ask more subtle questions and accept more tentative conclusions, but the historical process is essentially the same. Evidence of any kind, once recognized and appropriated by a historian, becomes a document to be used again and again by the historian and colleagues in the same field.

No historian, not even the beginning undergraduate, should remain a passive spectator. Each must ask questions and seek answers to them. At first, the student will be led to the written accounts of other historians. This approach, however, often results in confusion: historical accounts frequently differ from one another. Which is correct? At this point one should not become discouraged. Instead, the student should recognize in this confusion, frustration—and, yes, even anger—the maturing of a historian. Students who persevere will be led back first to the documents and evidence used by previous historians and then, hopefully, to new evidence. Along the way they ask their own questions and arrive at their own answers, with the same caution and confidence as other historians.

Each student of British history, who has now become a historian, needs the assistance of others; the task of historical research is too immense for a single person to investigate each aspect of the human experience. This collection of documents, as did our first edition, published in 1975, attempts to aid the beginning student in two ways.

1. We have included many of the documents generally agreed to be among the most important to an understanding of British history. To appreciate the British experience, you must know about the Bayeax Tapestry, Magna Carta, the Declaration of Arbroath, Shakespeare, the King James Bible, the Bill of Rights, and John Locke's *Two Treatises of Government*. These documents provide evidence that has been used, and will continue to be used, to answer the hardest and most persistent questions in British history.

2. We have presented a wide variety of documents to illustrate the diversity of historical evidence. Some of this evidence cannot be presented in a book: for example, a packet of soil analyzed by an agronomist to determine the location of

the pilings of a Neolithic building. Nevertheless, nonwritten documents such as the archeological sites of prehistoric Britain, the Sutton Hoo Ship-Burial, the Bayeux Tapestry, and medieval seals can be included, and they reveal the variety of historical documents. Most of the book appropriately consists of written documents, since the majority of historians still rely almost entirely on this type of evidence. Even here, however, we have included a wide variety. Chronicles, speeches, diaries, poetry, nursery rhymes, song lyrics, and governmental records and laws are examples of this variety. For a historian, imagination in both the framing of questions and the use of evidence is essential.

We have placed the documents in chronological order and have not attempted to group them topically. The division into two volumes has been done largely for reasons of cost and convenience of assignment. Each document in our volumes is a self-contained unit, sufficiently complete with its introduction to be understood and appreciated by itself. We have, however, been conscious of the place of each document in British history. The introductions provide a thread of continuity from one document to another, should you choose to read several documents in succession.

In this revised edition, we have sought to emphasize the British experience as opposed to that simply of England by including documents on Irish, Scottish, and Welsh history, such as St. Patrick's "Declaration," *The Massacre of Glenco,* and the Statute of Rhuddlan. We have strengthened the social and cultural dimension, especially the contribution of women. The reader can now find not only Izaak Walton's discussion of the joys of fishing, but Dorothy Osborne's view of love and marriage and a description of the civilizing impact of St. Margaret on Scotland. Finally, many of those who used the first edition, our wise and perceptive friends, have argued that some documents, most especially Chaucer's *Canterbury Tales* and Newton's *Principia,* required inclusion simply because of their importance to the concept of cultural literacy.

Many people have given us help in preparing *Documents in British History* as well as our 1975 *Documents in English History.* Patrick C. Lipscomb III, Brian C. Levack, and Stanford E. Lehmberg read the first manuscript and made recommendations for its improvement. C. Warren Hollister gave needed encouragement. For this edition, Joseph J. Mogan, Jr. and Marijane R. Davis provided valuable assistance. Derek Blakeley, our resourceful agent in London, was especially helpful. Wayne Anderson, history and political science editor at John Wiley & Sons, Inc., made preparation of our first edition more fun than it might have been. Sarah Touborg, Pamela Gordon, and Niels Aaboe, editors at McGraw-Hill, have done the same for this two-volume edition. John Beasley of the Wheetley Company, Inc., has taught us much about the craft of publishing. We also thank David Follmer. Finally, for their valuable suggestions we are grateful to the readers of this second edition: Lois Margaret Barnett, the University of Southern Mississippi; Eugene J. Bourgeois, Southwest Texas State University; David Cressy, California State University at Long

1
Prehistoric Britain in Pictures

Prehistory, often defined as the account of events and conditions prior to written or recorded history, is necessarily dependent on the work of archeologists. Through the careful search for and interpretation of surviving artifacts, we can learn much about the nature of prehistoric societies. In Britain archeologists have discovered simple stone tools dating from the Paleolithic (Old Stone Age), some as old as half a million years. It was not, however, until the Neolithic (New Stone Age), or about 3500 B.C., that people developed the social organization required to produce the impressive stone and earthen monuments that continue to attract not only scholars but wondering tourists.

Early Neolithic people left numerous large and impressive burial mounds, which in many areas resemble early cemeteries (Plate A). Most impressive are the East and West Kennet burial mounds and Silbury Hill (Plate B). The latter, 125 feet high and covering about 5 acres, is the largest artificial mound in Europe. Constructed as early as 2700 B.C., it was most likely a tomb, but a number of exploratory excavations have failed to produce a body. The most famous monument of this era is the great stone circle at Avebury (Plate C), which was completed in about 2600 B.C. Larger by far than even Stonehenge, Avebury serves as a reminder that these early peoples possessed definite religious beliefs, considerable wealth, and a sophisticated political and social structure. Tragically, Avebury and other monuments of this era later suffered vandalism at the hands of Christians and the "enlightened" Britons of the eighteenth century.

The Bronze Age Beaker People, so named because of the burial of drinking cups with their dead, arrived in Britain in time to participate in the latter stages of the construction of the early stone circles. Their greatest achievement, which reflected their ultimate domination of the Salisbury Plain, was Stonehenge (Plate D). Begun about 2500 B.C. as one of many stone circles, Stonehenge was remodeled over the centuries until it reached, as Stonehenge III, its final form in about 1450 B.C. Gerald S. Hawkins has confirmed and expanded the idea that Stonehenge was, at all phases of its construction, a means of determining the seasons of the year. Its exact civic and religious purposes and the details of its construction remain mysteries.

The Celts, who began to arrive in England about 1000 B.C., were more warlike than the earlier inhabitants, possessing by 500 B.C. the iron weapons that enabled them to conquer most of southern England. Their combative nature and their organized tribal government are reflected in their numerous hill forts, the most famous being Maiden Castle in Dorset (Plate E), enclosing almost 45 acres of land. The Celts were also artists. "White Horse" (Plate F), one of their greatest triumphs, is the figure of a horse 120 yards long, cut into the side of a chalk hill.

PLATE A
Prehistoric cemetery (Department of Antiquities, Ashmolean Museum).

PLATE B
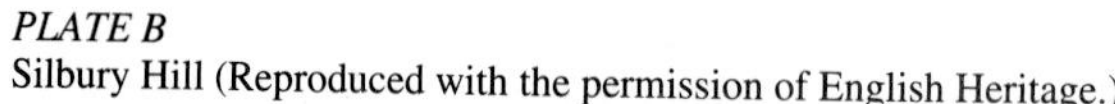
Silbury Hill (Reproduced with the permission of English Heritage.)

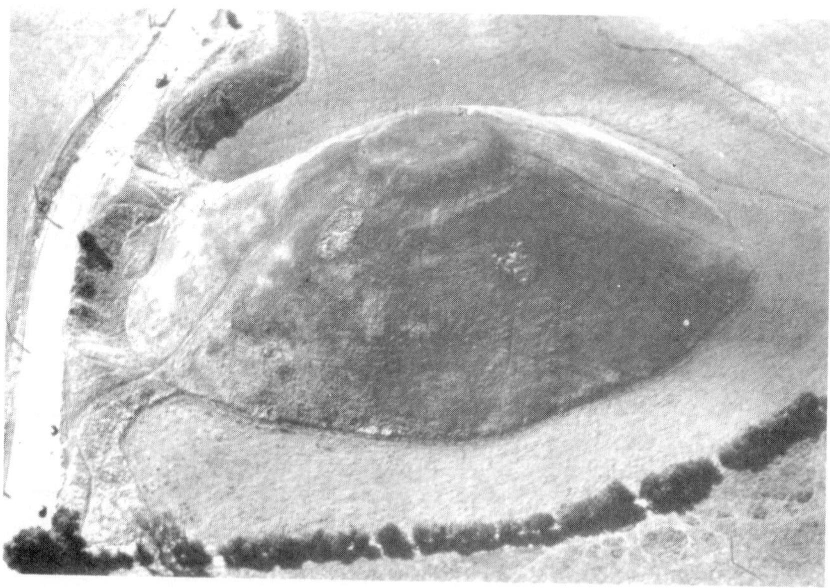

PLATE C
Avebury (Reproduced with the permission of English Heritage.)

PLATE D
Stonehenge (Cambridge University Collection, copyright reserved).

PLATE E
Maiden Castle (Reproduced with the permission of English Heritage.)

These prehistoric monuments are more than windows through which scholars can catch glimpses of civilizations long past. They remain among Britain's greatest national treasures. Most are in the custody of, or protected by, the Department of the Environment.

PLATE F
White Horse (Aerofilms Ltd.)

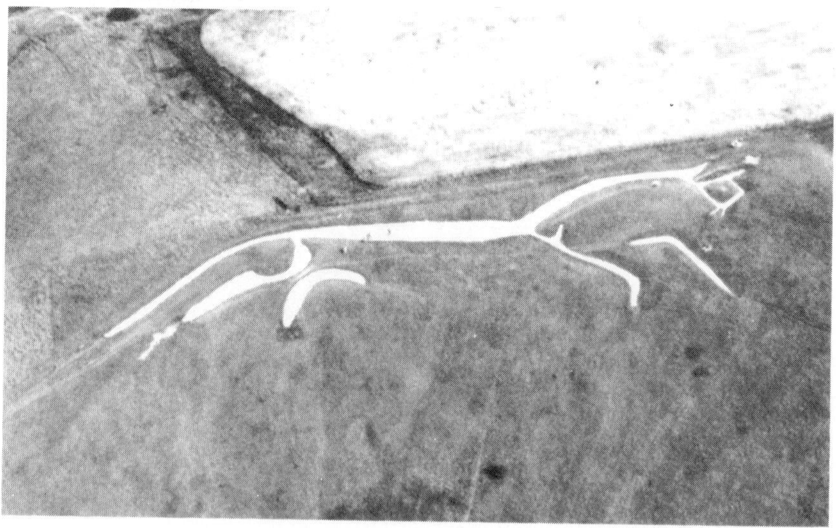

2

Tacitus, *Agricola* (A.D. 98). Roman Britain, A.D. 78–84

Rome's subjugation of Britain, initiated by Julius Caesar in 55 B.C. and completed following the Claudian invasion of A.D. 43, frees the historian from the restrictions imposed by the absence of written evidence. It must be remembered, nevertheless, that to the Romans, Britain was always an expendable frontier province, an outpost of Roman civilization, and that, consequently, few Roman writers treated it in much detail.

Much of our detailed knowledge of Roman Britain comes from P. Cornelius Tacitus's *Agricola,* a brief biography of Gnaeus Iulius Agricola, the most significant governor of Roman Britain (A.D. 78–84). Tacitus not only dealt with Agricola's conquests and his policy of Romanization, but he also included a valuable description of the geography and the people of Britain, part of which is reproduced below.

As with any document, the *Agricola* should not be accepted uncritically. It is difficult to test its accuracy against other written sources, as only one other Roman historian even mentions Agricola. Furthermore, Tacitus was Agricola's son-in-law, and the biography was not meant as an objective treatment of Britain's greatest governor but as a laudatory account of a good man. Finally, the *Agricola* (A.D. 98), Tacitus's first work, was penned during a period of great political turmoil and corruption in Rome. Most specialists argue that his portrayals of the civic-minded Agricola as well as of robust frontier peoples, in both the *Agricola* and his more famous *Germania,* were largely an appeal to the Romans to reassert their traditional virtues and to repudiate the corruption of their current "civilization." Whatever its limitations, Tacitus's account will obviously remain an essential document for the study of Roman Britain.

In view of the loss of portions of Tacitus's major works, the *Histories* and the *Annals,* it is fortunate, for both Agricola and later scholars, that four manuscript copies of the *Agricola* have survived, the oldest being from the tenth century. Although the

Source: Tacitus, *On Britain and Germany: A Translation of the "Agricola" and the "Germania,"* translated by H. Mattingly (Penguin Classics, 1948), pp. 61–63, 70–72.

Agricola was used by medieval writers working in the libraries at Fulda and Monte Cassino, Tacitus's writings were not highly regarded until modern times.

Who the first inhabitants of Britain were, whether natives or immigrants, remains obscure; one must remember we are dealing with barbarians. But physical characteristics vary, and that very variation is suggestive. The reddish hair and large limbs of the Caledonians proclaim a German origin, the swarthy faces of the Silures, the tendency of their hair to curl and the fact that Spain lies opposite, all lead one to believe that Spaniards crossed in ancient times and occupied the land. The peoples nearest to the Gauls are correspondingly like them. Perhaps the original strain persists, perhaps it is climatic conditions that determine physical type in lands that converge from opposite directions on a single point. On a general estimate, however, we may believe that it was Gauls who took possession of the neighboring island. In both countries you will find the same ritual, the same religious beliefs. There is no great difference in language, and there is the same hardihood in challenging danger, the same subsequent cowardice in shirking it. But the Britons show more spirit; they have not yet been softened by protracted peace. The Gauls, too, we have been told, had their hour of military glory; but then came decadence with peace, and valour went the way of lost liberty. The same fate has befallen such of the Britons as have long been conquered; the rest are still what the Gauls used to be.

Their strength is in their infantry. Some tribes also fight from chariots. The nobleman drives, his dependants fight in his defence. Once they owed obedience to kings; now they are distracted between the jarring factions of rival chiefs. Indeed, nothing has helped us more in war with their strongest nations than their inability to cooperate. It is but seldom that two or three states unite to repel a common danger; fighting in detail they are conquered wholesale. The climate is objectionable, with its frequent rains and mists, but there is no extreme cold. Their day is longer than is normal in the Roman world. The night is bright and, in the extreme North, short, with only a brief interval between evening and morning twilight. If no clouds block the view, the sun's glow, it is said, can be seen all night long. It does not set and rise, but simply passes along the horizon. The reason must be that the ends of the earth, being flat, cast low shadows and cannot raise the darkness to any height; night therefore fails to reach the sky and its stars. The soil can bear all produce, except the olive, the vine, and other natives of warmer climes, and it is fertile. Crops are slow to ripen, but quick to grow—both facts due to one and the same cause, the extreme moistness of land and sky. Britain yields gold, silver and other metals, to make it worth conquering. . . .

The Britons themselves submit to the levy, the tribute and the other charges of Empire with cheerful readiness, provided that there is no abuse. *That* they bitterly resent; for they are broken in to obedience, not to slavery. . . .

Agricola, however, understood the feelings of a province and had learned from the experience of others that arms can effect little if injustice follows in their train. He resolved to root out the causes of war. . . . He preferred to appoint to official positions and duties men whom he could trust not to transgress, rather than punish the transgressor. He eased the levy of corn and tribute by distributing the burden fairly, and cancelled those charges, contrived by profiteers, which were more bitterly resented than the tax itself. The provincials had actually been compelled to wait at the doors of closed granaries, buy back their own corn and pay farcical prices. Delivery was ordered to destinations off the map or at a great distance, and states that had permanent quarters of troops close by them had to send to remote and inaccessible spots, until a service that should have been easy for all ended by benefiting a few scoundrels only.

By checking these abuses in his very first year of office, Agricola gave men reason to love and honour peace. Hitherto, through the negligence or arbitrariness of former governors, it had been as much feared as war. . . .

The following winter was spent on schemes of the most salutary kind. To induce a people, hitherto scattered, uncivilized and therefore prone to fight, to grow pleasurably inured to peace and ease, Agricola gave private encouragement and official assistance to the building of temples, public squares and private mansions. He praised the keen and scolded the slack, and competition to gain honour from him was as effective as compulsion. Furthermore, he trained the sons of the chiefs in the liberal arts and expressed a preference for British natural ability over the trained skill of the Gauls. The result was that in place of distaste for the Latin language came a passion to command it. In the same way, our national dress came into favour and the toga was everywhere to be seen. And so the Britons were gradually led on to the amenities that make vice agreeable—arcades, baths and sumptuous banquets. They spoke of such novelties as "civilization," when really they were only a feature of enslavement.

3

St. Patrick, "Declaration" (c. 461), and Muirchu's "Life" (7th Century). The Conversion of Ireland

Though St. Patrick has been called (by Hugh Kearney) "the first clearly recognizable personality in British history," our knowledge of his life remains sketchy. He was born in about 399 on the island of Britain, though just where remains uncertain. At the age of sixteen, he was kidnapped by the Irish, becoming a slave and a herdsman. Escaping after six years, he became a priest, and in about 432 returned to Ireland as a missionary, surpassing in importance others, especially Palladius, who had preceded him.

Patrick gives the outline of his life in his "Declaration," part of which is printed below, and in his "Letter." These are "the only documents that have survived from the British Isles in the century after the fall of Rome" (John Morris). The Christian-monastic tradition begun by Patrick spread across Ireland and reached Scotland with the work of Columba (d. 597), centered at Iona, and then England with Aidan's founding of Lindisfarne on the North Sea coast of Northumberland in 635. In the seventh century, Muirchu, a priest in Leinster, wrote what is probably the first life of the saint, using the writings of Patrick and other sources now lost. His concern seems to have been to present Patrick as the representative of Rome in opposition to other, less orthodox traditions.

In the writings of both Patrick and Muirchu, some assertions define Patrick as an individual; others, following the tradition of medieval hagiographers, say things that could equally be said of any Christian saint. The writer's aim is only in part to relate the unique life of an individual; it is even more to tell a moral tale, miracles included, extolling the life of a saint and exhorting readers to emulate the same virtues. We should be particularly aware of what these writings tell us of the times in which they were written and of the authors who wrote them. We can learn far more from a document than merely the things that the author consciously intended to tell.

Source: St. Patrick, His Writings and Muirchu's Life, edited and translated by A. B. E. Hood. London and Chichester: Phillimore & Co., Ltd., 1978, pp. 41, 44–46, 53–54, 83, 85–86, 91–92. With permission of Phillimore & Co., Ltd.

Versions of Patrick's "Declaration" and of Muirchu's "Life" are found in several medieval manuscripts, some dating back to the ninth century. The first critical edition of Muirchu was published in 1882 by E. Hogan and the Bollandists, who pioneered the modern study of hagiography in the early nineteenth century.

DECLARATION

1 I, Patrick, a sinner, quite uncultivated and the least of all the faithful and utterly despicable to many, had as my father the deacon Calpurnius, son of the late Potitus, a priest, who belonged to the town of Bannavem Taburniae; he had a small estate nearby, and it was there that I was taken captive. I was then about sixteen years old. I did not know the true God and I was taken into captivity in Ireland with so many thousands; and we deserved it, because we drew away from God and did not keep His commandments and did not obey our priests who kept reminding us of our salvation; and the Lord brought on us the fury of His anger and scattered us among many peoples even to the ends of the earth, where now I in my insignificance find myself among foreigners.

2 And there the Lord opened up my awareness of my unbelief, so that I might, however late, remember my faults and turn with all my heart to the Lord my God, who had regard for my lowly estate and took pity on my youth and ignorance and watched over me before I knew Him and before I learned sense or could distinguish between good and evil and who protected me and comforted me as a father might his son.

3 And therefore I cannot keep silent—nor in fact would it be proper to do so—about the great benefits and grace which the Lord has deigned to confer on me in the land of my captivity. . . .

16 But after I reached Ireland . . . I pastured the flocks every day and I used to pray many times a day; more and more did my love of God and my fear of Him increase, and my faith grew and my spirit was stirred, and as a result I would say up to a hundred prayers in one day, and almost as many at night. . . .

17 One night while asleep I heard a voice saying to me: 'You do well to fast, since you will soon be going to your home country;' and again, very shortly after, I heard this prophecy: 'See, your ship is ready.' And it was not near at hand but was perhaps two hundred miles away, and I had never been there and did not know a living soul there. And then I soon ran away and abandoned the man with whom I had been for six years. . . .

23 And again a few years later I was in Britain with my kinsfolk, and they welcomed me as a son and asked me earnestly not to go off anywhere and leave them this time, after the great tribulations which I had been through. And it was there that I saw one night in a vision a man coming as it were from Ireland (his name was Victoricus), with countless letters, and he gave me one of them, and I read the heading of the letter, 'The Voice of the Irish.' and as I read these opening words aloud, I imagined at that very instant that I heard the voice of those who were beside the forest of Foclut which is near the western sea; and thus they cried, as though with one voice: 'We beg you, holy boy, to come and walk again among us;' and I was stung with remorse in my heart and could not read on, and so I awoke. Thanks be to God, that after so many years the Lord bestowed on them according to their cry.

61 See, over and over again I shall briefly set out the words of my declaration. I attest in truth and exultation of heart before God and His holy angels that I never had any cause, except His gospel and His promises, ever to return to that people from which I had previously escaped with such difficulty.

62 But I beg those who believe in and fear God, whoever deigns to look at or receive this document which the unlearned sinner Patrick drew up in Ireland, that no-one should ever say that if I have achieved anything, however trivial, or may have shown the way according to God's good pleasure, it was my ignorance at work, but consider and accept as the undeniable truth that it would have been God's gift. And this is my declaration before I die.

LIFE

These few items concerning St. Patrick's experience and miraculous powers were written down by Muirchu maccu Machtheni under the direction of Aed, bishop of the town of Sletty.

1 Patrick, who was also called Sochet, was of British nationality, born in Britain, the son of the deacon Calpurnius, whose father, as Patrick himself says, was the priest Potitus, who came from the town of Bannavem Taburniae, not far from our sea; we have discovered for certain and beyond any doubt that this township is Ventre; and the mother who bore him was named Concessa.

At the age of sixteen the boy, with others, was captured and brought to this island of barbarians and was kept as a slave in the household of a certain cruel pagan king. He spent six years in captivity, in accordance with the Jewish custom, in fear and trembling before God, as the psalmist says (*Psalms 54,6*), and in many vigils and prayers. He used to pray a hundred times a day and a hundred times a night, gladly giving to God what is due to God and to Caesar what is due to Caesar and beginning to fear God and to love the Lord Almighty; for up to that time he had no knowledge of the true God, but at this point the Spirit became fervent within him.

After many hardships there, after enduring hunger and thirst, cold and nakedness, after pasturing flocks, after visits from Victoricus, an angel sent to him by God, after great miracles known to almost everyone, after divine prophecies (of which I shall give just one or two examples: 'You do well to fast, since you will soon be going to your home country,' and again: 'See your ship is ready,' though it was not near at hand but was perhaps two hundred miles away, where he had never been to) after all these experiences, as we have said, which can hardly be counted by anyone, in the twenty-third year of his life he left the earthly, pagan king and his works, received the heavenly, eternal God and now sailed for Britain by God's command and accompanied by the Holy Spirit in the ship which lay ready for him. . . .

9 And so, when the word came of the death of St. Palladius in Britain, since Palladius' disciples, Augustine, Benedict and the others, returned to Ebmoria with the news of his death, Patrick and his companions turned aside to a wonderful man, a very important bishop called Amator, who lived nearby. And there St. Patrick, knowing what was to happen to him, received the rank of bishop from the holy bishop Amator, as also Auxilius and Iserninus and others received lesser orders on the same day as St. Patrick was consecrated. . . . Then in the name of the holy Trinity the venerable traveller went on board the ship which had been prepared and reached Britain; and as he made his way on foot he avoided all detours, except for the ordinary business of travelling (for no one seeks the Lord by idleness), and then he hurried across our sea with all speed and a favourable wind.

10 Now in the days in which these events took place in the aforesaid area there was a certain king, the fierce heathen emperor of the barbarians, who reigned in Tara, which was the Irish capital. His name was Loegaire, the son of Niall and the ancestor of the royal house of almost the whole of this island. He had had wise men, wizards, soothsayers, enchanters and inventors of every black art who were able in their heathen, idolatrous way to know and foresee everything before it happened; two of them were favoured above the rest, their names being Lothroch, also called Lochru, and Lucetmael, also known as Ronal.

These two repeatedly foretold by their magical arts that there would come to be a certain foreign practice like a kingdom, with some strange and troublesome doctrine; a practice brought from afar across the seas, proclaimed by a few, adopted by many and respected by all; it would overthrow kingdoms, kill kings who resisted, win over great crowds, destroy all their gods, and after driving out all the resources of their art it would reign for ever and ever. They also identified and foretold the man who would bring and urge this practice in the following words, often repeated by them in a sort of verse form, especially in the two or three years preceding Patrick's arrival. This is how the verse ran; the sense is less than clear because of the different character of the language:

'Adze-head shall come, with his crook-headed staff and his house with a hole in its head. He shall chant blasphemy from his table, from the eastern part of his house, and all his household will answer him: 'So be it, so be it!' (This can be expressed more clearly in our own language.) 'So when all these things happen, our kingdom, which is heathen, shall not stand.'

And this is just as it later turned out. For the worship of idols was wiped out on Patrick's arrival, and the catholic faith in Christ filled every corner of our land.

4
Sutton Hoo Ship-Burial

The Sutton Hoo ship-burial is a vivid example of archeology's role in the study of history. Since its excavation in 1939 from a barrow located 6 miles from the North Sea on Mrs. E. M. Pretty's Suffolk estate, Sutton Hoo, the ship-burial has been recognized as an archeological discovery of unprecedented importance.

PLATE A
The excavation (by permission of the Trustees of the British Museum).

PLATE B
The ceremonial whetstone (by permission of the Trustees of the British Museum).

The Sutton Hoo ship, an open rowing boat, measured 80 feet in length and 14 feet in the beam (Plate A). The discovery of its remains, together with a large number of seventh-century artifacts, caused considerable excitement among historians. Despite differences of opinion among specialists in Anglo-Saxon history, some tentative conclusions regarding the importance of the Sutton Hoo ship-burial have emerged. The ship-burial and its artifacts confirm what written evidence, such as *Beowulf,* has said about many of the institutions and practices of the period. The ceremonial whetstone (Plate B) is an emblem that supports the existence of the concept of royal sovereignty during this early period. The dishes, coins, and weaponry reveal extensive contact between the Anglo-Saxons and the rest of Europe, particularly Sweden. The elaborate gold-framed purse lid (Plate C) and the gold belt buckle (Plate D) have led to a new appreciation of the

PLATE C
Purse lid with gold frame (by permission of the Trustees of the British Museum).

artistic creativity and craftsmanship of the early Anglo-Saxons. Finally, the bronze fish and escutcheon (Plate E) confirm the influence of Christianity in East Anglia during the seventh century.

Sutton Hoo raises further historical questions. The date of the ship-burial is still a matter of some dispute, but the interment most likely corresponds with the

PLATE D
The gold belt buckle (by permission of the Trustees of the British Museum).

PLATE E
Bronze fish and escutcheon (by permission of the Trustees of the British Museum).

death of Raedwald (599–624), the greatest of the East Anglian kings and the first to convert to Christianity. Nevertheless, the absence of any evidence of a body permits debate to continue. Was the Sutton Hoo find really a burial, or was it simply a pagan cenotaph erected in adherence to older traditions? Or was it connected with the kings of East Anglia at all? It is, however, certain that Sutton Hoo, by forcing historians to explain its very existence, has added immeasurably to our understanding of the early Anglo-Saxon era.

Following storage in the Aldwich Underground Station during World War II, the Sutton Hoo artifacts received a permanent home in the British Museum. The most complete and accessible collection of photographs of the ship-burial is R. L. S. Bruce-Mitford's massive three-volume *The Sutton Hoo Ship-Burial* (London: British Museum, 1975, 1977, 1983).

5
Bede, *Ecclesiastical History* (731). Synod of Whitby, 664

The Venerable Bede (673–735) was in his time the greatest intellect in western Europe. He entered a monastery as a child and remained at Jarrow in Northumbria until his death, loved for his virtue and devotion and respected for his wisdom and learning. His *History,* which he completed in 731, is his most famous work and the first history of England.

The intellectual flowering of Northumbria in the seventh and eighth centuries, of which Bede is the chief product, was due largely to the mingling of the Celtic tradition, which had grown up and flourished in the isolation of Ireland while barbarian tribes were disrupting western Europe, and the Mediterranean tradition, which in 597 came with Augustine, the first Christian missionary sent by Rome to England. Bede's account of the introduction of Latin and Celtic Christianity into England and of the contest between the two traditions coming to a settlement at the Synod of Whitby in 664 is reproduced below.

In Bede's *History,* the Church occupies a central position, and its bringing of civilization as well as Christianity to the barbarian Anglo-Saxons is the theme. Not surprisingly, Bede acknowledges the role of God as prime mover in history and treats miracles as facts of life. It is noteworthy that Bede saw England as a unit, populated by one people despite its political division into the Heptarchy of seven kingdoms. Where he got this notion, how extensive it was, and the impact of his stating it are interesting questions. Also significant is Bede's role in initiating and making popular the new system of dating, *anno domini,* "in the year of our Lord." However, in recent years, the letters C.E. (for Common Era) have to some extent replaced the overtly Christian A.D.

Copies of Bede's original Latin manuscript soon found their way to all parts of Europe, attesting both to Bede's personal reputation and to the influence of Northumbrian learning. Its first partial translation into English was made in the reign of Alfred (871–899); its first printing was in 1475.

Source: Bede's *Ecclesiastical History of the English People*, eds. Bertram Colgrave and R. A. B. Mynors, pp. 69, 73, 75, 77, 221, 223, 225, 227, 231, 255, 295, 297, 299, 301, 305, 307. By permission of Oxford University Press.

In the year of our Lord 582, Maurice, the fifty-fourth from Augustus, became emperor; he ruled for twenty-one years. In the tenth year of his reign, Gregory, a man eminent in learning and in affairs, was elected pontiff of the apostolic see of Rome. . . . In the fourteenth year of this emperor and about 150 years after the coming of the Angles to Britain, Gregory, prompted by divine inspiration, sent a servant of God named Augustine and several more God-fearing monks with him to preach the word of God to the English race. In obedience to the pope's commands, they undertook this task and had already gone a little way on their journey when they were paralysed with terror. . . . Gregory, however, sent them an encouraging letter in which he persuaded them to persevere with the task of preaching the Word and trust in the help of God. . . .

So Augustine, strengthened by the encouragement of St. Gregory, in company with the servants of Christ, returned to the work of preaching the word, and came to Britain. At that time Aethelberht, king of Kent, was a very powerful monarch. The lands over which he exercised his suzerainty stretched as far as the great river Humber, which divides the northern from the southern Angles. Over against the eastern districts of Kent there is a large island called Thanet. . . . Here Augustine, the servant of the Lord, landed with his companions, who are said to have been nearly forty in number. They had acquired interpreters from the Frankish race according to the command of Pope St. Gregory. Augustine sent to Aethelberht to say that he had come from Rome bearing the best of news, namely the sure and certain promise of eternal joys in heaven and an endless kingdom with the living and true God to those who received it. On hearing this the king ordered them to remain on the island where they had landed and be provided with all things necessary until he had decided what to do about them. . . .

Some days afterwards the king came to the island and, sitting in the open air, commanded Augustine and his comrades to come thither to talk with him. He took care that they should not meet in any building, for he held the traditional superstition that, if they practised any magic art, they might deceive him and get the better of him as soon as he entered. But they came endowed with divine not devilish power and bearing as their standard a silver cross and the image of our Lord and Saviour painted on a panel. They chanted litanies and uttered prayers to the Lord for their own eternal salvation and the salvation of those for whom and to whom they had come. At the king's command they sat down and preached the word of life to himself and all his *gesiths* there present. Then he said to them: "The words and the promises you bring are fair enough, but because they are new to us and doubtful, I cannot consent to accept them and forsake those beliefs which I and the whole English race have held so long. But as you have come on a long pilgrimage and are anxious, I perceive, to share with us things which you believe to be true and good, we do not wish to do you harm; on the contrary, we will receive you hospitably and provide what is necessary for your support; nor do we forbid you to win all you can to your faith and religion by your preaching." So he gave them a dwelling in the city of Canterbury, which was the chief city of all his dominions. . . .

At last the king, as well as others, believed and was baptized, being attracted by the pure life of the saints and by their most precious promises, whose truth they confirmed by performing many miracles. Every day more and more began to flock to hear the Word, to forsake their heathen worship, and, through faith, to join the unity of Christ's holy Church. . . .

In the year of our Lord 565, when Justin the second took over the control of the Roman Empire after Justinian, there came from Ireland to Britain a priest and abbot named Columba, a true monk in life no less than habit; he came to Britain to preach the word of God to the kingdoms of the northern Picts. . . .

Columba turned them to the faith of Christ by his words and example and so received the island of Iona from them in order to establish a monastery there. . . .

This island always has an abbot for its ruler who is a priest, to whose authority the whole kingdom, including even bishops, have to be subject. This unusual arrangement follows the example of their first teacher, who was not a bishop but a priest and monk. Some written records of his life and teachings are said to have been preserved by his disciples. Whatever he was himself, we know this for certain about him, that he left successors distinguished for their great abstinence, their love of God, and their observance of the Rule. It is true that they used tables of doubtful accuracy in fixing the date of the chief festival, since they were so far away at the ends of the earth that there was none to bring them the decrees of the synods concerning the observance of Easter; but they diligently practised such works of religion and chastity as they were able to learn from the words of the prophets, the evangelists, and the apostles. . . .

Such was the island, such the community, from which Aidan was sent to give the English people instruction in Christ. . . . Aidan taught the clergy many lessons about the conduct of their lives but above all he left them a most salutary example of abstinence and self-control; and the best recommendation of his teaching to all was that he taught them no other way of life than that which he himself practised among his fellows. . . .

With such a man as bishop to instruct them, King Oswald, together with the people over which he ruled, learned to hope for those heavenly realms which were unknown to their forefathers; and also Oswald gained from the one God who made heaven and earth greater earthly realms than any of his ancestors had possessed. In fact he held under his sway all the peoples and kingdoms of Britain, divided among the speakers of four different languages, British, Pictish, Irish, and English. . . .

After Oswald had been translated to the heavenly kingdom, his brother Oswiu succeeded to his earthly kingdom in his place, as a young man of about thirty, and ruled for twenty-eight troubled years. . . .

In those days there arose a great and active controversy about the keeping of Easter. Those who had come from Kent or Gaul declared that the Irish observance of Easter Sunday was contrary to the custom of the universal church. . . .

It is said that in these days it sometimes happened that Easter was celebrated twice in the same year, so that the king had finished the fast and was keeping Easter Sunday, while the queen and her people were still in Lent and observing Palm Sunday. . . .

When this question of Easter and of the tonsure and other ecclesiastical matters was raised, it was decided to hold a council to settle the dispute at a monastery called *Streanaeshealh* (Whitby). . . .

King Oswiu began by declaring that it was fitting that those who served one God should observe one rule of life and not differ in the celebration of the heavenly sacraments, seeing that they all hoped for one kingdom in heaven; they ought therefore to inquire as to which was the truer tradition and then all follow it together. He then ordered his bishop Colman to say first what were the customs which he followed and whence they originated. Colman thereupon said, "The method of keeping Easter which I observe, I received from my superiors who sent me here as bishop; it was in this way that all our fathers, men beloved of God, are known to have celebrated it. Nor should this method seem contemptible and blameworthy seeing that the blessed evangelist John, the disciple whom the Lord specially loved, is said to have celebrated it thus, together with all the churches over which he presided." . . . Then Wilfrid, receiving instructions from the king to speak, began thus: "The Easter we keep is the same as we have seen universally celebrated in Rome, where the apostles St. Peter and St. Paul lived, taught, suffered, and were buried. We also found it in use everywhere in Italy and Gaul when we travelled through those countries for the purpose of study and prayer. We learned that it was observed at one and the same time in Africa, Asia, Egypt, Greece, and throughout the whole world, wherever the Church of Christ is scattered, amid various nations and languages. The only exceptions are these men and their accomplices in obstinacy, I mean the Picts and the Britons, who in these, the two remotest islands of the Ocean, and only in some parts of them, foolishly attempt to fight against the whole world."

"So far as your father Columba and his followers are concerned, whose holiness you claim to imitate and whose rule and precepts (confirmed by heavenly signs) you claim to follow, I might perhaps point out that at the judgment, many will say to the Lord that they prophesied in His name and cast out devils and did many wonderful works, but the Lord will answer that He never knew them. Far be it from me to say this about your fathers, for it is much fairer to believe good rather than evil about unknown people. So I will not deny that those who in their rude simplicity loved God with pious intent, were indeed servants of God and beloved by Him. Nor do I think that this observance of Easter did much harm to them while no one had come to show them a more perfect rule to follow. . . . But, once having heard the decrees of the apostolic see or rather of the universal Church, if you refuse to follow them, confirmed as they are by the holy Scriptures, then without doubt you are committing sin. For though your fathers were holy men, do you think that a handful of people in one corner of the remotest of islands is to be preferred to the universal Church of Christ which is spread throughout the world? And even if that Columba of yours—yes, and ours too, if he belonged to Christ—was a holy man of mighty works, is he to be preferred to the most blessed chief of the apostles, to whom the Lord said, 'Thou art Peter and upon this rock I will build my Church and the gates of hell shall not prevail against it, and I will give unto thee the keys of the kingdom of heaven'?"

When Wilfrid had ended, the king said, "It is true, Colman, that the Lord said these words to Peter?" Colman answered, "It is true, O King." Then the king went on, "Have you anything to show that an equal authority was given to your Columba?" Colman answered, "Nothing." Again the king said, "Do you both agree, without any dispute, that these words were addressed primarily to Peter and that the Lord gave him the keys of the kingdom of heaven?" They both answered, "Yes." Thereupon the king concluded, "Then, I tell you, since he is the doorkeeper I will not contradict him; but I intend to obey his commands in everything to the best of my knowledge and ability, otherwise when I come to the gates of the kingdom of heaven, there may be no one to open them because the one who on your own showing holds the keys has turned his back on me."

6
The Anglo-Saxon Chronicle

The Anglo-Saxon Chronicle is in fact seven related chronicles, which record in an annalistic fashion the events in England's history from the invasion of Julius Caesar, "Sixty years before Christ was born," to the death of Stephen in 1154. The *Chronicle* was initially compiled during the reign of Alfred (871–899), a result of his determination to revive learning. The earliest entries, often little more than identifying labels to help the memory distinguish one year from another, were similar to the brief remarks added by churches and monasteries to the column of years on an Easter table. Where written records such as Bede's History were available, entries were longer, and during a writer's own lifetime there was the possibility of considerable first hand information. Thus, Alfred's reign and the troubles produced by the invading Danes were emphasized. Copies of the initial compilation, added to with varying degrees of skill and imagin-

Source: The Anglo-Saxon Chronicle: A Revised Translation, ed. Dorothy Whitelock with David C. Douglas and Susie I. Tucker, New Brunswick, N.J.: Rutgers University Press, 1961, pp. 6–7, 9, 14, 22, 26, 28, 35–36, 42, 46–47, 49–50, 52, 58. Reprinted by permission of Methuen London.

ation, became the several versions, especially of the later period.

Not only does the *Chronicle* give the historian a wealth of information, but the long period of its composition by a number of scribes in different locations makes it an equally valuable source of information for the student of the Old English or Anglo-Saxon language. Its very existence, a vernacular chronicle spanning several centuries, is as unique in the field of letters as the Domesday survey is in the field of royal administration.

1 Octavian reigned 66 years and in the 52nd year of his reign Christ was born.

2 The three astrologers came from the East in order to worship Christ, and the children in Bethlehem were slain because of the persecution of Christ by Herod.

6 Five thousand and two hundred years had passed from the beginning of the world to this year.

47 In this year Claudius came to Britain, the second of the kings of the Romans to do so, and obtained the greater part under his control, and likewise subjected the island of Orkney to the rule of the Romans.

410 In this year Rome was destroyed by the Goths, eleven hundred and ten years after it was built. Then after that the kings of the Romans no longer reigned in Britain. Altogether they had reigned there 470 years since Gaius Julius first came to the land.

596 In this year Pope Gregory sent Augustine to Britain with a good number of monks, who preached God's word to the English people.

671 In this year there was the great mortality of birds.

715 In this year Ine and Ceolred fought at "Woden's barrow."

733 In this year Aethelbald occupied Somerton, and there was an eclipse of the sun.

734 In this year the moon looked as if it were suffused with blood, and Tatwine and Bede died.

789 In this year King Brihtric married Offa's daughter Eadburh. And in his days there came for the first time three ships of Northmen and then the reeve rode to them and wished to force them to the king's residence, for he did not know what they were; and they slew him. Those were the first ships of Danish men which came to the land of the English.

793 In this year dire portents appeared over Northumbria and sorely frightened the people. They consisted of immense whirlwinds and flashes of lightning, and fiery dragons were seen flying in the air. A great famine immediately followed those signs, and a little after that in the same year, on 8 June, the ravages of heathen men miserably destroyed God's church on Lindisfarne, with plunder and slaughter. And Sicga died on 22 February.

851 In this year Ealdorman Ceorl with the contingent of the men of Devon fought against the heathen army at *Wicganbeorg,* and the English made a great slaughter there and had the victory. And for the first time, heathen men stayed through the winter on Thanet. And the same year 350 ships came into the mouth of the Thames and stormed Canterbury and London and put to flight Brihtwulf, king of the Mercians, with his army, and went south across the Thames into Surrey. And King Aethelwulf and his son Aethelbald fought against them at *Aclea* with the army of the West Saxons, and there inflicted the greatest slaughter [on a heathen army] that we ever heard of until this present day, and had the victory there.

871 In this year the army came into Wessex to Reading, and three days later two Danish earls rode farther inland. Then Ealdorman Aethelwulf encountered them at Englefield, and fought against them there and had the victory, and one of them, whose name was Sidroc, was killed there. Then four days later King Ethelred and his brother Alfred led a great army to Reading and fought against the army; and a great slaughter was made on both sides and Ealdorman Aethelwulf was killed, and the Danes had possession of the battle-field. . . . And afterwards, after Easter, King Ethelred died, and he had reigned five years. . . .

Then his brother Alfred, the son of Aethelwulf, succeeded to the kingdom of the West Saxons. And a month later King Alfred fought with a small force against the whole army at Wilton and put it to flight far on into the day; and the Danes had possession of the battle-field. And during that year nine general engagements were fought against the Danish army in the kingdom south of the Thames. . . . And that year nine (Danish) earls were killed and one king. And the West Saxons made peace with the army that year.

878 In this year in midwinter after twelfth night the enemy army came stealthily to Chippenham, and occupied the land of the West Saxons and settled there, and drove a great part of the people across the sea, and conquered most of the others; and the people submitted to them, except King Alfred. He journeyed in difficulties through the woods and fen-fastnesses with a small force.

And afterwards at Easter, King Alfred with a small force made a stronghold at Athelney, and he and the section of the people of Somerset which was nearest to it proceeded to fight from that stronghold against the enemy. Then in the seventh week after Easter he rode to "Egbert's stone" east of Selwood, and there came to meet all the people of Somerset and of Wiltshire and of that part of Hampshire which was on this side of the sea, and they rejoiced to see him. And then after one night he went from that encampment to Iley, and after another night to Edington, and there fought against the whole army and put it to flight, and pursued it as far as the fortress, and stayed there a fortnight. And then the enemy gave him preliminary hostages and great oaths that they would leave his kingdom, and promised also that their king should receive baptism, and they kept their promise. Three weeks later King Guthrum with 30 of the men who were the most important in the army came [to him] at Aller, which is near Athelney, and the king stood sponsor to him at his baptism there; and the unbinding of the chrism took place at Wedmore. And he was twelve days with the king, and he honoured him and his companions greatly with gifts.

886 In this year the Danish army which had gone east went west again, and then up the Seine, and made their winter quarters there at the town of Paris.

That same year King Alfred occupied London; and all the English people that were not under subjection to the Danes submitted to him. . . .

900 In this year Alfred the son of Aethelwulf died, six days before All Saints' day. He was king over the whole English people except for that part which was under Danish rule, and he had held the kingdom for one and a half years less than thirty; and then his son Edward succeeded to the kingdom.

7

Anglo-Saxon Dooms of Wihtred (695) and Alfred (871–899)

The Anglo-Saxon's readiness to resort to violence was limited only by his knowledge that a victim's family would return in kind any injury or insult received. This tension produced a vast body of unwritten law and custom that governed the conduct of the folkmoot, or court, where responsibility or guilt and an appropriate monetary compensation was determined. A killing required the payment of a wergild, a lesser physical injury a bot, and other injuries, such as breaking the peace of a man's household, brought other fines. These procedures were both very formal and ancient. Stresses appeared in the system, however, as kings became more powerful, as the solidarity of the family declined, and as outside influences, such as Christianity and commerce, produced conditions for which the customary laws made no provision.

Dooms were written laws issued by a king and his council of wise men, the witenagemot, mainly for the purpose of adapting existing customs to new conditions. The first dooms, those of Ethelbert of Kent (560–616), date from shortly after Augustine's arrival in England in 597. The Church no doubt contributed the idea that laws should be written. The dooms reproduced below were issued by Wihtred of Kent in 695 and by Alfred of Wessex (871–899). The former illustrate the continuing attempt to accommodate the law to the Christian Church, as well as the perennial need to keep the peace. The dooms of Alfred indicate not only his wide-ranging interests but also the profound difficulties he faced during his reign.

The dooms were written in Anglo-Saxon and have survived in various manuscripts, none of which dates back to its original promulgation.

THESE ARE THE DECREES OF WIHTRED, KING OF THE PEOPLE OF KENT.

Prologue

When the most gracious king of the people of Kent, Wihtred, was reigning, in the fifth year of his reign . . . there was collected a deliberate assembly of lead-

Source: English Historical Documents, Vol. 1, c. 500–1042, ed. Dorothy Whitelock, 1955, Oxford University Press, Inc., pp. 362–364, 373, 377–380. Reprinted by permission of Methuen London.

ing men. . . . There, with the consent of all, the leading men devised these decrees and added them to the lawful usages of the people of Kent, as it says and declares hereafter.

1. The Church [is to be] free from taxation.

2. The [breach of] the Church's protection is to be 50 shillings like the king's.

9. If a servant, against his lord's command, do servile work between sunset on Saturday evening and sunset on Sunday evening, he is to pay 80 *sceattas* to his lord.

16. The word of the bishop and the king without an oath is to be incontrovertible.

17. The head of a monastery is to clear himself with a priest's exculpation.

18. A priest is to purge himself with his own asseveration in his holy vestments before the altar, saying thus: "I speak the truth in Christ, I do not lie." Similarly a deacon is to purge himself.

20. A stranger is to purge himself with his own oath on the altar; similarly a king's thegn;

21. A *ceorl* with three of the same class on the altar; and the oath of all these is to be incontrovertible.

25. If anyone kill a man who is in the act of thieving, he is to lie without wergild.

26. If anyone captures a freeman with the stolen goods on him, the king is to choose one of three things; he is either to be killed or sold across the sea or redeemed with his wergild.

26.1. He who discovers and captures him, is to have the right to half of [the payment for] him; if he is killed, 70 shillings is to be paid to them.

28. If a man from a distance or a foreigner goes off the track, and he neither shouts nor blows a horn, he is to be assumed to be a thief, to be either killed or redeemed.

THE DOOMS OF ALFRED

Int. 43. Judge thou very fairly. Do not judge one judgment for the rich and another for the poor; nor one for the one more dear and another for the one more hateful.

Int. 49.6. A man can think on this one sentence alone, that he judges each one rightly; he has need of no other law-books. Let him bethink that he judge to no man what he would not that he judged to him, if he were giving the judgment on him.

Int. 49.9. Then I, King Alfred, collected these together and ordered to be written many of them which our forefathers observed, those which I liked; and many of those which I did not like, I rejected with the advice of my councillors, and ordered them to be differently observed. For I dared not presume to set in writing at all many of my own, because it was unknown to me what would please those who should come after us. But those which I found anywhere, which seemed to me most just, either of the time of my kinsman, King Ine, or Offa, king of the Mercians, or of Ethelbert, who first among the English received baptism, I collected herein, and omitted the others.

Int. 49.10. Then I, Alfred, king of the West Saxons, showed these to all my councillors, and they then said that they were all pleased to observe them.

26 (29). If anyone with a band of men kills an innocent man of a two-hundred wergild, he who admits the slaying is to pay the wergild and the fine, and each man who was in that expedition is to pay 30 shillings as compensation for being in that band.

27 (30). If it is a man of a six-hundred wergild, each man [is to pay] 60 shillings as compensation for being in that band, and the slayer the wergild and full fine.

28 (31). If he is a man of twelve-hundred wergild, each of them [is to pay] 120 shillings, and the slayer the wergild and the fine.

34. Moreover, it is prescribed for traders: they are to bring before the king's reeve in a public meeting the men whom they take up into the country with them, and it is to be established how many of them there are to be; and they are to take with them men whom they can afterwards bring to justice at a public meeting. . . .

35. If anyone binds an innocent *ceorl*, he is to pay him six shillings compensation.

35.1. If anyone scourges him, he is to pay him 20 shillings compensation.

35.2. If he places him in the stocks, he is to pay him 30 shillings compensation.

35.3. If in insult he disfigures him by cutting his hair, he is to pay him 10 shillings compensation.

35.4. If, without binding him, he cuts his hair like a priest's, he is to pay him 30 shillings compensation.

35.5. If he cuts off his beard, he is to pay 20 shillings compensation.

35.6. If he binds him and then cuts his hair like a priest's, he is to pay 60 shillings compensation.

36. Moreover, it is established: if anyone has a spear over his shoulder, and a man is transfixed on it, the wergild is to be paid without the fine.

36.1. If he is transfixed before his eyes, he is to pay the wergild; if anyone accuses him of intention in this act, he is to clear himself in proportion to the fine, and by that [oath] do away with the fine,

36.2. if the point is higher than the butt of the shaft. If they are both level, the point and the butt end, that is to be [considered] without risk.

38. If anyone fights in a meeting in the presence of the king's ealdorman, he is to pay wergild and fine, as is fitting, and before that, 120 shillings to the ealdorman as a fine.

38.1. If he disturbs a public meeting by drawing a weapon, [he is to pay] 120 shillings to the ealdorman as a fine.

38.2. If any of this takes place before the deputy of the king's ealdorman, or before the king's priest, [there shall be] a fine of 30 shillings.

39. If anyone fights in the house of a *ceorl,* he is to pay six shillings compensation to the *ceorl.*

39.1. If he draws a weapon and does not fight, it is to be half as much.

42. Moreover we command: that the man who knows his opponent to be dwelling at home is not to fight before he asks justice for himself.

42.1. If he has sufficient power to surround his opponent and besiege him there in his house, he is to keep him seven days inside and not fight against him, if he will remain inside; and then after seven days, if he will surrender and give up his weapons, he is to keep him unharmed for 30 days, and send notice about him to his kinsmen and his friends.

42.2. If he, however, reaches a church, it is then to be [dealt with] according to the privilege of the church, as we have said above.

42.3. If he [the attacker] has not sufficient power to besiege him in his house, he is to ride to the ealdorman and ask him for support; if he will not give him support, he is to ride to the king, before having recourse to fighting.

42.5. Moreover we declare that a man may fight on behalf of his lord, if the lord is being attacked, without incurring a vendetta. Similarly the lord may fight on behalf of his man.

42.6. In the same way, a man may fight on behalf of his born kinsman, if he is being wrongfully attacked, except against his lord; that we do not allow.

42.7. And a man may fight without incurring a vendetta if he finds another man with his wedded wife, within closed doors or under the same blanket, or with his legitimate daughter or his legitimate sister, or with his mother who was given as a lawful wife to his father.

8

"The Battle of Maldon," 991

This Anglo-Saxon poem, a 325-line fragment missing the beginning and end, describes a battle fought at Maldon in Essex in 991. *The Anglo-Saxon Chronicle* relates the incident simply: "Ealdorman Brihtnoth came against him there with his army and fought against him; and they killed the ealdorman there and had control of the field." Thus, Maldon was one of many skirmishes in the renewed onslaught of the Danes against the faltering resistance of King Ethelred the Unready (978–1016).

The poem, however, gives a far more vivid impression of the battle—the personal defiance of Byrhtnoth in the face of the Danes' invitation to submit, allowing the Danes to cross the river defending his position, and the resolution of the slain Byrhtnoth's followers to avenge his death or to die on the field by him. The poem, demonstrating poetic artistry of the highest quality, gives a unique touch of individual sentiment and action and forces the historian to see real people and real emotions behind the chronicler's brief catalog of events.

Our understanding of the tenth century would be much different without this invaluable evidence. Part of England's oral heroic tradition that included *Beowulf,* it differs from that epic in its brevity, its lateness of composition, and its description of a recent historical event instead of a story remembered dimly from the past. Like *Beowulf,* "Maldon" owed its survival to its being written, the result perhaps of a monastery's regard for a dead benefactor or a widow's devotion for her dead husband. The poem apparently went unnoticed during the Middle Ages. It is first mentioned in the 1696 cataloging of the manuscripts of the Cottonian Library, works rescued when the monasteries were dissolved, and later left to the nation by its owner John Cotton. Thomas Hearne, seemingly for no particular reason, included the poem among the appendices of the *Chronicle of John of Glastonbury,* which he edited and printed in 1726. A transcript, probably that used by Hearne, came to light in the 1930s. Thus although the manuscript burned in 1731, the poem survived, illus-

Source: Margaret Ashdown, *English and Norse Documents, Relating to the Reign of Ethelred the Unready*, Cambridge University Press, 1930, pp. 23, 25, 29, 31, 33, 35, 37. Reprinted by permission of Cambridge University Press.

trating the role of good fortune in the historian's quest for knowledge of the past.

Then he bade each warrior leave his horse, drive it afar and go forth on foot, and trust to his hands and to his good intent.

Then Offa's kinsman first perceived that the earl would suffer no faintness of heart; he let his loved hawk fly from his hand to the wood and advanced to the fight. By this it might be seen that the lad would not waver in the strife now that he had taken up his arms.

With him Eadric would help his lord, his chief in the fray. He advanced to war with spear in hand; as long as he might grasp his shield and broad sword, he kept his purpose firm. He made good his vow, now that the time had come for him to fight before his lord.

Then Byrhtnoth began to array his men; he rode and gave counsel and taught his warriors how they should stand and keep their ground, bade them hold their shields aright, firm with their hands and fear not at all. When he had meetly arrayed his host, he alighted among the people where it pleased him best, where he knew his body-guard to be most loyal.

Then the messenger of the Vikings stood on the bank, he called sternly, uttered words, boastfully speaking the seafarers' message to the earl, as he stood on the shore. "Bold seamen have sent me to you, and bade me say, that it is for you to send treasure quickly in return for peace, and it will be better for you all that you buy off an attack with tribute, rather than that men so fierce as we should give you battle." . . .

Byrhtnoth lifted up his voice, grasped his shield and shook his supple spear, gave forth words, angry and resolute, and made him answer: "Hear you, searover, what this folk says? For tribute they will give you spears, poisoned point and ancient sword, such war gear as will profit you little in the battle. Messenger of the seamen, take back a message, say to your people a far less pleasing tale, how that there stands here with his troop an earl of unstained renown, who is ready to guard this realm, the home of Ethelred my lord, people and land; it is the heathen that shall fall in the battle." . . .

Then Byrhtnoth drew his blade, broad and of burnished edge, and smote upon his mail. All too quickly one of the seamen checked his hand, crippling the arm of the earl. Then his golden-hilted sword fell to the earth; he could not use his hard blade nor wield a weapon. Yet still the white-haired warrior spoke as before, emboldened his men and bade the heroes press on. He could no longer now stand firm on his feet. The earl looked up to heaven and cried aloud: "I thank thee, Ruler of Nations, for all the joys that I have met with in this world. Now I have most need, gracious Creator, that thou grant my spirit grace, that my soul may fare to thee, into thy keeping, Lord of Angels, and pass in peace. It is my prayer to thee that fiends of hell may not entreat it shamefully."

Then the heathen wretches cut him down, and both the warriors who stood near by, Aelfnoth and Wulfmaer, lay overthrown; they yielded their lives at their lord's side. . . .

All the retainers saw how their lord lay dead. Then the proud thanes pressed on, hastened eagerly, those undaunted men. All desired one of two things, to lose their lives or to avenge the one they loved.

With these words Aelfric's son urged them to go forth, a warrior young in years, he lifted up his voice and spoke with courage. Aelfwine said: "Remember the words that we uttered many a time over the mead, when on the bench, heroes in hall, we made our boast about hard strife. Now it may be proved which of us is bold! I will make known my lineage to all, how I was born in Mercia of a great race. Ealhelm was my grandfather called, a wise ealdorman, happy in this world's goods. Thanes shall have no cause to reproach me among my people that I was ready to forsake this action, and seek my home, now that my lord lies low, cut down in battle. This is no common grief to me, he was both my kinsman and my lord."

Then he advanced (his mind was set on revenge), till he pierced with his lance a seaman from among the host, so that the man lay on the earth, borne down with his weapon.

Then Offa began to exhort his comrades, his friends and companions, that they should press on. . . .

Leofsunu lifted up his voice and raised his shield, his buckler to defend him, and gave him answer: "This I avow, that I will not flee a footspace hence, but will press on and avenge my liege-lord in the fight." . . .

Dunhere spoke and shook his lance; a simple churl, he cried above them all, and bade each warrior avenge Byrhtnoth: "He that thinks to avenge his lord, his chief in the press, may not waver nor reck for his life." Then they went forth, and took no thought for life. . . .

They prayed God that they might take vengeance for their lord, and work slaughter among their foes. . . .

Then Offa smote a seaman in the fight, so that he fell to the earth. . . . Offa himself was quickly cut to pieces in the fray. Yet he had compassed what he had promised his chief, as he bandied vows with his generous lord in days gone by, that they should both ride home to the town unhurt or fall among the host, perish of wounds on the field. He lay, as befits a thane, at his lord's side.

Then came a crashing of shields; seamen pressed on, enraged by war; the spear oft pierced the life-house of the doomed. . . .

That was a fierce encounter; warriors stood firm in the strife. Men were falling, worn out with their wounds; the slain fell to the earth.

Oswold and Eadwold all the while, that pair of brothers, urged on the men, prayed their dear kinsmen to stand firm in the hour of need, and use their weapons in no weak fashion.

Byrhtwold spoke and grasped his shield (he was an old companion); he shook his ash-wood spear and exhorted the men right boldly: "Thoughts must be the braver, heart more valiant, courage the greater as our strength grows less. Here lies our lord, all cut down, the hero in the dust. Long may he mourn who thinks now to turn from the battle-play. I am old in years; I will not leave the field, but think to lie by my lord's side, by the man I held so dear."

9
William of Poitiers, *The Deeds of William* (c. 1071). Background to the Norman Conquest, 1064–1066

William of Poitiers's *Gesta Willelmi ducis Normannorum et regis Anglorum,* written about 1071, is one of several "chronicles" surviving from the Norman period. Unlike a pure chronicle, which simply attempts to remind the reader of past events, William's work begins the transition toward a more topically organized "history," which assists the reader to understand, as well as to recall, the past. William stands somewhere between the writers of *The Anglo-Saxon Chronicle* and later historians such as William of Newburgh.

William of Poitiers based his work in part on other chronicles and, possibly, on the Bayeux Tapestry (see Document 10). Oral evidence was, however, his most important source. As chaplain to Duke William of Normandy, he was a product of Norman feudalism, a warrior-priest like Bishop Odo of Bayeux, who commissioned the Bayeux Tapestry. Although he did not fight at Hastings, William knew many who did, and he undoubtedly gained much knowledge from them in conversation. His Latin account of the background to the invasion and the Battle of Hastings is, together with the Bayeux Tapestry, the source of much of our detailed knowledge of this central event in English history. The chronicle was almost lost; it survived only because of a copy made in 1619 from a manuscript then in the possession of Sir Robert Cotton.

Because William of Poitiers was a Norman and an admirer of

Source: English Historical Documents, Vol. II, 1042–1189, eds. David C. Douglas and George W. Greenaway. 1953, Oxford University Press, Inc., pp. 217–219. Reprinted by permission of Methuen London.

Duke William, later William I (1066–1087), he did not write an unbiased account. In the selection that follows he attempted to justify William's invasion of England, asserting that William was always Edward the Confessor's choice to succeed to the throne of England. Furthermore, the chronicle stresses Harold's debt to William and insists that Harold's oath taken in 1064 was voluntary. When Harold later broke his vow, this treachery rightly brought William widespread sympathy and support. Anglo-Saxons, in general, were assumed to act with "accustomed perfidy." This account differs sharply from that of *The Anglo-Saxon Chronicle.* The latter omits any mention of the oath taken by Harold and stresses that Edward the Confessor had chosen Harold as his successor. Thus, as is often the case, the historian must analyze the data critically and arrive at an independent judgment not wholly in agreement with any single source of evidence.

About the same time, Edward, king of the English, who loved William as a brother or a son, established him as his heir with a stronger pledge than ever before. The king, who in his holy life showed his desire for a celestial kingdom, felt the hour of his death approaching, and wished to anticipate its inevitable consequences. He therefore dispatched Harold to William in order that he might confirm his promise by an oath. This Harold was of all the king's subjects the richest and the most exhalted in honour and power, and his brother and his cousins had previously been offered as hostages in respect of the same succession. The king, indeed, here acted with great prudence in choosing Harold for this task, in the hope that the riches and the authority of this magnate might check disturbance throughout England if the people with their accustomed perfidy should be disposed to overturn what had been determined. Whilst travelling upon this errand Harold only escaped the perils of the sea by making a forced landing on the coast of Ponthieu where he fell into the hands of Count Guy, who threw him and his companions into prison. He might well have thought this a greater misfortune even than shipwreck, since among many peoples of the Gauls there was an abominable custom utterly contrary to Christian charity, whereby, when the powerful and rich were captured, they were thrown ignominiously into prison, and there maltreated and tortured even to the point of death, and afterwards sold as slaves to some magnate. When Duke William heard what had happened he sent messengers at speed, and by prayers and threats he brought about Harold's honourable release. . . . For the duke rejoiced to have so illustrious a guest in a man who had been sent him by the nearest and dearest of his friends: one, moreover, who was in England second only to the king, and who might prove a faithful mediator between him and the English. When they had come together in conference at Bonneville, Harold in that place swore fealty to the duke employing the sacred ritual recognized among Christian men. And as is testified by the most truthful and most honourable men who were there present, he took an oath of his own free will in the following terms: firstly that he would be the representative of Duke William at the court of his lord, King Edward, as long as the king lived; secondly that he would employ all his influence and wealth to ensure that after the death of King Edward the kingdom of England should be confirmed in the possession of the duke; thirdly that he would place a garrison of the duke's knights in the castle of Dover and maintain these at his own care and cost; fourthly that in other parts of England at the pleasure of the duke he would maintain garrisons in other castles and make complete provision for their sustenance. The duke on his part who before the oath was taken had received ceremonial homage from him, confirmed to him at his request all his lands and dignities. For Edward in his illness could not be expected to live much longer. . . . After this there came the unwelcome report that the land of England had lost its king, and that Harold had been crowned in his stead. This insensate Englishman did not wait for the public choice, but breaking his oath, and with the support of a few ill-disposed partisans, he seized the throne of the best of kings on the very day of his funeral, and when all the people were bewailing their loss. He was ordained king by the unhallowed consecration of Stigand, who had justly been deprived of his priesthood by the zeal and anathema of the apostolic see. Duke William therefore having taken counsel with his men resolved to avenge the insult by force of arms, and to regain his inheritance by war. . . . It would be tedious to tell in detail how by his prudent acts ships were made, arms and troops, provisions and other equipment assembled for war, and how the enthusiasm of the whole of Normandy was directed towards this enterprise. Nor did he neglect to take measures for the administration and the security of the duchy during his absence. Further, many warriors came to his support from outside the duchy, some being attracted by his well-known generosity, and all by confidence in the justice of his cause. . . .

At that time there sat in the seat of St. Peter at Rome Pope Alexander, who was worthy of the respect and obedience of the whole Church. . . . Wherever he could throughout all the world he corrected evil without compromise. The duke therefore sought the favour of this apostle for the project he had in hand, and gladly received from him the gift of a banner as a pledge of the support of St. Peter whereby he might the more confidently and safely attack his enemy. . . .

10

The Bayeux Tapestry. The Battle of Hastings, 1066

The Bayeux Tapestry, which is actually an embroidery, is a most unusual piece of historical evidence. It is unique not only because it survived but because it portrays a historical event of obvious importance—the Norman conquest of England. The tapestry is approximately 230 feet long and 20 inches wide. Its seventy-three panels begin with the mission of Harold to Normandy in 1064 and end with his death at Hastings. For the benefit of the largely illiterate population, it tells the story of the conquest in comic-strip fashion.

The tapestry was commissioned by Odo, bishop of Bayeux, William the Conqueror's half-brother, probably sometime between 1066 and 1082, most likely to adorn his new cathedral at Bayeux, which was dedicated in 1077. There is dispute on all of these points. Odo fought with William at Hastings, and the tapestry, although probably produced by Anglo-Saxon needlewomen, is a Norman version of these critical events. The account given by the Bayeux Tapestry is similar to that of William of Poitiers, although the two differ on points of detail. The tapestry also emphasizes the oath of 1064 as the justification for William's invasion. The panel depicting this oath (Plate A) appears near the middle of the tapestry and should be viewed as the central, climactic event. The portrayal of the coming of Halley's Comet (Plate B) was the designer's attempt to show divine displeasure with Harold's usurpation of the throne. The events shown in the rest of the tapestry, the invasion of England (Plates C and D) and the battle itself (Plates E and F), proceed as if the success of the Normans was inevitable. The tapestry is of particular value in studying the clothing, weaponry, and architecture of the eleventh century.

The tapestry itself has an interesting history. It is first referred to in an inventory of 1476, which revealed its occasional display in the nave of the cathedral. It was not mentioned again until the eighteenth century, when its historical importance was widely recognized. During the French Revolution it was on two occasions almost destroyed. In 1792 soldiers attempted unsuccessfully to use it to cover a wagon, and two years later it almost adorned a float honoring the revolution. In 1803 Napoleon exhibited the tapestry at the *Musée Napoléon* in Paris, perhaps hoping to draw attention to his own projected invasion of England. He later returned it to Bayeux, where it is now displayed in the former bishop's palace. It was first photographed in 1871.

Source: The Bayeux Tapestry: A Comprehensive Survey, gen. ed. Sir Frank Stenton, London: Phaidon Press, 1957, plates 29, 35, 43, 52, 67, 72. Reproduced with the permission of Phaidon Press.

PLATE A
Harold's oath (Phaidon Press, reproduced with permission of Phaidon Press).

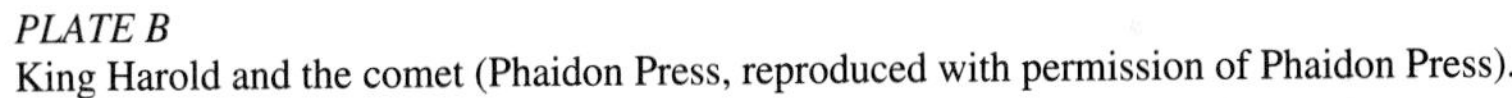

PLATE B
King Harold and the comet (Phaidon Press, reproduced with permission of Phaidon Press).

PLATE C
The invasion fleet (Phaidon Press, reproduced with permission of Phaidon Press).

PLATE D
Norman destruction in England (Phaidon Press, reproduced with permission of Phaidon Press).

PLATE E
The battle of Hastings (Phaidon Press, reproduced with permission of Phaidon Press).

PLATE F
The death of Harold (Phaidon Press, reproduced by permission of Phaidon Press).

11

Domesday Book (1086). Survey of Herefordshire

William the Conqueror (1066–1087), in the meeting of his great council at Christmas in 1085, ordered a survey of the kingdom of England. A rumored Norse invasion and a need for money probably prompted his action. Certainly, he wanted to learn the extent of his conquest and, particularly, to ascertain what taxes had gone to Edward the Confessor and should now come to him. *The Anglo-Saxon Chronicle,* not surprisingly, complains of the thoroughness of William's survey: "there was not a single hide or rood of land, nor even was there an ox or a cow or a pig left that was not set down in his writings."

Royal officials going through the shires, hundreds, and villages impaneled sworn inquests, requiring residents to reveal information on ownership, tenure, and taxation. This raw information, digested and reorganized according to feudal tenures within shires, was recopied into two bound volumes, which became known almost immediately as *Domesday Book.* The title has always been something of a curiosity: does it refer to doomsday, the day of Last Judgment, or to what?

The book is filled with specific detail regarding not only tenures and taxation but the incidental information so valuable to social and economic historians. Also interesting is the question of what it says of a king who could order such a project and the royal administration that could execute it so quickly and so well. *Domesday Book* is a unique document; no other kingdom in western Europe in the Middle Ages produced its like.

Domesday Book, originally kept in the Treasury at Winchester, is now in the Public Record Office in London. It was printed by the Record Commission in 1783.

In the city of Hereford, in the time of King Edward, there were 103 men dwelling together inside and outside the wall, and they had the customs hereinunder noted. If any of them wished to leave the city, he could, with the consent

Source: Sources of English Constitutional History, edited and translated by Carl Stephenson and Frederick George Marcham, pp. 41–44.

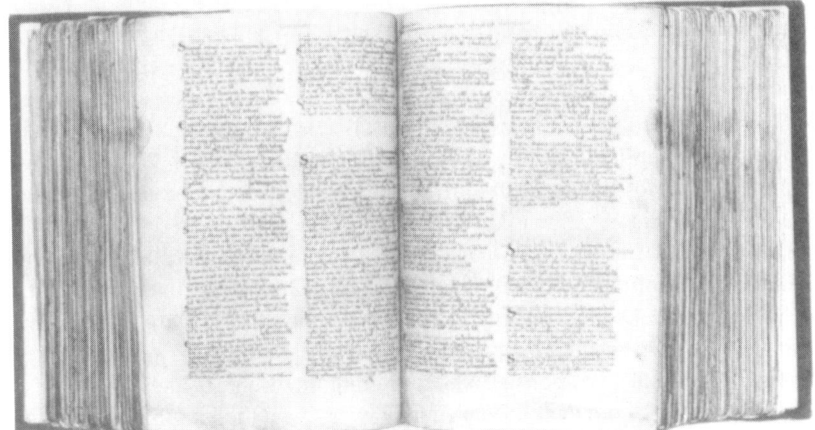

PLATE A
Domesday Book (permission of the Public Record Office, London).

of the reeve, sell his house to another man who was willing to perform the service owed from it, and the reeve got the third penny from this sale. But if any one, because of his poverty, could not perform the service, he gave up his house without payment to the reeve, who saw to it that the house did not remain vacant and that the king did not lose the service. Every entire messuage inside the wall rendered 7½*d.*, and [also] 4*d.* for the hire of horses; and [the holder] reaped for three days at Marden and spent one day gathering hay wherever the sheriff wished. Whoever had a horse went thrice a year with the sheriff to the pleas and the hundred [court] at Wormelow. When the king engaged in a hunting expedition, one man customarily went from each house to serve as a beater in the wood. Other men, who did not have entire messuages, found guards for the [royal] hall when the king was in the city. On the death of a burgess who served with a horse, the king had his horse and arms. From him who had no horse, when he died, the king had either 10*s.* or his land, together with the houses [on it]. If any one, overtaken by death, had not divided what he possessed, the king had all his chattels. These customs were had alike by those living in the city and by those dwelling outside the wall, except that an entire messuage outside the wall rendered only 3½*d.* The other customs were common [to both groups].

Any man's wife who brewed inside or outside the city gave 10*d.* according to custom. There were six smiths in the city, each of whom gave 1*d.* for his forge. Each of them made 120 shoes from the king's iron, and to each of them 3*d.* was customarily paid on that account, and these smiths were quit of all other custom. Seven moneyers were there; one of them was the bishop's moneyer. When the coinage was changed, each of them gave 18*s.*to obtain the dies, and from the day on which they returned each of them gave the king 20*s*. for one month; and in the same way the bishop had 20*s*. from his moneyer. When the king came to the city, the moneyers made for him as many pennies as he wished—that is to say, of the king's silver. And these seven had their *sac* and *soc*. When any moneyer of the king died, the king had 20*s*. as relief. But if he died without having divided his cash, the king had all of it. If the sheriff went into Wales with an army, these men [of Hereford] went with him. But if any one was summoned to go and did not do so, he paid 40*s*. fine to the king.

In this city Earl Harold had 27 burgesses enjoying the same customs as the other burgesses. From this city the reeve rendered £12 to King Edward and £6 to Earl Harold, and he had in his farm all the aforesaid customs. The king, however, had in his demesne three forfeitures: namely, breach of his peace, housebreaking, and assault by ambush. Whoever committed one of these [offenses] paid the king 100*s*. fine, whosesoever man he was. Now the king has the city of Hereford in demesne, and the English burgesses who dwell there have their previous customs. The French burgesses, however, are quit, through [payment of] 12*d*., of all forfeitures except the three aforesaid. This city renders to the king £ 60 by tale in assayed money. Between the city and the eighteen manors that render their farms in Hereford £335. 18*s*. are accounted for, besides the pleas of the hundred and county [courts] . . . .

Here are set down those holding lands in Herefordshire. . . .

The land of the king. . . . The king holds Leominster. Queen Edith held it. . . . In this manor . . . there were 80 hides, and in demesne 30 ploughs. In it were 8 reeves, 8 beadles, 8 ridingmen, 238 villeins, 75 bordars, and 82 serfs and bondwomen. These together had 230 ploughs. The villeins ploughed 140 acres of the lord's land and sowed it with their own seed grain, and by custom they paid £11. 52*d*. The ridingmen paid 14*s*. 4*d*. and 3 sesters of honey; and there were eight mills [with an income] of 73*s*. and 30 sticks of eels. The wood rendered 24*s*. besides pannage. Now in this manor the king has in demesne 60 hides and 29 ploughs; and 6 priests, 6 ridingmen, 7 reeves, 7 beadles, 224 villeins, 81 bordars, and 25 serfs and bondwomen. Among them all they have 201 ploughs. They plough and sow with their own grain 125 acres, and by custom they pay £7. 14*s*. 8½*d*.; also 17*s*. [worth] of fish, 8*s*. of salt, and 65*s*. of honey. In it are eight mills [with an income] of 108*s*. and 100 sticks of eels less 10. A wood 6 leagues long and 3 leagues wide renders 22*s*. Of these shillings 5 are paid for buying wood at Droitwich, and thence are obtained 30 mitts of salt. Each villein possessing ten pigs gives one pig for pannage. From woodland brought under cultivation come 17*s*. 4*d*. An eyrie of hawks is there. . . . Altogether this revenue, except the eels, is computed at £23. 2*s*. This manor is at farm for £60 in addition to the maintenance of the nuns. The county says that, if it were freed [of that obligation], this manor would be worth six score, that is to say, £120.

12

Turgot, *The Life of St. Margaret* (c. 1110). A Medieval British Woman

St. Margaret (c. 1046–1093) is important to the history of both England and Scotland. Through her daughter, Matilda, who married Henry I, the royal blood of the Anglo-Saxon line returned again to England, from whence it had been banished by the Norman Conquest. And Margaret's influence in Scotland brought a degree of culture and civility to that rough and backward kingdom. Her father, Edward the Exile, was the son of Edmund Ironside, who lost the kingdom of England to Canute after the death of his father, Ethelred the Unready (978–1016). Margaret, though born in Hungary of a German mother, from the age of about eleven was educated at the court of Edward the Confessor (1042–1066). After her brother, Edgar the Atheling, lost out to Harold Godwinson and then to William the Conqueror, Margaret and her family fled to Scotland in 1067. In 1069, she married the king of Scotland, Malcolm III, Canmore (meaning "great head or chief") (1057–1093), who became king in 1057 when he defeated and killed Macbeth, later made famous by William Shakespeare. Three of her sons, all of whom had English names, became kings of Scotland.

Thanks to Turgot, Margaret's confessor as well as the prior of Durham and later the bishop of St. Andrews, we probably know more about Margaret than any other woman so far back in British history. Though he wrote more in the fashion of a medieval hagiographer than a modern biographer, Margaret's character and her achievements stand out. She introduced Benedictine monks into the monastery at Dunfermline and helped push the Scottish church away from its Celtic past and into the mainstream of European Catholicism. She brought refinements to the court life of Scotland and helped bring Scotland more in line with England. She was proclaimed a saint in 1249. In Margaret we see a woman of education and culture playing an active role in the life of her time, neither a domestic drudge nor a mere ornament of court. Following the lead of Turgot, a twentieth-century biographer has

Source: Turgot, *The Life of St Margaret, Queen of Scotland,* edited by William Forbes-Leith, third edition, Edinburgh: David Douglas, 1896, pp. 27–29, 31–33, 37–40.

described Margaret as "one of those strong, interfering, pious and persistent women of whom England has successfully bred a considerable number."

§7 Whilst Margaret was yet in the flower of youth, she began to lead a very strict life, to love God above all things, to employ herself in the study of the Divine writings, and therein with joy to exercise her mind. Her understanding was keen to comprehend any matter, whatever it might be; to this was joined a great tenacity of memory, enabling her to store it up, along with a graceful flow of language to express it.

§8 While thus she was meditating upon the law of the Lord day and night, and, like another Mary sitting at His feet, delighted to hear His word, rather in obedience to the will of her friends than to her own, yea by the appointment of God, she was married to Malcolm, son of King Duncan, the most powerful king of the Scots. But although she was compelled to do as the world does, she thought it beneath her dignity to fix her affection upon the things of the world, and thus good works delighted her more than riches. By means of her temporal possession she earned for herself the rewards of heaven; for there, where her heart was, she had placed her treasure also. And since before all things she sought the kingdom of God and His justice, the bountiful grace of the Almighty freely added to her honours and riches in abundance. This prudent queen directed all such things as it was fitting for her to regulate; the laws of the realm were administered by her counsel; by her care the influence of religion was extended, and the people rejoiced in the prosperity of their affairs. Nothing was firmer than her fidelity, steadier than her favour, or juster than her decisions; nothing was more enduring than her patience, graver than her advice, or more pleasant than her conversation.

§9 She had no sooner attained this eminent dignity, than she built an eternal memorial of her name and devotion in the place where her nuptials had been held. The noble church which she erected there in honour of the Holy Trinity was to serve a threefold purpose; it was intended for the redemption of the king's soul, for the good of her own, and for securing to her children prosperity in the present life and in that which is to come. This church she beautified with rich gifts of various kinds. . . .

§10 These works were entrusted to certain women of noble birth and approved gravity of manners, who were thought worthy of a part in the queen's service. No men were admitted among them, with the exception only of such as she permitted to enter along with herself when she paid the women an occasional visit. No giddy pertness was allowed in them, no light familiarity between them and men; for the queen united so much strictness with her sweetness of temper, so great pleasantness even with her severity, that all who waited upon her, men as well as women, loved her while they feared her, and in fearing loved her. Thus it came to pass that when she was present no one ventured to utter even one unseemly word, much less to do aught that was objectionable. There was a gravity in her very joy, and something stately in her anger. With her, mirth never expressed itself in fits of laughter, nor did displeasure kindle into fury. Sometimes she chid the faults of others—her own always—using that commendable severity tempered with justice which the Psalmist directs us unceasingly to employ, when he says, "Be ye angry, and sin not." Every action of her life was regulated by the balance of the nicest discretion, which impressed its own distinctive character upon each single virtue. When she spoke, her conversation was seasoned with the salt of wisdom; when she was silent, her silence was filled with good thoughts. So thoroughly did her outward bearing correspond with the staidness of her character that it seemed as if she had been from her very birth the pattern of a virtuous life. In fact, I may say, every word which she uttered, every act which she performed, shewed that she was meditating upon the things of heaven.

§11 Nor was she less careful about her children than she was about herself. She took all heed that they should be well brought up, and especially that they should be trained in virtue. Knowing that it is written: "He that spareth the rod hateth his son," she charged the governor who had the care of the nursery to curb the children, to scold them, and to whip them whenever they were naughty, as frolicsome childhood will often be. Thanks to their mother's religious care, her children surpassed in good behaviour many who were their elders; they were always affectionate and peaceable among themselves, and everywhere the younger paid due respect to the elder. . . .

§12 Nor need we wonder that the queen governed herself and her household wisely when we know that she acted always under the wisest of masters, the guidance of the Holy Scriptures. I myself have had frequent opportunities of admiring in her how, even amidst the distractions of lawsuits, amidst the countless cares of state, she devoted herself with wonderful assiduity to the study of the word of God, respecting which she used to ask profound questions from the learned men who were sitting near her. But just as no one among them possessed a deeper intellect than herself, so none had the power of clearer expression. Thus it very often happened that these doctors went from her much wiser men than when they came. She sought with a religious earnestness for those sacred volumes, and oftentimes her affectionate familiarity with me moved me to exert myself to obtain them for her use. Not that in doing this she cared for her own salvation only; she desired that of others also.

§13 First of all in regard to King Malcolm: by the help of God she made him most attentive to the works of justice, mercy, almsgiving, and other virtues. From her he learnt how to keep the vigils of the night in constant prayer; she instructed him by her exhortation and example how to pray to God with groanings from the heart and abundance of tears. I was astonished, I confess, at this great miracle of God's mercy when I perceived in the king such a steady earnestness in his devotion, and I wondered how it was that there could exist in the heart of a man living in the world such an entire sorrow for sin. There was in him a sort of dread of offending one whose life was so venerable; for he could not but perceive from her conduct that Christ dwelt within her; nay, more, he readily obeyed her wishes and prudent counsels in all things. Whatever she refused, he refused also; whatever pleased her, he also loved for the love of her. Hence it was that, although he could not read, he would turn over and examine books which she used either for her devotions or her study; and whenever he heard her express especial liking for a particular book, he also would look at it with special interest, kissing it, and often taking it into his hands. Sometimes he sent for a worker in precious metals, whom he commanded to ornament that volume with gold and gems, and when the work was finished, the king himself used to carry the book to the queen as a loving proof of his devotion.

13
Establishment of the King's Household (c. 1135)

This document is what it appears to be: a list of the pay and allowances due various members of the king's household. Someone from the court of Henry I (1100–1135) prepared it for Stephen (1135–1154) shortly after he came to the throne. Its importance lies in the light it sheds on the king's management of his personal household and, more important, of his kingdom.

Norman kings had, like all feudal lords, a court that their tenants-in-chief were obliged to attend. This great council, meeting each year at Christmas, Easter, and Whitsuntide, discussed major problems and projects such as the Domesday survey. More obscure is the king's personal or household staff and its relationship to the small council, or curia regis, in theory indistinct from the great council but in practice containing only those men needed to run the government on a day-to-day basis. Between the small council and the household there was considerable overlap of personnel and functions; it was only natural for the king to rely on those who were at hand and whose talents he knew. Thus, the curia regis was formed largely from the household, and the household was the training ground for royal administrators. In time some officials left the household completely. For example, the chancellor began as the king's priest and confessor, later became his personal secretary, and eventually headed the secretarial staff of the royal government. This development produced conflicts between household officers who had already become public officials (e.g., the chancellor and the treasurer) and servants, specifically from the chamber and wardrobe, whose relationship with the king remained more personal. It was a problem in the Middle Ages, as well as now, to distinguish government officials from personal servants of the king.

Although the original manuscript has been lost, the document survived by being appended to two thirteenth-century copies of *The Dialogue of the Exchequer.*

Source: The Course of the Exchequer by Richard, Son of Nigel, translated and edited by Charles Johnson, London: Thomas Nelson and Sons, Ltd., 1950, pp. 129–130, 132–133. By permission of Oxford University Press.

THIS IS THE ESTABLISHMENT OF THE KING'S HOUSEHOLD PAY AND ALLOWANCES

Chancery and Chapel

Chancellor. 5*s.* a day, and one superior and two salt simnels, one sextary of dessert wine, and one of *vin ordinaire,* one large wax candle and forty candle-ends.

Master of the Writing-Chamber. Originally 10*d.* a day, and one salt simnel, and half a sextary of *vin ordinaire,* and one large candle and twenty-four candle-ends. But King Henry so increased Robert de Sigillo, that on the day of the King's death he had 2*s.*, and one sextary of *vin ordinaire,* and one salt simnel, and one small wax candle and twenty-four candle-ends.

Chaplain—in charge of the chapel and relics. Diet for two men. And four serjeants of the chapel, each double rations. And two sumpter-horses of the chapel, each 1*d.* a day, and a penny a month for shoeing them. For the chapel service, two wax candles on Wednesday and two on Saturday, and every night one wax candle before the relics, and thirty candle-ends, and one gallon of dessert wine for mass, and one gallon of *vin ordinaire* on Holy Thursday to wash the altar. On Easter day at communion, one sextary of dessert wine and one of *vin ordinaire.*

Steward's Department

Sewers. Sewers as the Chancellor, if they eat out. If indoors, 3*s.* 6*d.,* two salt simnels, one sextary of *vin ordinaire* and candles at discretion.

Clerk of the Spence of bread and wine. 2*s.* a day, and a salt simnel, and one sextary of *vin ordinaire,* and one small wax candle and twenty-four candle-ends.

Pantry

Dispensers of bread. The master-dispenser of bread, a permanent officer, if he eats out-of-doors, 2*s.* 10*d.* a day, and one salt simnel, one sextary of *vin ordinaire,* one small wax candle and twenty-four candle-ends. But if indoors, 2*s.*a day, half a sextary of *vin ordinaire* and candles at discretion.

Dispensers serving in turn. If out-of-doors, 19*d.* a day, one salt simnel, one sextary of *vin ordinaire,* one large candle and twenty candle-ends. If indoors, 10*d.,* half a sextary of *vin ordinaire* and candles at discretion.

Chamber

The *Master-Chamberlain's* livery is the same as that of a sewer. The *Treasurer* as the Master-Chamberlian, if he is at Court and serves in the Treasury. William

Mauduit 14*d.* a day; and shall eat permanently in the house, and have one large candle and fourteen ends, and two sumpter-horses with their liveries.

The *Bearer of the King's Bed* shall eat in the house, and have three halfpence a day for his man, and one sumpter-horse with its livery. A *Chamberlain* serving in his turn, 2*s.* a day, one salt simnel, and sextary of *vin ordinaire,* one small wax candle and twenty-four candle-ends. The *Chamberlain of the Chandlery:* 8*d.* a day, and half a sextary of *vin ordinaire.* The *King's Tailor* shall eat in his own house, and have three halfpence a day for his man. A *Chamberlain* without livery [i.e. not on duty] shall eat in the house, if he wishes. The *Ewer* has double diet; and when the King goes on a journey, 1*d.* for drying the King's clothes; and when the King bathes, 4*d.* except on the three great feasts of the year. The wages of the *Laundress* are in doubt.

14
The Assize of Clarendon (1166). Royal Justice in the Twelfth Century

The term "assize" means not only a sitting or session of a court or council, but also the enactment of that sitting. The Assize of Clarendon, produced by Henry II (1154–1189) and his great council in 1166, ordered members of the king's council acting as itinerant justices to convert the old Anglo-Saxon county courts into royal courts and thereby to enforce the king's will throughout the whole countryside. To strengthen the faltering Anglo-Saxon system of accusation by personal appeal, the assize expanded the use of the sworn inquest, now literally an accusation or grand jury. An indictment resulting from the action of a sworn inquest represented an accusation by the entire community. Those accused would still "make their law," that is, be tried by the traditional ordeal of hot water or hot iron.

This assize, extended and regularized by the Assize of Northampton (1176), was no doubt a product of the moment, a vigorous king's answer to immediate problems. The aptness of

Source: Sources of English Constitutional History, edited and translated by Carl Stephenson and Frederick George Marcham, pp. 76–79.

Henry's response is demonstrated by its immediate success and by the jury's becoming a fundamental part of the English legal system. The grand jury's accusations soon gained greater credence than the ordeal's acquittals. The rapidly expanding royal courts and a uniform law common to all of England quickly eroded the traditional jurisdictions not only of Anglo-Saxon courts but of the feudal courts as well. On the one hand, Henry's bold innovations promoted efficiency in government and provided law and order; on the other, they were an enhancement of royal power and revenue at the expense of ancient rights and privileges.

HERE BEGINS THE ASSIZE OF CLARENDON MADE BY KING HENRY, NAMELY THE SECOND, WITH THE ASSENT OF THE ARCHBISHOPS, BISHOPS, ABBOTS, EARLS, AND BARONS OF ALL ENGLAND

1 In the first place the aforesaid King Henry, by the counsel of all his barons, has ordained that, for the preservation of peace and the enforcement of justice, inquiry shall be made in every county and in every hundred through twelve of the more lawful men of the hundred and through four of the more lawful men of each vill, [put] on oath to tell the truth, whether in their hundred or in their vill there is any man accused or publicly known as a robber or murderer or thief, or any one who has been a receiver of robbers or murderers or thieves, since the lord king has been king. And let the justices make this investigation in their presence and the sheriffs in their presence.

2 And whoever is found by the oath of the aforesaid men to have been accused or publicly known as a robber or murderer or thief, or as a receiver of them since the lord king has been king, shall be seized; and he shall go to the ordeal of water and swear that, to the value of 5*s*., so far as he knows, he has not been a robber or murderer or thief, or a receiver of them, since the lord king has been king.

9 And let there be no one . . . who forbids the sheriffs to enter upon his jurisdiction or his land for view of frankpledge; and let all men be placed under sureties, and let them be sent before the sheriffs under frankpledge.

10 And within cities or boroughs no one shall have men, or shall receive [men] without his house or his land or his soke for whom he will not be sponsor, [guaranteeing] that he will bring them before the justice, should they be summoned, or that they are under frankpledge.

11 And let there be no persons . . . who forbid the sheriffs to enter upon their land or their soke for the purpose of seizing those who have been accused or publicly known as robbers or murderers or thieves, or receivers of them, or outlaws, or those accused under forest [law]; on the contrary, [the king] commands them to give assistance in seizing those [suspects].

12 And if any one is seized who possesses [the proceeds] of robbery or theft, should he be a notorious person and have a bad reputation, and should he not have a warrantor, let him not have his law. And if he is not notorious, let him, on account of his [suspicious] possessions, go to the [ordeal of] water.

13 And if any one, in the presence of lawful men or of a hundred [court], has confessed robbery or murder or theft, or the reception of those [who have committed such crimes], and should he then wish to deny it, let him not have his law.

14 The lord king also wills that those who make their law and are cleared by the law, if they are of very bad reputation, being publicly and shamefully denounced by the testimony of many lawful men, shall abjure the lands of the king, so that they shall cross the sea within eight days unless they are detained by the wind; then, with the first [favourable] wind that they have, they shall cross the sea and thenceforth not return to England, except at the mercy of the lord king; [so that] they shall there be outlaws and shall be seized as outlaws if they return.

19 And the lord king wills that, as soon as the sheriffs have received the summons of the itinerant justices to come before the latter together with [the courts of] their counties, they shall bring together [the courts of] their counties and make inquiry concerning all who recently, after this assize, have come into their counties; and they shall put those [newcomers] under pledge to appear before the justices, or they shall guard those [newcomers] until the justices come to them, and then they shall bring [the newcomers] before the justices.

15

William of Newburgh, *History of England* (c. 1198). The Becket Controversy, 1170

The struggle between Henry II (1154–1189) and Archbishop Thomas Becket, ending with Becket's murder in Canterbury Cathedral in 1170, captured and still holds the imagination of the general public. Their rivalry was largely the result of the conflict between the church and the state, in England going back to the Norman Conquest. Two major issues contributed to the conflict. First was the Investiture Controversy over who should appoint the bishops and invest them with the symbols of office. In England, this issue had been settled in 1107: the Church would invest those who, in fact, were selected by the king. Second was the question of the jurisdiction of church courts. In 1164, Henry II asserted in the Constitutions of Clarendon the power of royal courts over churchmen accused of secular crimes—the criminous clerks. Becket championed, and by his death won, the right of the Church to try its own. Fundamental to these specific disputes was the question of ultimate authority in medieval society. Viewed in this light, the Becket controversy represented one in a series of challenges to the growth of royal authority.

William of Newburgh (c. 1135–1198) was born in Yorkshire and was educated at the Augustinian priory at Newburgh, where he returned in 1182 after deserting his wealthy wife. There he wrote his justly famous *Historia Rerum Anglicarum,* a study of England from the Conquest to 1197. The most remarkable thing about William is not his accuracy or his style but the characteristics he shares with modern historians. He attempted to subject earlier writers and contemporary historical evidence to critical analysis. He sought to present his material topically rather than simply listing it chronologically. Finally, he tried to be impartial in his treatment of controversial events. In the following section he recognizes the underlying causes as well as the personality conflicts leading to the break between Henry II and Becket.

The Latin text of William's work was, like most important medieval chronicles, published in the Rolls Series.

Source: The History of William of Newburgh, translated by Joseph Stevenson, in *The Church Historians of England,* vol. IV, part II (London, Seeleys, 1856), pp. 478–481.

In the year one thousand one hundred and seventy from the delivery of the Virgin, which was the seventeenth of the reign of Henry the second, the king caused his son Henry, yet a youth, to be solemnly anointed and crowned king at London, by the hands of Roger, archbishop of York. For the king not being yet appeased, the venerable Thomas, archbishop of Canterbury, was still an exile in France, though the Roman pontiff and the king of France had interested themselves extremely to bring about a reconciliation. The moment Thomas heard of this transaction, jealous for his church, he quickly informed the pope of it (by whose favour and countenance he was supported), alleging that this had taken place to the prejudice of himself and his see: and he obtained letters of severe rebuke, for the purpose of correcting equally the archbishop of York, who had performed the office in another's province, and the bishops, who, by their presence, had sanctioned it. The king, however, continued but a short time in England after the coronation of his son, and went beyond sea; and when urged by the frequent admonitions of the pope, and the earnest entreaties of the illustrious king of France, that he would, at least, condescend to be reconciled to the dignified exile, after a seven years' banishment, he at length yielded; and a solemn reconciliation took place between them, which was the more desired and the more grateful in proportion to the time of its protraction. While the king, therefore, continued abroad, the archbishop, by royal grant and permission, returned to his diocese; having in his possession, unknown to the king, letters obtained from the pope against the archbishop of York, and the other prelates who had assisted at that most unfortunate coronation; which was the means of breaking the recently concluded peace, and had become the incentive to greater rage. . . .

The bishops, on account of the offence before mentioned (which I could wish to have remained unnoticed at the time), being suspended, at the instance of the venerable Thomas, from all episcopal functions, by the authority of the apostolic see, the king was exasperated by the complaints of some of them, and grew angry and indignant beyond measure, and losing the mastery of himself, in the heat of his exuberant passion, from the abundance of his perturbed spirit, poured forth the language of indiscretion. On which, four of the bystanders, men of noble race and renowned in arms, wrought themselves up to the commission of iniquity through zeal for their earthly master; and leaving the royal presence, and crossing the sea, with as much haste as if posting to a solemn banquet, and urged on by the fury they had imbibed, they arrived at Canterbury on the fifth day after Christmas, where they found the venerable archbishop occupied in the celebration of that holy festival with religious joy. Proceeding to him just as he had dined, and was sitting with certain honourable personages, omitting even to salute him, and holding forth the terror of the king's name, they commanded (rather than asked, or admonished him) forthwith to remit the suspension of the prelates who had obeyed the king's pleasure, to whose contempt and disgrace this act redounded. On his replying that the sentence of a higher power was not to be abrogated by an inferior one, and that it was not his concern to pardon persons suspended not by himself, but by the Roman pontiff, they had recourse to violent threats. Undismayed at these words, though uttered by men raging and extremely exasperated, he spoke with singular freedom and confidence. In consequence, becoming more enraged than before, they hastily retired, and bringing their arms, (for they had entered without them,) they prepared themselves, with loud clamour and indignation, for the commission of a most atrocious crime. The venerable prelate was persuaded by his friends to avoid the madness of these furious savages, by retiring into the holy church. When, from his determination to brave every danger, he did not acquiesce, on the forcible and tumultuous approach of his enemies, he was at length dragged by the friendly violence of his associates to the protection of the holy church. The monks were solemnly chanting vespers to Almighty God, as he entered the sacred temple of Christ, shortly to become an evening sacrifice. The servants of Satan pursued having neither respect as Christians to his holy order, nor to the sacred place, or season; but attacking the dignified prelate as he stood in prayer before the holy altar, even during the festival of Christmas, these truly nefarious Christians most inhumanly murdered him. Having done the deed, and retiring as if triumphant, they departed with unhallowed joy. Recollecting, however, that perhaps the transaction might displease the person in whose behalf they had been so zealous, they retired to the northern parts of England, waiting until they could fully discover the disposition of their monarch towards them.

The frequent miracles which ensued manifested how precious, in the sight of God, was the death of the blessed prelate, and how great the atrocity of the crime committed against him, in the circumstances of time, place, and person. Indeed, the report of such a dreadful outrage, quickly pervading every district of the western world, sullied the illustrious king of England, and so obscured his fair fame among Christian potentates, that, as it could scarcely be credited to have been perpetrated without his consent and mandate, he was assailed by the execrations of almost all, and deemed fit to be the object of general detestation. . . .

Whilst almost all persons then attributed the death of this holy man to the king, and more especially the French nobles, who had been jealous of his good fortune, were instigating the apostolical see against him, as the true and undoubted author of this great enormity, the king sent representatives to Rome, to mitigate, by submissive entreaty, the displeasure which was raging against him. When they arrived at Rome, (as all men joined in execrating the king of England,) it was with difficulty that they were admitted. Constantly affirming, however, that this dreadful outrage was not committed either by the command or concurrence of their master, they, at length, obtained, that legates *a latere* from the pope, vested with full power, should be sent into France, who, on carefully investigating, and ascertaining the truth of the matter, should admit the king either to the purgation of his fame, or punish him, if found guilty, by ecclesiastical censure, which was done accordingly. . . . Indeed, he did not deny that those murderers had, perhaps, taken occasion and daring to their excessive fury from some words of his too incautiously uttered; when, hearing of the suspension of the prelates, he became infuriated, and spake unadvisedly. "And, on this account," said he, "I do not refuse the discipline of the Church: I will submit devotedly to whatever you decree, and I will fulfil your injunction." Saying this, and casting off his clothes, after the custom of public penitents, he submitted himself naked to ecclesiastical discipline. The cardinals, overjoyed at the humility of so great a prince, and weeping with joy, while numbers joined their tears, and gave praise to God, dissolved the assembly,—the king's conscience being quieted, and his character in some measure restored. Richard, prior of Dover, then succeeded the blessed Thomas in the see of Canterbury.

16
Richard FitzNigel, *The Dialogue of the Exchequer* (c. 1179)

As treasurer of England, Richard FitzNigel was well qualified to play the part of the "Master" in his dialogue describing the form and function of the exchequer. The exchequer, which met at Easter and at Michaelmas to receive and to audit accounts due the king, had two parts. The lower exchequer received and assayed the monies and issued receipts in the form of wooden tallies (see Plate A), sticks notched to indicate pounds, shillings, and pence and then split to give the sheriff and the treasury identifiable, duplicate copies. These quaint tallies, stored in the basement of the House of Commons, were lost when that building burned in 1834. The upper exchequer, the exchequer of account, consisted of a table covered with a checkered cloth, around which sat members of the king's small council, special exchequer officials, and the sheriff whose account was being audited. The abacus-like tablecloth facilitated computations in Roman numerals and allowed even an illiterate sheriff readily to see the status of his account. The results of the audit became an entry in the Pipe Roll such as the following: "Miles of Gloucester accounts for 80 pounds and 14

Source: The Course of the Exchequer by Richard, Son of Nigel, translated and edited by Charles Johnson, London: Thomas Nelson and Sons, Ltd., 1950, pp. 3, 6–8, 24–25. By permission of Oxford University Press.

pence. . . . He has paid this in the Treasury. And he is quit." The exchequer's development can be seen from the surviving annual Pipe Rolls—one in 1130 under Henry I and then nothing until the nearly continuous series that began in 1155 under Henry II.

Besides the intriguing technical details of the exchequer's operations, the most interesting feature of its development is the role it played in the creation of a central royal bureaucracy. The upper exchequer, which began as a special function of the small council, soon split off to become a specialized department. This recurring process of development was confirmed by the central common law courts. The early history of the exchequer, as described by Richard FitzNigel, forms an important chapter in the creation of the best organized and most efficient government in western Europe.

Three basic manuscript copies of the *Dialogue,* once belonging to various officials of the exchequer, are now deposited in the Public Record Office and the British Library.

The Exchequer has its own rules. They are not arbitrary, but rest on the decisions of great men; and if they are observed scrupulously, individuals will get their rights, and Your Majesty will receive in full the revenue due to the Treasury, which your generous hand, obeying your noble mind, may spend to the best advantage. . . .

PLATE A
Exchequer tallies (by permission of the Public Record Office, London).

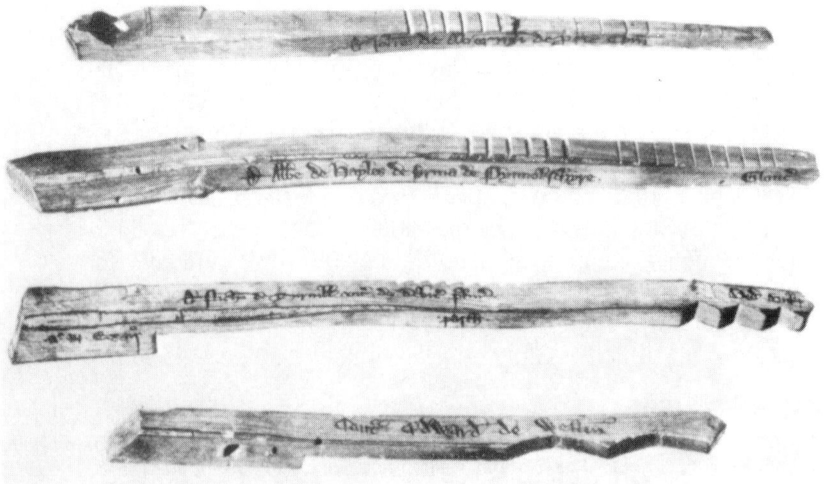

Scholar: What is the Exchequer?

Master: The exchequer [*chess-board*] is an oblong board measuring about ten feet by five, used as a table by those who sit at it, and with a rim round it about four finger-breadths in height, to prevent anything set on it from falling off. Over the [*upper*] exchequer is spread a cloth, bought in Eastern term, of a special pattern, black, ruled with lines a foot, or a full span, apart. In the spaces between them are placed the counters, in their ranks, as will be explained in another place. But though such a board is called "exchequer," the name is transferred to the Court in session at it; so that if a litigant wins his case, or a decision on any point is taken by common consent, it is said to have happened "at the Exchequer" of such a year. But where we now say "at the Exchequer," they used to say "at the Tallies."

Scholar: Why is the Court so called?

Master: I can think, for the moment, of no better reason than that it resembles a chess-board.

Scholar: Was its shape the only reason why our wise forefathers gave it that name? For they might equally well have called it a draught-board.

Master: I was justified in calling you "precise." There is another less obvious reason. For as on the chess-board the men are arranged in ranks, and move or stand by definite rules and restrictions, some pieces in the foremost rank and others in the foremost position; here, too, some [*the barons*] preside, others assist *ex officio*, and nobody is free to overstep the appointed laws, as will appear later. Again, just as on a chess-board, battle is joined between the kings; here too the struggle takes place, and battle is joined, mainly between two persons, to wit, the Treasurer and the Sheriff who sits at his account, while the rest sit by as judges to see and decide.

Scholar: Does the Treasurer really take the account when there are many present who appear by reason of their power to be more important?

Master: It is obvious that the Treasurer takes the account from the Sheriff, because it is from him that an account is required when the King so pleases. Nor would that be demanded of him unless he had received it. . . .

Scholar: Is the Exchequer where this conflict takes place the only Exchequer?

Master: No. For there is a Lower Exchequer, also called the Receipt, where the money received is counted and entered on rolls and tallies, in order that the account may be made up from them in the Upper Exchequer. But both spring from the same root, because whatever is found in the Upper Exchequer to be due, is paid in the Lower, and what is paid in the Lower is credited in the Upper. . . .

Master: [In the Upper Exchequer] sits the man who, by the King's command, makes out the account, using coins for counters. It is a confusing and laborious process, and without it the business of the Exchequer would be interminable, or nearly so. But it is not the specific duty of any officer sitting at the Exchequer unless the King or the Justiciar has committed the task to him. I call it laborious, because every other official duty is carried out by using the tongue or the hand or both. But in this:

Tongue, eyes, hand and restless brain
Work with all their might and main

But the system of this is according to the usual course of the Exchequer, not by the rules of Arabian arithmetic. You remember my saying, I imagine, that a cloth is laid on the Exchequer table ruled with lines, and that the coins used as counters are placed in the spaces between them. The Accountant sits in the middle of his side of the table, so that everybody can see him, and so that his hand can move freely at his work. In the lowest space, on the right, he places the heap of the pence, eleven or fewer. In the second the shillings, up to nineteen. In the third he puts the pounds; and this column should be directly in front of him, because it is the centre column in the Sheriff's usual accounts. In the fourth is the heap of the scores of pounds. In the fifth, hundreds, in the sixth, thousands, in the seventh, but rarely, tens of thousands. I say "rarely"; that is, when an account of the whole receipt of the realm is taken by the King, or by the magnates of the realm at his command from the Treasurer and Chamberlains. The Accountant may substitute a silver halfpenny for ten shillings, and a gold one for ten pounds for convenience in counting. But he must take care that his hand does not outrun his tongue or *vice versa;* but as he reckons, he must put out the counters and state the number simultaneously, lest there should be a mistake in the number. So, when the sum demanded of the Sheriff has been set out in heaps of counters, the payments made into the Treasury or otherwise are similarly set out in heaps underneath. If the demand made on him is for a farm or other debt payable "by tale," the lower line is simply subtracted from the upper, and the Sheriff will be liable for the remainder.

17

Rannulf Glanvill, *Treatise on the Laws and Customs of the Realm of England* (c. 1189)

Whether Rannulf Glanvill, Henry II's justiciar from 1180 to 1189, was the author of this *Treatise* is uncertain. Written late in his tenure as justiciar, it has been attributed to him for so long that it is commonly referred to simply as "Glanvill."

"Glanvill" is the first textbook on English common law. Where earlier there had been separate laws of Wessex, Mercia, and the Danelaw and a host of local peculiarities, by Glanvill's time a royal law common to all of England was rapidly taking shape. Unlike on the continent, where the emphasis was on the study of Roman and canon law, in England the major concern was the expansion of royal justice at the expense of old local and feudal courts, as in Henry II's Assizes of Clarendon and Northampton.

It was the purpose of the author of "Glanvill" to do for the judicial part of Henry II's administration what Richard FitzNigel had done for the fiscal, to describe its workings in a straightforward and intelligible manner. He stressed the importance of royal writs, in bringing cases before the courts and in enforcing their decisions, and of the jury, the sworn inquest, in presenting the facts and deciding the case. The passage below, which deals with one of the possessory assizes, illustrates this.

Also significant is Glanvill's assertion that the laws of England were unwritten. By describing the earliest processes and functions of the common law, he contributed both to its development and to its survival as a discrete system from that day to this. Anyone seeking to understand the original workings of the common law has of necessity begun with "Glanvill." More than 30 manuscript copies of the *Treatise* exist. The first printed edition appeared in 1554.

Here begins the treatise on the laws and customs of the realm of England, composed in the time of King Henry the Second when justice was under the direction

Source: *The Treatise on the Laws and Customs of the Realm of England, commonly called Glanvill,* ed. G. D. G. Hall, London: Nelson, in Association with the Selden Society, 1965, pp. 1–3, 148–153.

of the illustrious Rannulf Glanvill, the most learned of that time in the law and ancient customs of the realm.

Prologue

Not only must royal power be furnished with arms against rebels and nations which rise up against the king and the realm, but it is also fitting that it should be adorned with laws for the governance of subject and peaceful peoples; so that in time of both peace and war our glorious king may so successfully perform his office that, crushing the pride of the unbridled and ungovernable with the right hand of strength and tempering justice for the humble and meek with the rod of equity, he may both be always victorious in wars with his enemies and also show himself continually impartial in dealing with his subjects.

No one doubts how finely, how vigorously, how skillfully our most excellent king has practised armed warfare against the malice of his enemies in time of hostilities, for now his praise has gone out to all the earth and his mighty works to all the borders of the world. Nor is there any dispute how justly and how mercifully, how prudently he, who is the author and lover of peace, has behaved towards his subjects in time of peace, for his Highness's court is so impartial that no judge there is so shameless or audacious as to presume to turn aside at all from the path of justice or to digress in any respect from the way of truth. For there, indeed, a poor man is not oppressed by the power of his adversary, nor does favour or partiality drive any man away from the threshold of judgment. For truly he does not scorn to be guided by the laws and customs of the realm which had their origin in reason and have long prevailed; and, what is more, he is even guided by those of his subjects most learned in the laws and customs of the realm whom he knows to excel all others in sobriety, wisdom and eloquence, and whom he has found to be most prompt and clearsighted in deciding cases on the basis of justice and in settling disputes, acting now with severity and now with leniency as seems expedient to them.

Although the laws of England are not written, it does not seem absurd to call them laws—those, that is, which are known to have been promulgated about problems settled in council on the advice of the magnates and with the supporting authority of the prince—for this also is a law, that "what pleases the prince has the force of law." For if, merely for lack of writing, they were not deemed to be laws, then surely writing would seem to supply to written laws a force of greater authority than either the justice of him who decrees them or the reason of him who establishes them.

It is, however, utterly impossible for the laws and legal rules of the realm to be wholly reduced to writing in our time, both because of the ignorance of scribes and because of the confused multiplicity of those same laws and rules. But there are some general rules frequently observed in court which it does not seem to me presumptuous to commit to writing, but rather very useful for most people and highly necessary to aid the memory. I have decided to put into writing at least a small part of these general rules, adopting intentionally a commonplace style and words used in court in order to provide knowledge of them for those who are not versed in this kind of inelegant language.

[Book XIII]

THE VARIOUS KINDS OF RECOGNITION

So far the questions which most often arise in pleas about right have been dealt with. There remain for discussion those which are concerned with seisin only. By virtue of a constitution of the realm called an assize these questions are for the most part settled by recognition, and therefore the various kinds of recognition must now be considered.

One kind of recognition is called mort d'ancestor. Another concerns the last presentation of parsons to churches; another, whether a tenement is ecclesiastical or lay fee.

There is also the recognition called novel disseisin.

When anyone dies seised of a free tenement, if he was seised in his demesne as of fee, then his heir can lawfully claim the seisin which his ancestor had, and if he is of full age he shall have the following writ:

THE WRIT OF MORT D'ANCESTOR

The king to the sheriff, greeting. If G. son of O. gives you security for prosecuting his claim, then summon by good summoners twelve free and lawful men from the neighbourhood of such-and-such a vill to be before me or my justices on a certain day, ready to declare on oath whether O. the father of the aforesaid G. was seised in his demesne as of his fee of one virgate of land in that vill on the day he died, whether he died after my first coronation, and whether the said G. is his next heir. And meanwhile let them view the land; and you are to see that their names are endorsed on this writ. And summon by good summoners R., who holds that land, to be there then to hear the recognition. And have there the summoners and this writ. Witness, etc.

THE PROCEDURE LEADING TO THIS ASSIZE

When the sheriff has received the writ of mort d'ancestor and security for prosecuting the claim has been given in the county court, then the procedure leading to the assize is as follows. First, in accordance with the terms of the writ, twelve free and lawful men from the neighbourhood are to be elected in the presence of both demandant and tenant, or even in the absence of the tenant provided he has been summoned at least once to attend the election. He must be summoned once to come and hear who are elected to make the recognition, and he can if he wishes reject some of them for reasonable cause so that they are excluded from the recognition. If, however, he has not come when the first summons is properly attested in court, then he shall be waited for no longer, and in his absence the twelve jurors shall be elected and sent by the sheriff to view the land or other tenement of which seisin is claimed. Here again the tenant shall have one summons only. The sheriff shall see that the name of the elected twelve are endorsed on the writ.

Then the sheriff shall arrange for the tenant to be summoned to be before the king or his justices on the day stated in the writ of the king or his justices, to hear the recognition. If the demandant is of full age, the tenant can essoin himself on the first and second return days but not on the third day, for then the recognition shall be taken whether the tenant comes or not, because no more than two essoins are allowed in any recognition which concerns only seisin. Indeed, in the recognition of novel disseisin no essoin is allowed. On the third return day, then, as stated above, the assize shall be taken whether the tenant has come or not. And if the jurors declare in favour of the demandant, seisin shall be adjudged to him and the sheriff ordered by the following writ to have put in seisin:

THE WRIT FOR DELIVERING SEISIN AFTER THE RECOGNITION

The king to the sheriff, greeting. Know that N. has proved in my court, by a recognition concerning the death of a certain ancestor of his, his right against R. to the seisin of so much land in such-and-such a vill. And therefore I command you to have him put in seisin without delay. Witness, etc.

18
Charter for Bristol (1189). The Rights of Medieval Towns

The charter, first used in Anglo-Saxon times, was a legal instrument granting a privilege or recognizing a right. It is the most important type of document for the study of Anglo-Norman feudalism. Royal charters, usually issued by the chancery, were of two basic kinds: the *diploma,* a long document normally in Latin describing in a formal, stylized manner a grant of great importance, and the *writ* or *writ-charter,* a simpler, more efficient document usually in the vernacular and dealing with a more routine matter. Private charters assumed a variety of forms. Both royal and private charters normally began with an introduction or greeting, proceeded to the terms of the grant itself, and concluded by stating the agreement of all parties. Finally, there was usually a list of witnesses, not necessarily present, and a seal or seals to authenticate the grant.

The charter below, issued in 1189 by John, then count of Mortain (Moreton) but later king (1199–1216), confirmed the privileges Henry II had given to the city of Bristol in 1155. It is typical of the charters granted to the rising towns of the twelfth century, a recognition by the monarch of the importance of their goodwill and wealth, a counterweight to an unruly baronage. The rights and privileges guaranteed to the burgesses of Bristol were those essential for them to carry out their mercantile functions—a separate system of justice, the right to regulate their own economic affairs, and freedom from many of the traditional feudal obligations. Because towns had common needs, their charters tended to be similar. In England, the privileges of Newcastle-upon-Tyne, dating from the reign of Henry I, became a model for other towns, although local conditions inevitably led to many modifications.

A large number of royal and private charters from the twelfth century have been preserved. In 1199 the chancery, in order to have a complete record of grants made, initiated the Charter Rolls, on which all royal charters were copied. In 1201 the *writ-charters,* now called letters patent, were inscribed on the Patent Rolls. These rolls, plus others, such as the Close Rolls (1204), are not

Source: Bristol Charters, 1155–1373, edited by N. Dermott Harding, Bristol Record Society, 1930, pp. 9, 11, 13. First printed by Bristol Record Society.

only of great value to the historian but are another indication of the sophistication of royal government in medieval England.

John, Count of Moreton, to all men and to his friends, French and English, Welsh and Irish, present and to come, greeting. Know ye that I have granted and by this present charter have confirmed to my burgesses of Bristol dwelling within the walls and without the walls unto the metes of the town, to wit, between Sandbrook and Bewell and Brightneebridge and the spring in the way near Aldebury of Knowle, all their liberties and free customs, as well, freely and entirely, or more so, as ever they had them in my time or in the time of any of my predecessors. Now the liberties which have been granted to them are these, to wit:— That no burgess of Bristol shall plead without the walls of the town concerning any plea except pleas of exterior tenements which do not pertain to the Hundred of the town. And that they shall be quit of murder within the metes of the town. And that no burgess shall wage battle except he have been appealed concerning the death of a foreign man who has been killed in the town and who was not of the town. And that no one shall take a hospice within the walls by assize or by livery of the marshals against the will of the burgesses. And that they shall be quit of Toll and Lastage and Passage and Pontage and of all other customs throughout all my land and power. . . . And that the Hundred shall be held only once in the week. . . .

And that they shall have justly their lands and tenures and their pledges and debts throughout all my land whosoever shall owe to them. And that concerning lands and tenures which are within the town, right shall be done to them according to the custom of the town. And that concerning debts which have been contracted in Bristol and concerning pledges made in the same place pleas shall be held in the town, according to the custom of the town. And that if anyone anywhere in my land shall take Toll of the men of Bristol if he have not restored it after he shall have been required to restore [it], the Prepositor of Bristol shall take thereupon a distress at Bristol and shall destrain to restore [it]. And that no strange merchant shall buy within the town of any strange man hides or corn or wool except of the burgesses. And that no stranger shall have a tavern except in a ship, nor shall he sell cloths for cutting except in the fair. And that no stranger shall tarry in the town with his wares in order to sell his wares except for forty days. And that no burgess anywhere in my land or power shall be attached or destrained for any debt except he be debtor or pledge. And that they shall be able to marry themselves and their sons and daughters and widows without license of their lords. And that none of their lords on account of foreign lands shall have custody or gift of their sons or daughters or widows, but only custody of their tenements which are of their fee until they shall be of age. . . . And that they shall be able to grind their corn wheresoever they will. And that they shall have all their reasonable gilds as well as, or better than, they had them in the time of Robert and William his son, Earls of Gloucester. . . . I have granted also that everyone of them shall be able to make improvement as much as he be able in making edifices everywhere upon the bank and elsewhere without damage to the borough and town. And that they shall have and possess all lands and void places which are contained within the aforesaid metes to be built on at their will. Wherefore, I will and firmly command that my aforesaid burgesses of Bristol and their heirs shall have and shall hold all their aforesaid liberties and free customs as is above written of me and my heirs as well and entirely, or more so, as ever they had them at what time they have been effectual, well and in peace and honourably without all impediment or molestation which any one shall do to them thereupon.

19
Magna Carta (1215)

Magna Carta is universally recognized as England's most important constitutional document. Disaffected barons and churchmen, fearing the growth of royal authority and exasperated with King John personally, reacted in the only way they knew. By force of arms, they extracted in June 1215 John's promise to acknowledge the freedom of the Church, to respect the traditional laws and customs of England and the feudal system, and to recognize a makeshift grievance committee established to ensure that his promise was kept. Charters of liberties had been issued by earlier kings for political purposes, the most important being that of Henry I in 1100, but Magna Carta was the first actually imposed by force.

Pope Innocent III's nullification of Magna Carta revived the civil war, which continued until John's death in October 1216. The barons accepted John's nine-year-old son Henry as king, but took advantage of his youth to have a shortened version of Magna Carta confirmed in 1216, 1217, and 1225 (in the text below the words deleted are indicated by italics). This version was subsequently confirmed more than 50 times, the last being in 1416. The most noteworthy confirmation was in 1297 when Edward I had it copied onto the Statute Rolls. Almost forgotten during the fifteenth and sixteenth centuries, Magna Carta was revived in the seventeenth by lawyers like Sir Edward Coke to counter the Stuart kings' theory of divine right and to support the general idea that the gov-

Source: Sources of English Consititutional History, edited and translated by Carl Stephenson and Frederick George Marcham, pp. 115–121, 123, 125–126.

ernment as well as the governed must obey the law. It was now regarded as a guarantee of liberty in general, an implication that can be found in the original but which was hardly intended by either the barons in 1215 or the kings who later confirmed it.

Another feature of Magna Carta was the need seen for a means to enforce its terms. The barons' solution was a collective *diffidatio,* a formalization of a vassal's right to resort to arms if his lord violated the feudal contract. But as the centuries passed, those who feared royal oppression gradually evolved more effective machinery—control of taxation in Parliament and, ultimately, responsible government.

Both the significance of Magna Carta and the historian's difficulty in understanding it result from its being a fundamental part of a living, developing constitution. Its role and its meaning (see clauses 12, 14, and especially 39, dealing with due process) have changed as times and occasions demanded. Its specific provisions have, to a great extent, been repealed and forgotten. However, the conviction, inherent in its feudal beginnings, that it guaranteed the people's liberties has evolved along with the understanding of those liberties.

The 1215 version of Magna Carta, although it disappeared when the shortened version replaced it, was found again in the seventeenth century and in 1759 was published by William Blackstone. What is believed to be the original manuscript to which John affixed his seal is in the British Library.

1 We have in the first place granted to God and by this our present charter have confirmed, for us and our heirs forever, that the English Church shall be free and shall have its rights entire and its liberties inviolate. . . . We have also granted to all freemen of our kingdom, for us and our heirs forever, all the liberties hereinunder written, to be had and held by them and their heirs of us and our heirs.

2 If any one of our earls or barons or other men holding of us in chief dies, and if when he dies his heir is of full age and owes relief, [that heir] shall have his inheritance for the ancient relief: namely, the heir or heirs of an earl £100 for the whole barony of an earl. . . . And let whoever owes less give less, according to the ancient custom of fiefs.

3 If, however, the heir of any such person is under age and is in wardship, he shall, when he comes of age, have his inheritance without relief and without fine.

4 The guardian of the land of such an heir who is under age shall not take from the land of the heir more than reasonable issues and reasonable customs and reasonable services, and this without destruction and waste of men or things. . . .

6 Heirs shall be married without disparagement; *yet so that, before the marriage is contracted, it shall be announced to the blood-relatives of the said heir.*

7 A widow shall have her marriage portion and inheritance immediately after the death of her husband and without difficulty. . . .

8 No widow shall be forced to marry so long as she wishes to live without a husband. . . .

9 Neither we nor our bailiffs will seize any land or revenue for any debt, so long as the chattels of the debtor are sufficient to repay the debt; nor shall the sureties of that debtor be distrained so long as the chief debtor is himself able to pay the debt. . . .

10 *If any one has taken anything, whether much or little, by way of loan from Jews, and if he dies before that debt is paid, the debt shall not carry usury so long as the heir is under age. . . .*

12 *Scutage or aid shall be levied in our kingdom only by the common counsel of our kingdom, except for ransoming our body, for knighting our eldest son, and for once marrying our eldest daughter; and for these* [*purposes*] *only a reasonable aid shall be taken. . . .*

13 And the city of London shall have all its ancient liberties and free customs, *both by land and by water.* Besides we will and grant that all the other cities, boroughs, towns, and ports shall have all their liberties and free customs.

14 *And in order to have the common counsel of the kingdom for assessing aid other than in the three cases aforesaid, or for assessing scutage, we will cause the archbishops, bishops, abbots, earls, and greater barons to be summoned by our letters individually; and besides we will cause to be summoned in general, through our sheriffs and bailiffs, all those who hold of us in chief—for a certain day, namely, at the end of forty days at least, and to a certain place. And in all such letters of summons we will state the cause of the summons; and when the summons has thus been made, the business assigned for the day shall proceed according to the counsel of those who are present, although all those summoned may not come.*

17 Common pleas shall not follow our court, but shall be held in some definite place.

18 Assizes of novel disseisin, of mort d'ancestor, *and of darrein presentment* shall be held onlyin their counties [of origin] and in this way: we, or our chief justice if we are out of the kingdom, will send two justices through each county *four times a year; and they, together with four knights of each county elected by the county* [*court*], *shall hold the aforesaid assizes in the county, on the day and at the place* [*set for the meeting*] *of the county* [*court*].

28 No constable or other bailiff of ours shall take grain or other chattels of any one without immediate payment therefor in money. . . .

32 We will hold the lands of those convicted of felony only for a year and a day, and the lands shall then be given to the lords of the fiefs [concerned].

35 There shall be one measure of wine throughout our entire kingdom, and one measure of ale; also one measure of grain, namely, the quarter of London. . . . With weights, moreover, it shall be as with measures.

36 Nothing henceforth shall be taken or given for the writ of inquisition concerning life and limbs, but it shall be issued gratis and shall not be denied.

39 No freeman shall be captured or imprisoned or disseised or outlawed or exiled or in any way destroyed, nor will we go against him or send against him, except by the lawful judgment of his peers or by the law of the land.

40 To no one will we sell, to no one will we deny or delay right or justice.

41 All merchants may safely and securely go away from England, come to England, stay in and go through England, by land or by water, for buying and selling under right and ancient customs and without any evil exactions, except in time of war if they are from the land at war with us.

54 No one shall be seized or imprisoned on the appeal of a woman for the death of any one but her husband.

60 Now all these aforesaid customs and liberties, which we have granted, in so far as concerns us, to be observed in our kingdom toward our men, all men of our kingdom, both clergy and laity, shall, in so far as concerns them, observe toward their men.

61 *Since moreover for* [*the love of*] *God, for the improvement of our kingdom, and for the better allayment of the conflict that has arisen between us and our barons, we have granted all these* [*liberties*] *aforesaid, wishing them to enjoy those* [*liberties*] *by full and firm establishment forever, we have made and granted them the following security: namely, that the barons shall elect twenty-five barons of the kingdom, whomsoever they please, who to the best of their ability should observe, hold, and cause to be observed the peace and liberties that we have granted to them and have confirmed by this our present charter; so that, specifically, if we or our justiciar or our bailiffs or any of our ministers are in any respect delinquent toward any one or transgress any article of the peace or the security, and if the delinquency is shown to four barons of the aforesaid twenty-five barons, those four barons shall come to us, or to our justiciar if we are out of the kingdom, to explain to us the wrong asking that without delay we cause this wrong to be redressed. And if within a period of forty days, counted from the time that notification is made to us, or to our justiciar if we are out of the kingdom, we do not re-*

dress the wrong, or, if we are out of the kingdom, our justiciar does not redress it, the four barons aforesaid shall refer that case to the rest of the twenty-five barons, and those twenty-five barons, together with the community of the entire country, shall distress and injure us in all ways possible—namely, by capturing our castles, lands, and possessions and in all ways that they can—until they secure redress according to their own decision, saving our person and [*the person*] *of our queen and* [*the persons*] *of our children. And when redress has been made, they shall be obedient to us as they were before. . . .*

20
Royal Seals of the Thirteenth and Fourteenth Centuries

Seals were used by both private and official persons in the Middle Ages to authenticate documents, much as personal signatures are today. The practice was begun in Carolingian France. Edward the Confessor (1042–1066) was probably the first English king to use a Great Seal, so called not only for its importance but for its size, 3 or more inches in diameter. The Great Seal in Plate A is that used by John in 1215 to attest to his acceptance of the Articles of the Barons during the negotiations preliminary to Magna Carta. Plate B, showing an authenticated copy of the Magna Carta of 1225, indicates how the wax seal, impressed on both sides, was suspended from the bottom of the document. The possession of the Great Seal and its use when instructed by the king were duties of the chancellor. The obvious importance of these functions made the chancellor, following the decline of the justiciar after the loss of Normandy, the most important official of the royal government.

The creation and use of the privy seal (Plate C) as early as the reign of Henry II (1154–1189) indicate the enlargement of the royal government. Following the chancery's establishment at Westminster, the king still needed in his immediate household a means of authenticating documents. By the privy seal he could instruct the chancellor to use the Great Seal, or even bypass the Great Seal entirely. In the thirteenth and fourteenth centuries, especially in the reigns of Henry III (1216–1272) and Edward II (1307–1327), the barons endeavored, by gaining

PLATE A
The Great Seal of King John, obverse and reverse (by courtesy of the Trustees of the British Museum).

PLATE B
Exemplification of King Henry III's reissue of Magna Carta, 1225 (by courtesy of the Trustees of the British Museum).

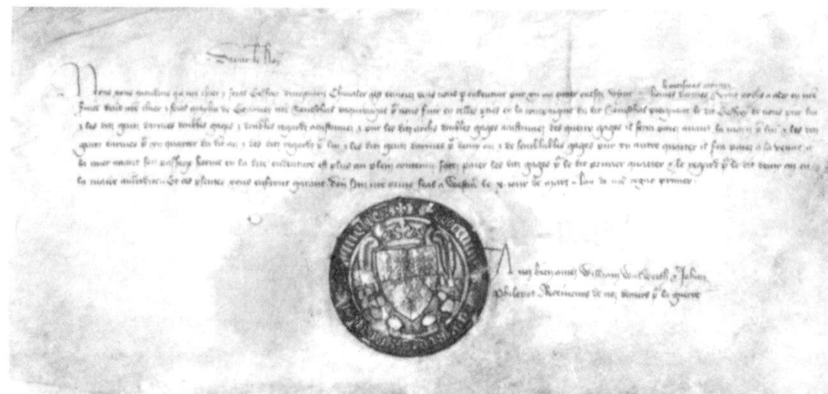

PLATE C
Privy seal of Richard II (by permission of the Public Record Office, London).

PLATE D
Signet seal of Richard II (by permission of the Public Record Office, London).

possession of the king's major officers and by controlling his council, to dominate his government. When they discovered that the king could by means of the privy seal circumvent the officers they controlled, specifically the chancellor, they attempted to make the keeper of the privy seal a public officer, as was the chancellor. Richard II (1377–1399) later resorted to his yet more personal signet seal (Plate D), his ring kept by himself or later by his personal secretary. In the reign of Henry VIII (1509–1547), this household officer became the principal secretary, eclipsing the chancellor and becoming the original of the several secretaries of state of the modern cabinet.

The history of royal seals tells much about the origins and development of government, especially the household, the fertile breeding ground of royal servants who often became officers, and indeed offices, of the royal government.

21
Statutes of Edward I: Gloucester (1278), Mortmain (1279), and Quia Emptores (1290)

When Edward I (1272–1307) became king, two centuries had passed since the Conquest and the introduction of feudalism, and one century since the beginning of the development of the common law. The curia regis had recently, with the requirement that its members take a specified oath of office, become a distinct body with identifiable members. The great council was evolving into a parliament consisting of representatives from the shires and boroughs as well as of the traditional great barons and churchmen. The statute was becoming distinct from the royal ordinance, the latter a minor or temporary order issued by the king and his small council, the former a permanent enactment or promulgation for which the king needed the support of a great council, or parliament. Amidst this development and change, Edward saw the opportunity to refurbish and strengthen many features of his royal government, and he recognized the statute as the appropriate means.

Source: Sources of English Constitutional History, edited and translated by Carl Stephenson and Frederick George Marcham, pp. 169–170, 174.

The statutes reproduced below are typical of the many from Edward's reign dealing with a wide range of matters from the promotion of trade (Statute of Acton Burnell, 1283) to the incorporation of the principality of Wales into the legal system of England (Statute of Rhuddlan, 1284). The Statute of Gloucester (1278) gave direction to the royal policy of retrieving the private jurisdictions of vassals unable to show "by what warrant" they held them. The readiest warrant was of course a charter, but long-term possession was also acknowledged. In 1290 the term of possession was set at Richard I's coronation in 1189, a date soon recognized as the limit of legal memory beyond which no precedent need be traced. Mortmain (1279), by which the "dead hand" of the Church holds fast to its land, attempted to prevent vassals from subinfeudating or granting land to the Church by terms that would financially injure the lord. Quia Emptores (1290), which means "whereas the buyers," attempted to prevent a lord's loss of reliefs and other feudal incidents by a vassal's careless or malicious subinfeudation. The solution that the buyer (feoffee) of land should assume the feudal obligations of the seller (feoffor) and that no new tenure be created, was a drastic remedy which, in fact, ended all subinfeudation and proved an important step in the ultimate decline of the feudal system.

By means of statutes, Edward built a sounder administration and provided the foundation on which the common law would develop for the next five centuries. The statute, thus employed, became a powerful new instrument of governmental initiative, not only strengthening the king but enhancing the role of a developing Parliament.

STATUTE OF GLOUCESTER (1278)

In the year of grace 1278, the sixth of the reign of King Edward, son of King Henry, at Gloucester in the month of August, the same king, having summoned the more discreet men of his kingdom, both greater and lesser, has made provision for the betterment of his kingdom and the fuller administration of justice, as is demanded by the kingly office. . . .

The sheriffs shall have it commonly proclaimed throughout their bailiwicks—that is to say, in cities, boroughs, trading towns, and elsewhere—that all those who claim to have any franchises by charters of the king's predecessors, kings of England, or by other title, shall come before the king or before the itinerant justices on a certain day and at a certain place to show what sort of franchises they claim to have, and by what warrant [they hold them]. . . . And if those who claim to have such franchises do not come on the day aforesaid, those franchises shall then be taken into the king's hand by the local sheriff in the name of distress; so that they shall not enjoy such franchises until they come to receive justice. . . .

STATUTE OF MORTMAIN (1279)

The king to his justices of the bench, greeting. Whereas it was formerly enacted that men of religion should not enter upon the fiefs of any persons without the consent and license of the principal lords from whom those fiefs were immediately held; and whereas since then men of religion have nevertheless entered upon the fiefs of others as well as their own—by appropriating them, buying them, and sometimes by receiving them through gifts of other men—whereby the services which are owed from fiefs of this sort, and which were originally established for the defence of the kingdom, are wrongfully withheld and the principal lords [are caused to] lose their escheats: [therefore] we, seeking in this connection to provide a suitable remedy for the good of the kingdom, by the counsel of the prelates, earls, and other faithful men of our kingdom who are members of our council, have enacted, established, and ordained that no man of religion or any other whatsoever shall buy or sell lands or tenements, or under colour of donation, lease, or other title of any sort shall receive them from any one, or presume artfully and craftily to appropriate them in any way whatsoever, whereby land and tenements of this sort may somehow come into mortmain—under pain of forfeiting the same [lands or tenements]. . . . And so we command you to have the aforesaid statute read in your presence and henceforth strictly held and observed.

STATUTE OF QUIA EMPTORES (1290)

Whereas the buyers of lands and tenements belonging to the fiefs of magnates and other men have in times past frequently entered upon their fiefs to the prejudice of the same [lords], because the freeholders of the same magnates and other men have sold their lands and tenements to such purchasers to be held in fee by themselves and their heirs of the feoffors and not of the principal lords of the fiefs, whereby those same principal lords have often lost the escheats, marriages, and wardships of lands and tenements belonging to their fiefs; and whereas this has seemed very hard and burdensome to those magnates and other lords, being in such cases manifest disinheritance: [therefore] the lord king in his parliament at Westminister [held] after Easter in the eighteenth year of his reign . . . , at the suggestion of the magnates of his realm, has granted, provided, and established that henceforth every freeman shall be permitted to sell his land or tenement, or a part of it, at pleasure; yet so that the feoffee shall hold that land or tenement of the same principal lord [of whom the feoffor held] and by the same services and customs by which the feoffor earlier held. . . .

22

The Statute of Rhuddlan (1284). The English Conquest of Wales

The creation of the United Kingdom of Great Britain and Ireland is reflected in the design of the Union Jack. The red cross of St. George on a white field represents England. The white diagonal cross of St. Andrew on a blue field is for Scotland, which entered the union in 1707, and the red diagonal of St. Patrick on a white field stands for Ireland, which was brought in in 1800. Only Wales, the first to be conquered and incorporated (provided one is willing to ignore Cornwall), is overlooked.

The Anglo-Saxon conquest of Britain stopped at the Welsh frontier, King Offa of Mercia (757–796) reputedly building his Dyke to mark the place. The relations between the English and the Cymry (the Welsh) were seldom smooth. At the time of the Norman Conquest, some of William's barons conquered the eastern and southern parts of Wales. These "Marcher Lords" held their land as fiefs under the king, but their power was so great that in their Marches the king's writ did not run. The unconquered remainder of Wales, the northwest, centering on Mount Snowdon, was the Welsh Principality, the land of the native Welsh princes. Early in the thirteenth century, Llywellyn the Great (c. 1173–1240) established himself as the sole Prince of Wales. When his grandson, Llywellyn ap Gruffudd (d. 1282), refused to do homage to Edward I, the English king proceeded to subdue the Principality and to incorporate it into England, while building great stone castles such as those at Conway, Carnarvon, and Harlech and discovering the usefulness of the Welsh longbow.

The Statute of Rhuddlan created counties, provided for the appointment of English royal officials such as sheriff and coroner, and introduced many features of English law. The great Marcher Lords retained their administrative semi-independence until 1536, when Henry VIII's Act of Union, superseding Rhuddlan, fully incorporated all of Wales into the kingdom of England.

Source: English Historical Documents, Volume III, 1189–1327, edited by Harry Rothwell, pp. 422–423, 426–427.

Edward by the grace of God king of England, lord of Ireland and duke of Aquitaine to all his faithful of his land of Snowdon and of all his other lands in Wales greeting in the Lord. Divine providence, which is unerring in its dispositions, among other gifts of its dispensation with which it has deigned to honour us and our kingdom of England has now of its grace wholly and entirely converted the land of Wales previously subject to us by feudal right with its inhabitants into a dominion of our ownership, every obstacle being overcome, and has annexed and united it to the crown of the said kingdom as a constituent part of it. . . .

[II] We have provided and in our wisdom ordained that the justice of Snowdon shall have the keeping and administration of our royal peace in Snowdon and our adjacent lands of Wales, and do justice to anyone whatsoever in accordance with royal original writs and with the underwritten laws and customs. We will also and ordain that there shall be sheriffs, coroners and commote-bailiffs in Snowdon and our lands of those parts; a sheriff of Anglesey, under whom shall be the whole land of Anglesey with its cantreds, metes and bounds; a sheriff of Carnarvon. . . . a sheriff of Merioneth. . . . A sheriff of Flint, under whom shall be the cantred of Englefield, the land of Maelor Saesneg, the land of Hope and all the land attached to our castle and town of Rhuddlan, as far as the town of Chester, shall in future under us be subordinate to our justice of Chester and answer for the issues of that commote at our exchequer of Chester. There shall be coroners in those shires, to be chosen by a writ of the king. . . . A sheriff of Carmarthen with its cantreds, commotes and ancient metes and bounds. A sheriff of Cardigan and Llampeter with its cantreds, commotes and metes and bounds. There are to be coroners in these shires and commote-bailiffs as before.

[III] The sheriff ought to execute his office in this manner, namely . . . And it should be known that a shire-court ought to be held in this way. . . .

[IV] The sheriff shall make his tourn twice a year in each of his commotes. . . .

[XII] And because women have not hitherto had dower in Wales, the king grants that they shall have it. A woman's dower is of two kinds. One is the assignment of a third part of the whole of the land which was her husband's in his lifetime. . . . The other dower is when a son endows his wife with his father's consent. . . .

[XIII] Because the custom is otherwise in Wales than in England with regard to succession to an inheritance inasmuch as the inheritance is partible among the heirs male and has been partible from a time whereof the memory of man is not to the contrary, the lord king does not wish that custom to be abrogated but inheritances to remain partible among like heirs as used to be, and the partition of the inheritance shall be made as it used to be made; with this exception, that bastards shall not in future inherit and also shall not in future have purparties with the lawful heirs or without them. And if perchance from now on any inheritance for lack of heir male descends to females as lawful heirs of their ancestor last seised thereof, we will of our special grace that those law-worthy females shall have their purparties thereof assigned to them in our court, although this is contrary to Welsh custom used up to now. . . .

We command you to observe strictly the aforementioned in all things from now on, on condition however that we can as often as and whensoever and wheresoever we like clarify, interpret, add to or take away from the aforesaid statutes and every part of them at our pleasure and as seems to us expedient for our security and that of our aforesaid land.

In witness of which thing our seal has been affixed to these presents. Given at Rhuddlan on Sunday in mid-Lent, in the twelfth year of our reign.

23 Memorandum of Parliament (1306). Parliament's Membership and Activities

Parliament was initially not an institution, but an event, a meeting where men came together to talk—thus the word *parliament,* from the French word *parler,* "to talk." More specifically, it was a meeting of the great council at which a number of functions were performed. It acted as a high court; it assisted in the formulation of statutes; it approved grants of taxation; not least, it served as a useful tool for a king seeking support for unpopular actions. By the reign of John (1199–1216), it was occasionally useful to have knights of the shire meet with the great barons and churchmen. In 1265, at the climax of the troubles between Henry III and the barons, Simon de Montfort had in addition summoned representatives from boroughs to broaden support for the baronial party.

Edward I (1272–1307) inherited and exploited these constitutional experiments. In 1295, he called what has become known as the Model Parliament, containing all the elements of which Parliament was ultimately to be composed: barons, prelates, and two representatives from each shire, city, and borough. In 1297, Ed-

Source: Sources of English Constitutional History, edited and translated by Carl Stephenson and Frederick George Marcham, pp. 167–169.

ward promised in the Confirmation of the Charters to collect no taxes other than the three feudal aids "except by the common assent of the whole kingdom." Whatever the original intention of these words, they were soon interpreted to mean the consent of Parliament with all the elements present.

It is an old argument whether Parliament in the early stage of its development was simply the king's small council temporarily made large or a completely different institution, the product of an ancient custom that the king must consult the kingdom. There is also debate over whether Parliament's primary function was judicial, as a court of law, or legislative, as an assembly giving advice and granting taxation. Answers to these questions must come, at least in part, from study of the *Rotuli Parliamentorum,* the Parliament Rolls, on which parliamentary proceedings were recorded. The passage below, from the Memorandum for 1306, indicates that Parliament was beginning to assume a definite membership and that taxation was an important item of its business. On the other hand, there is still no indication of a division into two houses, barons and prelates in one, and the commons in the other. In fact, the knights were still clearly associated with the barons, and the citizens and burgesses made their grant separately, almost as a separate estate.

Memorandum that, after the lord king had recently ordered that Edward, his first-born son, should be decorated with the belt of knighthood at the feast of Pentecost in the thirty-fourth year of his reign, mandates were issued for the archbishops, bishops, abbots, priors, earls, barons, and other magnates to come before the lord king and his council at Westminster on the morrow of Holy Trinity next following, in order to deliberate and ordain with regard to giving the king an aid for the knighting aforesaid and in order to consent to those matters which should further be ordained in that connection, or for them then and there to send procurators or attorneys with sufficient instructions to carry out the aforesaid matters in their place; also each of the sheriffs of England was commanded to cause two knights from his county to come to the said place at the said time, and from each city of his bailiwick two citizens and from each borough of the same bailiwick two burgesses or one, etc., in order to deliberate, ordain, and consent as aforesaid. . . . And when all the aforesaid persons had assembled before the aforesaid council of the king, and it had been explained to them by the same council on behalf of the king that by right of the royal crown aid should be given the lord king on the occasion aforesaid, and besides, that the lord king had incurred multifarious expenses and many other obligations toward suppressing the rebellion and malice of Robert Bruce, traitor to the same lord king, and of his adherents in the parts of Scotland, who were then presuming to make war against the king in those parts; the same prelates, earls, barons, and other magnates, as well as the knights of the shires, having discussed the matter with deliberation, and considering that aid was owed as aforesaid and that the king had incurred many obligations on account of the aforesaid war, at length unanimously granted to the lord king on behalf of themselves and the whole community of the land a thirtieth of all their movable temporal goods which they should happen to possess on Michaelmas next following, to be taken as a competent aid to the lord king for the knighting of his aforesaid son and also as an aid toward the expenditures that should be made in connection with the aforesaid war. This grant, however, [was made] on condition that it should in no way be held to their own prejudice or to that of their successors or heirs in future times, and that it should never be taken as a precedent in a case of this kind; also that in assessing the aforesaid goods all should be excepted which had been excepted in assessing the fifteenth granted by the community of the kingdom to the lord king in the eighteenth year of his reign for exiling the Jews. Moreover, the citizens and burgesses of the cities and boroughs aforesaid and others of the king's demesnes, being assembled and holding a discussion on the said matters, in consideration of the obligations incurred by the lord king as aforesaid, unanimously granted the lord king for the reasons aforesaid the twentieth of their movable goods, to be taken as aforesaid.

24

The Declaration of Arbroath (1320). Scottish Nationalism

This declaration, or diplomatic dispatch, was a product of the series of wars between the kingdoms of England and Scotland that began in the reign of Edward I (1272–1307) and continued until 1328, when England finally recognized Scotland's independence. By 1320, the date of the declaration, the Scots had survived several defeats and had, under the leadership of Robert Bruce (1306–1329), crushed the English decisively at Bannockburn in 1314 and driven them out of Scotland. England, by far the greater power, refused, however, to admit that the war was over as, indeed, in the border counties it was not. To achieve peace, Robert needed to maintain a solid political and military front in Scotland, and, more important, to bring outside pressure to bear on Edward II of England (1307–1327). This dispatch was Robert's attempt to enlist the help of Pope John XXII.

The Declaration of Arbroath is noteworthy for its moving prose, its expression of national feeling supported by the trappings of a national mythology, and its breadth of popular support. Indeed, it enlists "the whole community of the realm." It remains a problem the extent to which such expressions of national sentiment should be taken literally rather than merely as diplomatic rhetoric. And to what extent does the seeming participation of the small freemen reflect their actual role in the royal government rather than simply the king's need of such men's economic and military support in the wars against England?

It must not be forgotten that this is a Scottish—not an English—document. It is a valuable reminder to the British historian that evidence must be sought in books and archives throughout the British Isles.The "file copy" of the Declaration, written in Latin, is in the Scottish Record Office, H.M. General Register House, Edinburgh.

To the most holy father and lord in Christ, lord John, by divine providence supreme pontiff of the holy Roman and universal church, his humble and devout

Source: Reproduced from "The Nation of Scots and the Declaration of Arbroath," by A. A. M. Duncan, published by the Historical Association, London, 1970, pp. 34–37.

sons Duncan, earl of Fife, Thomas Randolph, earl of Moray . . . and the other barons and freeholders and the whole community of the realm of Scotland send all manner of filial reverence, with devout kisses of his blessed feet.

Most holy father and lord, we know, and we gather from the deeds and books of the ancients, that among other distinguished nations our own nation, namely of Scots, has been marked by many distinctions. It journeyed from Greater Scythia by the Tyrrhenian Sea and the Pillars of Hercules, and dwelt for a long span of time in Spain among the most savage peoples, but nowhere could it be subjugated by any people, however barbarous. From there it came, twelve hundred years after the people of Israel crossed the Red Sea and, having first driven out the Britons and altogether destroyed the Picts, it acquired, with many victories and untold efforts, the places which it now holds, although often assailed by Norwegians, Danes and English. As the histories of old time bear witness, it has held them free of all servitude ever since. In their kingdom one hundred and thirteen kings of their own royal stock have reigned, the line unbroken by a single foreigner. Their high qualities and merits, if they were not otherwise manifest, shine out sufficiently from this: that the king of kings and lord of lords, our lord Jesus Christ, after his passion and resurrection, called them, even though settled in the uttermost ends of the earth, almost the first to his most holy faith. Nor did he wish to confirm them in that faith by anyone but by the first apostle by calling (though second or third in rank)—namely the most gentle Andrew, the blessed Peter's brother, whom he wished to protect them as their patron for ever.

The most holy fathers your predecessors gave careful heed to these things and strengthened this same kingdom and people, as being the special charge of the blessed Peter's brother by many favours and numerous privileges. Thus our people under their protection did heretofore live in freedom and peace until that mighty prince Edward, king of the English, father of the present one, when our kingdom had no head and our people harboured no malice or treachery and were then unused to wars or attacks, came in the guise of friend and ally to invade them as an enemy. His wrongs, killings, violence, pillage, arson, imprisonment of prelates, burning down of monasteries, despoiling and killing of religious, and yet other innumerable outrages, sparing neither age nor sex, religion nor order, no one could fully describe or fully understand unless experience had taught him.

But from these countless evils we have been set free, by the help of him who though he afflicts yet heals and restores, by our most valiant prince, king and lord, the lord Robert, who, that his people and his heritage might be delivered out of the hands of enemies, bore cheerfully toil and fatigue, hunger and danger, like another Maccabeus or Joshua. Divine providence, the succession to his right according to our laws and customs which we shall maintain to the death, and the due consent and assent of us all have made him our prince and king. We are bound to him for the maintaining of our freedom both by his rights and his merits, as to him by whom salvation has been wrought unto our people, and by him, come what may, we mean to stand. Yet if he should give up what he has begun, seeking to make us or our kingdom subject to the king of England or to the English, we would strive at once to drive him out as our enemy and a subverter of his own right and ours, and we would make some other man who was able to defend us our king; for, as long as a hundred of us remain alive, we will never on any conditions be subjected to the lordship of the English. For we fight not for glory, nor riches, nor honours, but for freedom alone, which no good man gives up except with his life.

Therefore it is, reverend father and lord, that we beseech your holiness . . . will look with paternal eyes on the troubles and anxieties brought by the English upon us and upon the church of God; that you will deign to admonish and exhort the king of the English, who ought to be satisfied with what he has, since England used once to be enough for seven kings or more, to leave in peace us Scots, who live in this poor little Scotland, beyond which there is no dwelling-place at all, and who desire nothing but our own. . . .

But if your Holiness giving too much credence to the tales of the English will not give sincere belief to all this, nor refrain from favouring them to our confusion, then the slaughter of bodies, the perdition of souls, and all the other misfortunes that will follow inflicted by them on us and by us on them, will, we believe, be imputed by the most high to you. . . .

Given at the monastery of Arbroath in Scotland on the sixth day of the month of April in the year of grace thirteen hundred and twenty and the fifteenth year of the reign of our aforesaid king.

25

Statute of York (1322). Assertion of Parliamentary Responsibility

In the decades that followed Magna Carta, the barons turned from attempting to restrain royal government by means of military force and a grievance committee to efforts to dominate the king's administration directly by appointments to the curia regis and the other major offices. The first real effort in this direction, the Provisions of Oxford, sponsored by Simon de Montfort in 1258, came to a violent end in 1265 in the battle of Evesham. A second attempt came when Edward II (1307–1327) was forced to accept the Ordinances of 1311, by which the barons in Parliament would dominate his royal government. This also failed. The barons, beset by disagreements among themselves and confronted by the king's greater reserve of power and authority, found that even though they personally filled the offices of the king's council they still could not control his government. The barons, the Lords Ordainers as they were called, were defeated in 1322 at the battle of Boroughbridge, and a few weeks later the Statute of York repealed the Ordinances of 1311, the basis of their attempted takeover of the government.

The Statute of York is highly controversial because of what it says, or seems to say, about Parliament. There is, for instance, no consensus among scholars as to the meaning of the phrases, "the whole community of the realm" and "the commonalty of the kingdom." Do they refer to the commons, the representatives of the shires and boroughs, or to the kingdom in general? The intention of the last sentence of the statute is also unclear. Was it the establishment of a new and greater power of legislation for Parliament? Was it a statement of what was already thought to be fact? Or was it simply a rhetorical flourish? Nevertheless, it is clear that Edward used this statute to sanction what had already been accomplished on the field of battle. Although Parliament was used by the king against the barons in 1322, five years later it was used to sanction Edward's abdication. The continued use of Parliament to justify major governmental decisions, even those of dubious legali-

Source: B. Wilkinson, *Constitutional History of Medieval England, 1216–1399,* Volume II: *Politics and the Constitution, 1307–1399,* London: Longmans, Green and Co., 1952, pp. 155–156. Reprinted by permission of Longmans Group U.K.

ty, strengthened it and made it a recognized part of the English constitution.

Our lord King Edward, son of King Edward, on March 16, in the third year of his reign, granted to the prelates, earls and barons of his realm . . . power to make ordinances. The archbishop of Canterbury, primate of all England, and the bishops, earls and barons chosen for the purpose, drew up certain ordinances . . . , which ordinances our said lord the king caused to be rehearsed and examined in his parliament at York three weeks after Easter in the fifteenth year of his reign. . . . Through that examination in the said parliament, it was found that, by the ordinances thus decreed, the royal power of our said lord the king was wrongfully limited in many respects, to the injury of his royal lordship and contrary to the estate of the crown. Furthermore, through such ordinances and provisions made by subjects in times past against the royal authority of our lord the king's ancestors, the kingdom has incurred troubles and wars, whereby the land has been imperilled. [Therefore] it is agreed, and established at the said parliament by our lord the king, by the said prelates and earls and barons, and by the whole community of the realm assembled in this parliament, that everything ordained by the said Ordainers and contained in the said ordinances shall henceforth and forever cease [to be valid], losing for the future all title, force, virtue, and effect; and that the statutes and establishment duly made by our lord the king and his ancestors prior to the said ordinances shall remain in force. And [it is decreed] that, henceforth and forever at all times, every kind of ordinance or provision made under any authority or commission whatsoever, by subjects of our lord the king or of his heirs, relative to the royal power of our lord the king or of his heirs, or contrary to the estate of the lord king or of his heirs or contrary to the estate of the crown, shall be null and shall have no validity or force whatever; but that matters which are to be determined for [i.e. favourable to] the estate of the king and of his heirs, and for the estate of the kingdom and of the people, shall be "treated," granted, and established in parliament by our lord the king and with the consent of the prelates, earls, and barons, and of the commonalty of the kingdom, as has been accustomed in times past.

26

Articles of the Spurriers (1345). Guilds in Medieval London

The growth of commerce and industry fostered in England, as elsewhere, the formation of guilds, organizations to protect the interests of certain economic groups. The most powerful were merchant guilds, consisting of the important merchants in a town, but, by the thirteenth century, strong craft or industrial guilds had also developed. In 1351 the most powerful craft guilds in London included the fishmongers, mercers, grocers, ironmongers, vintners, and woolmongers. There were also numerous smaller guilds, such as the glovers, cobblers, and spurriers, creating by 1422 a total of 111 organizations of this kind in London alone.

The craft guilds had useful functions. Initially, at least, they provided stability to the various trades and guaranteed the consumer a certain level of craftsmanship and honesty. They also established schools and charitable relief, maintained law and order in the absence of a regular police force, fought the frequent fires, and provided their members such special services as a dignified burial. In fact, some guilds began as religious or charitable organizations, resembling the friendly societies of the nineteenth century.

Guilds that fell under the control of a few master craftsmen could, however, easily become oppressive and monopolistic. For example, were the spurriers, in the regulations reprinted below, interested in protecting the consumer or were they simply using the excuse of quality control to restrict membership in their guild? Apprentices, finding it increasingly difficult to qualify as master craftsmen, often spent their entire lives as wage-earning journeymen. Eventually they formed their own guilds or unions. As guilds became more powerful, they also sought, usually successfully, to dominate municipal government. A royal charter often permitted the mercantile oligarchy to become a self-perpetuating corporation, controlling not only a town's social and economic life but its politics as well. It is not surprising that later generations increasingly viewed guilds as obstructions to political liberty and economic progress.

Source: Memorials of London and London Life in the XIIIth, XIVth, and XVth Centuries, edited by Henry Thomas Riley, London: Longmans, Green, and Co., 1868, pp. 226–228.

Surviving guild records, like manorial records, are very numerous and widely scattered. Most of those relating to London are found in the Corporation of London Records Office and the Guildhall Library.

Be it remembered, that on Tuesday, the morrow of St. Peter's Chains [1 August], in the 19th year of the reign of King Edward the Third etc., the Articles underwritten were read before John Hamond, Mayor, Roger de Depham, Recorder, and the other Aldermen; and seeing that the same were deemed befitting, they were accepted and enrolled, in these words.—

"In the first place,—that no one of the trade of Spurriers shall work longer than from the beginning of the day until curfew rung out at the Church of St. Sepulchre, without Neugate; by reason that no man can work so neatly by night as by day. And many persons of the said trade, who compass how to practise deception in their work, desire to work by night rather than by day: and then they introduce false iron, and iron that has been cracked, for tin, and also, they put gilt on false copper, and cracked. And further,—many of the said trade are wandering about all day, without working at all at their trade; and then, when they have become drunk and frantic, they take to their work, to the annoyance of the sick and of all their neighbourhood, as well as by reason of the broils that arise between them and the strange folks who are dwelling among them. And then they blow up their fires so vigorously, that their forges begin all at once to blaze; to the great peril of themselves and of all the neighbourhood around. And then too, all the neighbours are much in dread of the sparks, which so vigorously issue forth in all directions from the mouths of the chimneys in their forges. By reason whereof, it seems unto them that working by night [should be put an end to,] in order such false work and such perils to avoid; and therefore, the Mayor and Aldermen do will, by assent of the good folks of the said trade, and for the common profit, that from henceforth such time for working, and such false work made in the trade, shall be forbidden. And if any person shall be found in the said trade to do the contrary hereof, let him be amerced, the first time in 40*d.,* one half thereof to go to the use of the Chamber of the Guildhall of London, and the other half to the use of the said trade; the second time, in half a mark, and the third time, in 10*s.,* to the use of the same Chamber and trade; and the fourth time, let him forswear the trade for ever.

"Also,—that no one of the said trade shall hang his spurs out on Sunday, or on other days that are Double Feasts; but only a sign indicating his business: and such spurs as they shall so sell, they are to shew and sell within their shops, without exposing them without, or opening the doors or windows of their shops, on the pain aforesaid.

"Also,—that no one of the said trade shall keep a house or shop to carry on his business, unless he is free of the City; and that no one shall cause to be sold, or exposed for sale, any manner of old spurs for new ones; or shall garnish them, or change them for new ones.

"Also,—that no one of the said trade shall take an apprentice for a less term than seven years; and such apprentice shall be enrolled, according to the usages of the said city.

"Also,—that if any one of the said trade who is not a freeman, shall take an apprentice for a term of years, he shall be amerced, as aforesaid.

"Also,—that no one of the said trade shall receive the apprentice, serving-man, or journeyman, of another in the same trade, during the term agreed upon between his master and him; on the pain aforesaid.

"Also,—that no alien of another country, or foreigner of this country, shall follow or use the said trade, unless he is enfranchised before the Mayor, Aldermen, and Chamberlain; and that, by witness and surety of the good folks of the said trade, who will undertake for him as to his loyalty and his good behavior.

"Also,—that no one of the said trade shall work on Saturdays, after None has been rung out in the City; and not from that hour until the Monday morning following."

27

Jean Froissart, *Chronicles*. The Battle of Crécy, 1346

Froissart is undoubtedly the most widely read medieval chronicler. A native of northern France, he went to England in 1361, becoming secretary to Edward III's wife, Philippa of Hainault. Queen Philippa, a patron of the arts, encouraged Froissart to write his famous *Chronicles of England, France, Spain,* etc. Covering the years from 1307 to 1400, his chronicle is based largely on oral evidence gathered at the court of Edward III (1327–1377). Froissart, despite his inaccuracies, has remained popular because of his forceful style and his preoccupation with the violence and pageantry of the Hundred Years' War (1337–1453). Better than any other writer, he captures the spirit of medieval feudalism; he is, as one recent historian has remarked, "a faithful echo of the feelings of chivalrous society."

It is ironic that Froissart wrote when feudalism was declining. Although there were many reasons for the demise of feudalism, one factor was the eclipse of the armored knight as the premier instrument of warfare. From Froissart's description of the battle of Crécy (1346), it is obvious that England's victory resulted not from the heroic exploits of her nobility but from the quiet efficiency of her lowborn archers. The Welsh longbow, used effectively for the first time in Edward I's Scottish campaigns, revolutionized English warfare. Good archers firing ten to twelve arrows a minute at a maximum range of almost 400 yards threatened the existence of the medieval knight. It was, however, very difficult for the nobility of England or France to accept the implications of Crécy. The question posed was simple. If a feudal elite trained for war was no longer a military necessity, how could knights justify their existence, to say nothing of their special standing in society? The French nobility, refusing to accept its obsolescence, repeated the mistakes made at Crécy, and suffered the same disastrous results at the battles of Poitiers (1356) and Agincourt (1415). Only then did the nobility accept the inevitable. By the fifteenth century the military aspect of feudalism had become the pageantry of the tourna-

Source: Jean Froissart, *The Chronicles of England, France, Spain and the Adjoining Countries*, translated by Thomas Johnes, rev. ed., New York and London: The Cooperative Publication Society, 1901, pp. 39–41,42, 44–45.

ment, and the place of the mounted knight in the royal arsenal had been taken not only by the longbow but increasingly by the pike and by cannon and gunpowder.

There is no man, unless he had been present, that can imagine or describe truly the confusion of that day, especially the bad management and disorder of the French, whose troops were out of number. What I know, and shall relate in this book, I have learned chiefly from the English, and from those attached to Sir John of Hainault, who was always near the person of the King of France. The English, who, as I have said, were drawn up in three divisions, and seated on the ground, on seeing their enemies advance, rose up undauntedly, and fell into their ranks. The prince's battalion, whose archers were formed in the manner of a portcullis, and the men-at-arms in the rear, was the first to do so. The Earls of Northampton and Arundel, who commanded the second division, posted themselves in good order on the prince's wing to assist him if necessary.

You must know that the French troops did not advance in any regular order, and that as soon as their King came in sight of the English his blood began to boil, and he cried out to his marshals, "Order the Genoese forward and begin the battle in the name of God and St. Denis." There were about 15,000 Genoese cross-bow men; but they were quite fatigued, having marched on foot that day six leagues, completely armed and carrying their cross-bows, and accordingly they told the constable they were not in a condition to do any great thing in battle. The Earl of Alençon hearing this, said, "This is what one gets by employing such scoundrels, who fall off when there is any need for them." During this time a heavy rain fell, accompanied by thunder and a very terrible eclipse of the sun; and, before this rain, a great flight of crows hovered in the air over all the battalions, making a loud noise; shortly afterward it cleared up, and the sun shone very bright; but the French had it in their faces, and the English on their backs. When the Genoese were somewhat in order they approached the English and set up a loud shout, in order to frighten them; but the English remained quite quiet and did not seem to attend to it. They then set up a second shout, and advanced a little forward; the English never moved. Still they hooted a third time, advancing with their cross-bows presented, and began to shoot. The English archers then advanced one step forward, and shot their arrows with such force and quickness that it seemed as if it snowed. When the Genoese felt these arrows, which pierced through their armor, some of them cut the strings of their cross-bows, others flung them to the ground, and all turned about and retreated quite discomfited.

The French had a large body of men-at-arms on horseback to support the Genoese, and the King, seeing them thus fall back, cried out, "Kill me those scoundrels, for they stop up our road without any reason." The English continued shooting, and some of their arrows falling among the horsemen, drove them upon the Genoese, so that they were in such confusion they could never rally again.

In the English army there were some Cornish and Welsh men on foot, who had armed themselves with large knives; these advancing through the ranks of the men-at-arms and archers, who made way for them, came upon the French when they were in this danger, and falling upon earls, barons, knights, and squires, slew many, at which the King of England was exasperated. . . .

This battle, which was fought on Saturday, between La Broyes and Cressy, was murderous and cruel; and many gallant deeds of arms were performed that were never known; toward evening, many knights and squires of the French had lost their masters, and, wandering up and down the plain, attacked the English in small parties; but they were soon destroyed, for the English had determined that day to give no quarter, nor hear of ransom from anyone. . . .

This Saturday the English never quitted their ranks in pursuit of anyone, but remained on the field guarding their position and defending themselves against all who attacked them. The battle ended at the hour of vespers, when the King of England embraced his son and said to him, "Sweet son, God give you perseverance; you are my son; for most loyally have you acquitted yourself; you are worthy to be a sovereign." The prince bowed very low, giving all honor to the King, his father. The English during the night made frequent thanksgivings to the Lord for the happy issue of the day; and with them there was no rioting, for the King had expressly forbidden all riot or noise.

On the following day, which was Sunday, there were a few encounters with the French troops; however, they could not withstand the English, and soon either retreated or were put to the sword. When Edward was assured that there was no appearance of the French collecting another army, he sent to have the number and rank of the dead examined. This business was entrusted to Lord Reginald Cobham and Lord Stafford, assisted by three heralds to examine the arms, and two secretaries to write down the names. They passed the whole day upon the field of battle, and made a very circumstantial account of all they saw: according to their report it appeared that 80 banners, the bodies of 11 princes, 1,200 knights, and about 30,000 common men were found dead on the field. After this very successful engagement, Edward marched with his victorious army to Wisant, and having halted there one whole day, arrived on the following Thursday before the strong town of Calais, which he had determined to besiege.

28

Henry Knighton, *Chronicle.* The Black Death, 1348–1350

Little is known of the life of Henry Knighton except that he was a canon of St. Mary-of-the-Meadows Abbey, an Augustinian house at Leicester. Although noted neither for its style nor its analysis, the last portion of his chronicle contains the most important contemporary narrative of the constitutional conflicts of the reign of Richard II (1377–1399). The beginning, based largely on well-known sources, also drew on local chronicles since lost. Using these sources effectively, Knighton wrote what is regarded today as the best description of the Black Death and its effect on the population of England. Part of this is reprinted below.

The Black Death, a highly infectious form of the bubonic plague, struck England with great force in 1348 to 1349, returning in 1361 to 1362 and again in 1369. The death of approximately one-third of the entire population could at the time be explained only in terms of God's wrath. Few historians, even today, would argue that the death and social dislocation resulting from the plague was a "good thing," but it seems likely that in the long run the plague did improve, if only slightly, the position of the English peasant. Surviving peasants took advantage of the labor shortage to bargain with their landlords for better terms. The attempt by the landed classes to freeze wages and to maintain their own status by a Statute of Labourers (1351) led to a number of local disturbances and eventually contributed to the Peasants' Revolt of 1381.

A Latin edition of the *Chronicon Henrici Knighton* was published in the Rolls Series, 1889 to 1895.

In this and the following year (1348–9) there was a general mortality among men throughout the whole world. It began first in India, and spread thence into Tharsis, thence to the Saracens, and at last to the Christians and Jews; so that in the space of a single year, namely from Easter to Easter, as it was rumored at the court of Rome, 8000 legions of men perished in those distant regions, besides Christians. . . .

Then the dreadful pestilence made its way along the coast by Southampton

Source: *The Peasants' Revolt of 1381*, edited by R. B. Dobson, London: Macmillan and Co., 1970, pp. 59–63. Reprinted by the permission of Macmillan, London and Basingstoke.

and reached Bristol, where almost the whole strength of the town perished, as it were surprised by sudden death; for few kept their beds more than two or three days, or even half a day. Then this cruel death spread on all sides, following the course of the sun. And there died at Leicester, in the small parish of St. Leonard's, more than 380 persons, in the parish of Holy Cross, 400, in the parish of St. Margaret's, Leicester, 700; and so in every parish, in a great multitude. Then the bishop of Lincoln sent notice throughout his whole diocese giving general power to all priests, both regulars and seculars, to hear confessions and give absolution with full episcopal authority to all persons, except only in case of debt. In such a case, the debtor was to pay the debt, if he were able, while he lived, or others were to be appointed to do so from his goods after his death. In the same way the Pope gave plenary remission of all sins (once only) to all receiving absolution at the point of death, and granted that this power should last until Easter next following, and that every one might choose his own confessor at will.

In the same year there was a great plague among sheep everywhere in the kingdom, so that in one place more than 5000 sheep died in a single pasture; and they rotted so much that neither bird not beast would touch them. . . . Sheep and oxen strayed at large through the fields and among the crops, and there were none to drive them off or herd them; but for lack of keepers they perished in remote by-ways and hedges in inestimable numbers throughout all districts, because there was such a great scarcity of servants that no one knew what he ought to do. For there was no recollection of so great and terrible a mortality since the time of Vortigern, king of the Britons, in whose day, as Bede testifies, in his book concerning the deeds of the English, the living did not suffice to bury the dead.

In the following autumn a reaper was not to be had for less than 8*d,* with his food, a mower for less than 12*d,* with food. Therefore many crops rotted in the fields for lack of men to gather them. But in the year of the pestilence, as has been said above of other things, there was so great an abundance of all kinds of corn that virtually no one cared for it. . . .

At this time there was everywhere so great a scarcity of priests that many churches were left destitute, without divine service, masses, matins, vespers or sacraments. A chaplain was scarcely to be had to serve any church for less than £10 or 10 marks; and whereas when there was an abundance of priests before the pestilence a chaplain could be had for 4, 5 or even 2 marks with his board, at this time there was scarcely one willing to accept any vicarage at £20 or 20 marks. . . .

Meanwhile the king sent notice into all counties of the realm that reapers and other labourers should not receive more than they used to take, under a penalty defined by statute; and he introduced a statute for this reason. But the labourers were so arrogant and hostile that they took no notice of the king's mandate; and if anyone wanted to employ them he was obliged to give them whatever they asked, and either to lose his fruits and crops, or satisfy at will the labourers' greed and arrogance. When it became known to him that they did not observe his ordinance and gave higher stipends to their labourers, the king levied heavy amercements upon abbots, priors, knights of greater and lesser degree, and others great and small throughout the countryside, taking 100*s* from some, 40*s* or 20*s* from others, according as they were able to pay. . . .

In the following winter there was such a shortage of servants for all sorts of labour as it was believed had never been before. For the sheep and cattle strayed in all directions without herdsmen, and all things were left with no one to care for them. Thus necessaries became so dear that what had previously been worth 1*d* was now worth 4*d* or 5*d*. Moreover the great men of the land and other lesser lords who had tenants, remitted the payment of their rents, lest their tenants should go away, on account of the scarcity of servants and the high price of all things—some half their rents, some more, some less, some for one, two, or three years according as they could come to an agreement with them. Similarly, those who had let lands on yearly labour-services to tenants as is the custom in the case of villeins, were obliged to relieve and remit these services, either excusing them entirely, or taking them on easier terms, in the form of a small rent, lest their houses should be irreparably ruined and the land should remain completely uncultivated. And all sorts of food and necessities became excessively dear.

29

The Statutes of Kilkenny (1366). England and Her Other Island

The Statutes of Kilkenny (1366) stand as a monument to the failure of English-Irish relations. The frustrations of the Irish were readily apparent. Despite her cultural and educational achievements, beginning with Patrick (c. 389–c. 461) and continuing through the building of monasteries in northern Britain and in western Europe in the sixth through the eighth centuries, Ireland suffered misery piled upon misery. The Norwegians (counterparts to the Danes in England), came to plunder in the ninth and tenth centuries but remained to found such trading towns as Dublin, Waterford, and Limerick. Brian Boru, the High King, led the Irish in repelling the Norse in the battle of Clontarf in 1014, in a sense attempting to duplicate what Alfred had done for Wessex and England in 878. After Brian's death in that battle, the clans and the kings of Leinster, Munster, Ulster, and Connaught fell to fighting again. Ireland became a Celtic backwater, tempting intervention by the burgeoning Anglo-Norman kingdom of England. The English conquest, begun during the reign of Henry II (1154–1189), at one time dominated as much as two-thirds of Ireland.

The English suffered frustrations almost as great as those of the Irish. Though they controlled the Pale, where they had introduced English institutions such as Parliament and the common law, the area "beyond the Pale" remained the home of the "wild Irish." Even more disturbing was the realization that not even the Pale was secure. The relatively small number of English, further reduced by the Black Death in 1349, faced the threat of cultural absorption. Familiarity with the vastly more numerous native Irish could easily erode one's Englishness. This was especially true if marriage or, as the Statutes of Kilkenny put it, "concubinage or amour" occurred between the two races. As early as the reign of Edward I, those adopting Irish culture were referred to as "degenerate English."

The Statutes of Kilkenny, written in French and passed by the Irish parliament in 1366, attempted to force the English conquerors

Source: *Irish Historical Documents, 1172–1922*, edited by Edmund Curtis and R. B. McDowell. Published by Methuen & Co. Ltd., 1943, pp. 52–55. Reprinted by permission of Methuen & Co.

to retain their English identity. The effort was a failure, as were similar statutes passed again and again. The last, in 1495, abandoned as useless all efforts to restrict the speaking of Gaelic. The Statutes of Kilkenny tell much about the attitude of the English toward themselves as well as their opinion of subject peoples. The assertion that Britain's overseas empire began, and ended, with England's experiences in Ireland is not without foundation in fact.

Whereas at the conquest of the land of Ireland and for a long time after, the English of the said land used the English language, mode of riding and apparel and were governed and ruled, they and their subjects called *Betaghes,* by the English law. . . . But now many English of the said land, forsaking the English language, fashion, mode of riding, laws, and usages, live and govern themselves according to the manners, fashion and language of the Irish enemies, and also have made divers marriages and alliances between themselves and the Irish enemies aforesaid; whereby. . . the English laws there are put in subjection and decayed and the Irish enemies exalted and raised up contrary to right. Now therefore our lord the King, considering the mischiefs aforesaid, in consequence of the grievous complaints of the commons of his said land summoned to his Parliament held at Kilkenny the Thursday next after Ash Wednesday in the fortieth year of his reign [February 18, 1366], before his well-beloved son Lionel, Duke of Clarence, his Lieutenant in Ireland, to the honour of God and of his glorious Mother and of Holy Church and for the good government of the said land and quiet of the people and for the better observance of the laws and the punishment of evil doers, there are ordained and established by our said lord the King and his said Lieutenant and council there with the assent of the archbishops, bishops, abbots and priors (in that which appertains to them to assent to), the Earls, barons, and others the commons of the said land at the said parliament there assembled the ordinances and articles under-written to be held and kept perpetually, upon the penalties contained therein.

Firstly, it is ordained, agreed, and established that Holy Church be free and have all her franchises without infringement. . . .

Also it is ordained and established that no alliance by marriage, gossipred, fostering of children, concubinage or amour or in any other manner be henceforth made between the English and Irish on the one side or on the other. And that no Englishman or other person being at peace shall give or sell to any Irish in time of peace or war horses or armour or any manner of victuals in time of war. And if any do to the contrary and thereof be attaint, that he shall have judgment of life and limb as a traitor to our lord the King.

Also it is ordained and established that every Englishman shall use the English language and be named by an English name, leaving off entirely the manner of naming used by the Irish; and that every Englishman use the English custom, fashion, mode of riding and apparel according to his estate; and if any English or Irish living amongst the English use the Irish language amongst themselves contrary to this ordinance and thereof be attaint, that his lands and tenements, if he have any, be seized. . . .

In case that such person have not lands or tenements, then his body shall be taken by some of the officers of our lord the King and committed to the next gaol, there to remain until he or another in his name find sufficient surety in the manner aforesaid. And that no Englishman who has to the value of one hundred shillings of lands or tenements or of rent by the year shall ride otherwise than on a saddle in the English fashion, and he that shall do the contrary and be thereof attaint his horse shall be forfeited to our lord the King and his body committed to prison until he make fine according to the King's pleasure for the contempt aforesaid. And also that beneficed persons of Holy Church living amongst the English shall use the English language; and if they do not, then their ordinaries shall have the issues of their benefices until they use the English language as aforesaid; and they shall have respite in order to learn the English language and to provide saddles between this and the feast of Saint Michael next coming.

Also, whereas diversity of government and divers laws in one land cause diversity of allegiance and disputes among the people, it is agreed and established that no English having disputes with other English henceforth make distraint or take pledge, distress, or vengeance against any other whereby the people may be troubled, but that they shall sue each other at the common law, and that no English be governed in the settlement of their disputes by March or Brehon law, which by right ought not to be called law but bad custom; but that they be governed by the common law of the land as the lieges of our lord the King; and if any do to the contrary and thereof be attaint then he shall be taken and imprisoned and adjudged as a traitor. And that no difference of allegiance henceforth be made between the English born in Ireland and the English born in England by calling them 'English hobbe' or 'Irish dog,' but that all shall be called by one name [viz] the English lieges of our lord the King. . . .

Also, whereas a land which is at war requires that every person do render himself able to defend himself, it is ordained and established that the commons of the said land of Ireland who are in divers marches of war use not henceforth the games which men call 'hurlings' with great clubs at ball upon the ground, from which great evils and maims have arisen to the weakening of the defence of the said land. . . but that they apply and accustom themselves to use and draw bows and throw lances and other gentle games which appertain to arms, whereby the Irish enemies may be the better checked. . . .

Also it is ordained that no Irish of the nations [septs] of the Irish shall be admitted into any cathedral or collegiate church by provision, collation, or presentation of any person whatsoever or to any benefice of Holy Church amongst the English of the land. . . .

Also it is agreed and established that no house of religion which is situate among the English, whether it be exempt or not, shall henceforth receive any Irishmen [to their] profession but shall receive Englishmen, without taking into consideration that they be born in England or in Ireland. . . .

Also, whereas the Irish minstrels coming among the English spy out the secrets, customs and policies of the English whereby great evils have often happened, it is agreed and forbidden that any Irish minstrels, that is to say tympanours, poets, story-tellers, babblers, rymours, harpers or any other Irish minstrels [in the original, 'tympanours, fferdanes, skelaghes, bablers, rymours, clarsaghours'] shall come amongst the English; and that no English receive them or make gift to them.

30
John of Arderne, *Treatises of Fistula in Ano* (1376). A Surgeon's Code of Behavior

Medicine was in the fourteenth century a part of the curricula of many universities. Its study, however, had advanced little beyond the work of Galen, a second-century Greek physician. This was due, at least in part, to the reluctance of physicians to operate. Because surgery was manual labor and was inclined to be messy and even dangerous, doctors felt that it was beneath their dignity. As a result, most experimental work was done outside the universities by "surgeons," who necessarily received their training at first as apprentices and then at the expense of their early patients. There were both ordinary surgeons, or barbers, who performed common treatments such as leeching and pulling teeth, and master surgeons, such as John of Arderne (1306–1390?), who specialized in more delicate operations. Competition for business led ultimately to the creation of rival professional organizations, the Barber Guilds and the Surgeon Guilds.

Little is known of John of Arderne's life. He apparently received a good education and then acquired his practical skills as a sur-

Source: *English Historical Documents, Volume IV, 1327–1485*, edited by A. R. Myers, pp. 1184–1186.

geon during the Hundred Years' War. In his most famous work, *Treatises of Fistula in Ano* (1376), he made advances in the treatment of fistulas (abscesses) and gout and in the use of clysters (enemas). The large number of surviving translations of his Latin treatise indicates that his work was highly regarded. Although ahead of his colleagues, he was still a product of the fourteenth century, believing in astrology and, therefore, including in his book a section on the influence of the moon on surgery.

It is apparent from the following section that John of Arderne regarded medical practice as more than a matter of correct diagnosis and efficient treatment. He was concerned that surgeons maintain a code of conduct that would produce confidence in the patient's mind and money in the surgeon's pocket. The surgeon must always be aware of the social status of his patient. He must learn to set the correct fee. He must have a good bedside manner. And, he must be professionally responsible and not criticize his colleagues.

First, it behoves a surgeon who wishes to succeed in this craft always to put God first in all his doings, and always meekly to call with heart and mouth for his help, and sometimes give of his earnings to the poor, so that they by their prayers may gain him grace of the Holy Ghost. And he must not be found rash or boastful in his sayings or in his deeds; and he must abstain from much speech, especially among great men; and he must answer cautiously to all questions, so that he may not be trapped by his own words. For if his works are known to disagree often with his words and his promises, he will be held more unworthy, and he will tarnish his own good fame. . . . A surgeon should not laugh or joke too much; and as far as he can without harm, he should avoid the company of knaves and dishonest persons. He should be always occupied in things that belong to his craft, whether reading, studying, writing, or praying; the study of books is of great advantage to the surgeon, both by keeping him occupied and by making him wiser. Above all, it helps him much to be found always sober; for drunkenness destroys all wisdom and brings it to nought. In strange places he should be content with the meats and drinks which he finds there, using moderation in all things. . . . He must scorn no man. . . . If anyone talks to him about another surgeon, he must neither set him at nought nor praise nor commend him too much, but he may answer courteously thus: "I have no real knowledge of him, but I have neither learnt nor heard anything of him but what is good and honest." . . . A surgeon should not look too boldly at the lady or the daughters or other fair women in great men's houses, nor offer to kiss them, nor to touch them secretly or openly . . . lest he arouses the indignation of the lord or one of his household. . . . If sick men or any of their friends come to the surgeon to ask help or advice, let him be neither too brusque nor too familiar, but adjust his manner according to the character of the person; to some respectful, to some friendly. . . . Also it is a help for him to have excuses ready for not being able to undertake a case so that he does not hurt or anger some great man or friend, and does not interrupt some necessary work. Otherwise he could pretend to be hurt or ill or give some other likely excuse if he does not want to undertake a case. If he does undertake a case, he should make a clear agreement about payment and take the money in advance. But the surgeon should be sure not to make any definite pronouncement in any illness, unless he has first seen the sickness and the signs of it. When he has made an examination, even though he may think that the patient may be cured, he should warn the patient in his prognosis of the perils to come if treatment should be deferred. And if he sees that the patient is eager for the cure, then the surgeon must boldly adjust his fee to the man's status in life. But the surgeon should always beware of asking too little, for this is bad both for the market and the patient. Therefore for a case of fistula in ano, when it is curable, the surgeon may reasonably ask of a great man 100 marks or £40 with robes and fees to the value of 100 shillings each year for the rest of his life. From lesser men he may ask £40 or 40 marks without fees; but he must never take less than forty shillings. Never in my life have I taken less than 100 shillings for the cure of this disease; but of course every man must do what he thinks is right and most expedient. And if the patient or his friends and servants asks how long the cure will take, the surgeon had better always say twice as long as he really thinks; thus if a surgeon hopes to heal the patient in twenty weeks, which is the common period, let him add another twenty. For it is better to name a longer term for recovery than that the cure should drag on, a thing which might cause the patient to despair at the very time when confidence in the doctor is the greatest aid to recovery. For if the patient should later wonder or ask why the surgeon estimates so long for recovery when he was able to cure the patient in half the time, the surgeon should answer that it was because the patient had a strong heart and bore pain well and that he was of good complexion (that is, having such a combination of the four humours as would speed recovery) and that his flesh healed quickly; and he must think of other causes that would please the patient, for by such words are patients made proud and glad. And a surgeon should always be soberly dressed, not likening himself in clothing or bearing to minstrels, but rather after the manner of a clerk; for any discreet man clad in clerk's dress may sit at a gentleman's table. A surgeon must also have clean hands and well shaped nails, free from all blackness and dirt. And he should be courteous at the lord's table, and not displease the guests sitting by either in word or deed; he should hear many things but speak only a few. . . . A young doctor should also learn good proverbs relating to his craft to comfort his patients. . . . It is also expedient for the surgeon to be able to tell good honest tales that may make the patient laugh, both from the Bible and from other great books; and also any other stories that are not too dubious which may make the patient more cheerful. A surgeon should never betray inadvertently the confidences of his patients, either men or women, nor belittle one to another, even if he should have cause . . . for if men see that you can keep other men's confidences, they will have more confidence in you.

31
Rolls of the Prior and Convent of Durham (1378). Life of the Medieval Peasant

The traditional, and most readily accessible, historical evidence dealing with medieval England has one great failing: it ignores the peasants, who made up the bulk of the population. Chroniclers seldom referred to the peasants but concentrated instead on describing the activities of the secular and ecclesiastical leaders of society. Charters and related documents originating in the royal chancery dealt almost exclusively with relations between the king and his most important subjects. The popular literature of the period, mostly in French, was written to please the lords and ladies, not their serfs and hired laborers. The lower classes, if depicted in these writings at all, appeared almost subhuman.

Today, historians recognize that a vast amount of information dealing with the lower classes actually does exist. The most important new material consists of manorial court proceedings, records of financial and land transactions between peasants and landlords, and inventories of the landholdings and property of manors. Most of this material is now deposited in county record offices. Although some of it is well organized and indexed, much of it is still difficult for the historian to use.

Such evidence as the records of the manorial court of the Prior and Convent of Durham, reprinted below, give the historian a broader perspective on life in late medieval England. English histo-

Source: *English Historical Documents, Volume !V, 1327–1485*, edited by A. R. Myers, pp. 997–1000.

ry did not consist solely of endless feudal wars, developing legal institutions, and continuous constitutional conflicts, but also of the lives of ordinary people. For most village life revolved around the seasons of the year and the holidays of the church, not events taking place in distant London. In 1378 John Akke was, for example, undoubtedly more concerned about keeping his dogs from chasing his lord's sheep and thus staying out of court than he was about the composition of the council of the new king, Richard II.

At Bellyngham [Billingham] before the lords William Aslakbe, terrar, and Thomas Legat, bursar [i.e. officials of the convent] on Tuesday before the feast of the Purification of the Blessed Virgin Mary [28 January].

Billingham. . . . From all the tenants of the village because they did not repair the wethercot, as they were told to do in various halmotes—And they were ordered to repair the wethercot before the next meeting of the court on penalty of 40*s*. . . . All the tenants of the village were ordered not to follow an unjust path across the land called Litilmeres in the holding of Henry of the Neuraw, on penalty of 12*d.* It was ordered that everyone shall help to look after the pigs, and that everyone of them shall guard them, when his turn comes, until they have a common piggery, on penalty of 12*d.* It was ordered that none of them should dig in the high street in the village of Billyngham, on pain of 40*d.*

Neuton Vieuluve [Newton Beaulieu or Bewley]. Robert Smith came into court and took 1 cottage and 6 acres last in the tenure of John de Neuton, who lost it, because the aforesaid John was unwilling to stay there as he was ordered to do in several halmotes for the last three years. Robert is to have it for the term of his life, rendering for it the ancient rent. . . .

Acley. It was found by the oath of [8 jurors named] that John Clerk of Acley at the time when he killed Walter Tailliour had goods and chattels to the value of 26*s* 8*d* and they were given a day to show what goods and chattels of John came into the hands of John Tours the coroner and into whose hands the rest have come, within two weeks. The constable and all the tenants of the village were told not to let the chattels of felons or other fugitives be removed from the village; they were told to keep these chattels and cause them to be valued at their true value, until they should receive further orders from the prior and the bishop's official, on pain of 40*s.* It was ordered by common agreement that none of them should let any cattle trample down corn nor eat grass in any other place than is customary, on pain of half a mark.

Fery [Ferryhill]. All the tenants of the village and of the villages of East, West, and Mid Merrington and Chilton were ordered that none of them should play at ball [?football—*ad pilas*] henceforth on penalty of paying 40*s*. . . .

West Merrington. A day was given to John de Heswell to make his law with six hands at the next court [i.e. to exonerate himself with six oath-helpers], that he does not owe John of Galleway, chaplain, 16*s* 6*d* for the corn, which he ought to have paid him for two years past, to the injury of John, 6*s* 8*d*. . . .

Jarrow. Thomas, son of Simon Fig of Jarrow, came into court and took 3 cottages and 36 acres of land last held by Agnes widow of John Hewet, of which land 12 acres belong to each cottage. He has them for the term of his life, to pay the ancient rent, and to do proper service and fulfil all the other burdens.

Suthwyk [Southwick]. A day was given to Thomas son of Alan [and eleven others] to inquire about the boundaries between the lands of the lord prior which John son of Adam junior holds and the free land, formerly of Thomas Ayer, which John de Thornton now holds and they are to place the boundary marks. . . .

Wyvestowe. The tenants of Wyvestow were told that they must get the mill pond repaired, each for his part as much as is needed, on penalty of 40*d* and also that they do not hold the way beyond Caldwelmedowe, on pain of 40*d*. . . .

Schelles [Shields]. From Thomas son of Henry, 6*d* John Hilton junior [6*d* pardoned by the terrar], John Akke [6*d* pardoned by the terrar] because his dogs chased the lord's sheep and bit them as is presented by the shepherd. . . .

Estraynton [East Rainton]. All the tenants of the village were told to make a well near the spring, on account of the shares of the ploughs breaking up the ground, so that the spring can be kept clean, on pain of paying 12*d* by the man who works at the forge, from anyone who is unwilling to do this.—Richard Widouson was chosen reeve of the village and swore to do what belongs to the office and John Freman will be the collector of the rents. . . .

Pittyngton [Pittington]. It was presented that Robert of the Kiln of Cokon took two hares, Ralph of Malteby took 1 hare; Thomas Menenyl took 1 hare. William Ayr of Houghton is a common poacher, also Alan Bouer and John Gray.

Mid-Merrington. All the tenants of the village were told that no one should defame any other in words or deeds on pain of paying 40*s*. And a day was given for William Currour, John Smith, John de Fery, Roger Arowsmith, and William Byng, to inquire and present to the terrar at Durham who defamed Robert Robson and Mariot his wife and also night wanderers [i.e. presumably they were defamed of being night-wanderers and therefore suspect] on the Sunday next before Palm Sunday, on penalty of 20*s*, and also if John de Fery defamed the wife of John Doket calling her a whore and a thief.

Dalton. All the tenants of the village were told that none of them must allow any of their beasts to enter gardens to trample down crops nor any other necessary things within the gardens of neighbors, on pain of paying 12*d*.

32

Thomas Walsingham, *English History* (c. 1395). John Ball and the Peasants' Revolt, 1381

Thomas Walsingham (d. 1422?) was for many years the superintendent of the scriptorium of St. Albans, a Benedictine abbey noted for its scholarship, especially in the writing of chronicles. His most famous work, *Historia Anglicana,* from which the passage below is taken, covers the years 1372 to 1422. Although in places it follows the work of previous chroniclers, for the early years of Richard II's reign (1377–1399) it reflects Walsingham's original work.

The Peasants' Revolt of 1381, larger and more violent than earlier such disturbances, was the result of social dislocation caused by the plague, specific financial grievances such as the poll taxes levied by Parliament and, as is revealed below, growing resentment at the privileges claimed by landlords. Although the revolt led by Wat Tyler and John Ball failed, its violence caused great fear and alarm among the propertied classes. In their search for a scapegoat, chroniclers like Walsingham gave prominence to the influence of John Ball, who is portrayed as a subversive seeking to "corrupt" the people by preaching "the perverse doctrines of the perfidious John Wycliffe."

This description of John Ball raises a number of questions. How widespread, for example, were Ball's ideas? Some recent scholars argue that his egalitarianism was fairly common in the fourteenth century. Also, was Ball associated with Wycliffe's Lollardy, or were the ecclesiastical chroniclers simply attempting to discredit the Lollards by identifying them with the social radicalism of Ball? Since the chroniclers of this period were all biased against the ideas of Ball and Tyler, their descriptions of these men must be subjected to the greatest scrutiny.

All of Walsingham's manuscripts were published in the Rolls Series in the late nineteenth century.

Moreover, on that day [Saturday 13 July] the same Robert [Tresilian] sentenced John Balle, priest, after hearing of his scandalous and confessed crimes,

Source: The Peasants' Revolt of 1381, edited by R. B. Dobson, London: Macmillan and Co., 1970, pp. 373–375. Reprinted by the permission of Macmillan, London and Basingstoke.

to drawing, hanging, beheading, disembowelling and—to use the common words—quartering: he had been taken by the men of Coventry and on the previous day brought to St. Albans and into the presence of the king whose majesty he had insulted so gravely. His death was postponed until the following Monday [15 July] by the intervention of Lord William [Courtenay] bishop of London, who obtained a short deferment so that Balle could repent for the sake of his soul.

For twenty years and more Balle had been preaching continually in different places such things as he knew were pleasing to the people, speaking ill of both ecclesiastics and secular lords, and had rather won the goodwill of the common people than merit in the sight of God. For he instructed the people that tithes ought not to be paid to an incumbent unless he who should give them were richer than the rector or vicar who received them; and that tithes and offerings ought to be withheld if the parishioner were known to be a man of better life than his priest; and also that none were fit for the Kingdom of God who were not born in matrimony. He taught, moreover, the perverse doctrines of the perfidious John Wycliffe, and the insane opinions that he held, with many more that it would take long to recite. Therefore, being prohibited by the bishops from preaching in parishes and churches, he began to speak in streets and squares and in the open fields. Nor did he lack hearers among the common people, whom he always strove to entice to his sermons by pleasing words, and slander of the prelates. At last he was excommunicated as he would not desist and was thrown into prison, where he predicted that he would be set free by twenty thousand of his friends. This afterwards happened in the said disturbances, when the commons broke open all the prisons, and made the prisoners depart.

And when he had been delivered from prison, he followed them, egging them on to commit greater evils, and saying that such things must surely be done. And, to corrupt more people with his doctrine, at Blackheath, where two hundred thousand of the commons were gathered together, he began a sermon in this fashion:

"Whan Adam dalf, and Eve span,
Wo was thanne a gentilman?"

And continuing his sermon, he tried to prove by the words of the proverb that he had taken for his text, that from the beginning all men were created equal by nature, and that servitude had been introduced by the unjust and evil oppression of men, against the will of God, who, if it had pleased Him to create serfs, surely in the beginning of the world would have appointed who should be a serf and who a lord. Let them consider, therefore, that He had now appointed the time wherein, laying aside the yoke of long servitude, they might, if they wished, enjoy their liberty so long desired. Wherefore they must be prudent, hastening to act after the manner of a good husbandman, tilling his field, and uprooting the tares that are accustomed to destroy the grain; first killing the great lords of the realm, then slaying the lawyers, justices and jurors, and finally rooting out everyone whom they knew to be harmful to the community in future. So at last they would obtain peace and security, if, when the great ones had been removed, they maintained among themselves equality of liberty and nobility, as well as of dignity and power.

And when he had preached these and many other ravings, he was in such high favour with the common people that they cried out that he should be archbishop and Chancellor of the kingdom, and that he alone was worthy of the office, for the present archbishop was a traitor to the realm and the commons, and should be beheaded wherever he could be found.

33
Geoffrey Chaucer, *The Canterbury Tales* (c. 1387–1400). The Wife of Bath

Geoffrey Chaucer (c. 1343–1400) was England's first literary giant. Born in London, he spent a lifetime serving kings and princes. In the Hundred Years' War, he was captured by the French in 1359 and ransomed in 1360. He traveled to Italy for King Edward III, and if he did not meet Boccaccio and Petrarch, he certainly became acquainted with their writing. He married the sister of Katherine Swynford, who later married John of Gaunt, the most powerful man in England and Chaucer's patron. Chaucer was buried in Westminster Abbey in what was to become the Poets' Corner.

The Canterbury Tales was probably begun in 1387, when Chaucer was temporarily out of royal service. In the General Prologue, he describes some two dozen pilgrims wending their way to the shrine of St. Thomas Becket at Canterbury. To while away the time, each tells a tale. There is a cross-section of medieval society: a gallant knight, a loud and lusty miller, a university student, and a handful of clerics, from the worldly prioress to the admirable parson. Perhaps most memorable of all is the Wife of Bath, a comic character who can be compared to Shakespeare's Falstaff.

Source: Geoffrey Chaucer, *The Canterbury Tales*, translated into Modern English by Nevill Coghill, Revised Edition (Baltimore: Penguin Books, 1977), pp. 31–32, 276–278, 281–283, 290.

The passage below begins with the General Prologue's description of the Wife of Bath. Passages from the long prologue to the Wife's tale describe her attitude toward marriage and her five husbands. Written by Chaucer, a man, the prologue reflects traditional antifeminist attitudes, both comic and serious. But it is almost as if the Wife herself takes over the telling, demonstrating the inadequacy of the tradition, pointing out the foibles of men and women alike, and becoming literature's first feminist. According to Charles Muscatine, the Wife of Bath is "an antagonist in three parallel medieval controversies: she represents practical experience as against received authority, female freedom as against male domination, and unblushing sensuality as against emotional austerity."

The Canterbury Tales can be read in the original Middle English only with difficulty, as shown by the famous opening lines of the General Prologue:

> Whan that Aprill with his shoures soote
> The droghte of March hath perced to the roote.

The tales are written in the dialect of the East Midlands and London, the immediate parent of the modern English, which came into being a century later.

FROM THE GENERAL PROLOGUE

A worthy *woman* from beside *Bath* city
Was with us, somewhat deaf, which was a pity.
In making cloth she showed so great a bent
She bettered those of Ypres and of Ghent.
In all the parish not a dame dared stir
Towards the altar steps in front of her,
And if indeed they did, so wrath was she
As to be quite put out of charity.
Her kerchiefs were of finely woven ground;
I dared have sworn they weighted a good ten pound,
The ones she wore on Sunday, on her head.
Her hose were of the finest scarlet red
And gartered tight; her shoes were soft and new.
Bold was her face, handsome, and red in hue.
A worthy woman all her life, what's more
She'd had five husbands, all at the church door,
Apart from other company in youth;
No need just now to speak of that, forsooth.

And she had thrice been to Jerusalem,
Seen many strange rivers and passed over them;
She'd been to Rome and also to Boulogne,
St James of Compostella and Cologne,
And she was skilled in wandering by the way.
She had gap-teeth, set widely, truth to say.
Easily on an ambling horse she sat
Well wimpled up, and on her head a hat
As broad as is a buckler or a shield;
She had a flowing mantle that concealed
Large hips, her heels spurred sharply under that.
In company she liked to laugh and chat
And knew the remedies for love's mischances,
An art in which she knew the oldest dances.

THE WIFE OF BATH'S PROLOGUE

'IF there were no authority on earth
Except experience; mine, for what it's worth,
And that's enough for me, all goes to show
That marriage is a misery and a woe;
For let me say, if I may make so bold,
My lords, since when I was but twelve years old,
Thanks be to God Eternal evermore,
Five husbands have I had at the church door;
Yes, it's a fact that I have had so many,
All worthy in their way, as good as any.
'Someone said recently for my persuasion
That as Christ only went on one occasion
To grace a wedding—in Cana of Galilee—
He taught me by example there to see
That it is wrong to marry more than once.
Consider, too, how sharply, for the nonce,
He spoke, rebuking the Samaritan
Beside the well, Christ Jesus, God and man.
"Thou hast had five men husband unto thee
And he that even now thou hast," said He,
"Is not thy husband." Such the words that fell;
But what He meant thereby I cannot tell.
Why was her fifth—explain it if you can—
No lawful spouse to the Samaritan?
How many might have had her, then, to wife?

I've never heard an answer all my life
To give the number final definition.
People may guess or frame a supposition,
But I can say for certain, it's no lie,
God bade us all to wax and multiply.
That kindly text I well can understand.
Is not my husband under God's command
To leave his father and mother and take me?
No word of what the number was to be,
Then why not marry two or even eight?
And why speak evil of the married state?
'Take wise King Solomon of long ago;
We hear he had a thousand wives or so.
And would to God it were allowed to me
To be refreshed, aye, half so much as he!
He must have had a gift of God for wives,
No one to match him in a world of lives!
This noble king, one may as well admit,
On the first night threw many a merry fit
With each of them, he was so much alive.
Blessed be God that I have wedded five!
Welcome the sixth, whenever he appears.
I can't keep continent for years and years.
No sooner than one husband's dead and gone
Some other christian man shall take me on,
For then, so says the Apostle, I am free
To wed, o' God's name, where it pleases me.
Wedding's no sin, so far as I can learn.
Better it is to marry than to burn.
'Now, gentlemen, I'll on and tell my tale
And as I hope to drink good wine and ale
I'll tell the truth. Those husbands that I had,
Three of them were good and two were bad.
The three that I call 'good' were rich and old.
They could indeed with difficulty hold
The articles that bound them all to me;
(No doubt you understand my simile).
So help me God, I have to laugh outright
Remembering how I made them work at night!
And faith I set no store by it; no pleasure
It was to me. They'd given me their treasure,
I had no need to do my diligence
To win their love or show them reverence.

They loved me well enough, so, heavens above,
Why should I make a dainty of their love?
'A knowing woman's work is never done
To get a lover if she hasn't one,
But as I had them eating from my hand
And as they'd yielded me their gold and land,
Why then take trouble to provide them pleasure
Unless to profit and amuse my leisure?
I set them so to work, I'm bound to say;
Many a night they sang, "Alack the day!" . . .
I governed them so well and held the rein
So firmly they were rapturously fain
To go and buy me pretty things to wear;
They were delighted if I spoke them fair.
God knows how spitefully I used to scold them.
'Listen, I'll tell you how I used to hold them,
You knowing women, who can understand.
First put them in the wrong, and out of hand.
No one can be so bold—I mean no man—
At lies and swearing as a woman can.
This is no news, as you'll have realized,
To knowing ones, but to the misadvised.
A knowing wife if she is worth her salt
Can always prove her husband is at fault,
And even though the fellow may have heard
Some story told him by a little bird
She knows enough to prove the bird is crazy
And get her maid to witness she's a daisy,
With full agreement, scarce solicited.
'Now of my fifth, last husband let me tell.
God never let his soul be sent to Hell!
And yet he was my worst, and many a blow
He struck me still can ache along my row
Of ribs, and will until my dying day.
'But in our bed he was so fresh and gay,
So coaxing, so persuasive. . . . Heaven knows
Whenever he wanted it—my *belle chose*—
Though he had beaten me in every bone
He still could wheedle me to love, I own.
I think I loved him best, I'll tell no lie.
He was disdainful in his love, that's why.
We women have a curious fantasy
In such affairs, or so it seems to me.

When something's difficult, or can't be had,
We crave and cry for it all day like mad.
Forbid a thing, we pine for it all night,
Press fast upon us and we take to flight;
We use disdain in offering our wares.
A throng of buyers sends prices up at fairs,
Cheap goods have little value, they suppose;
And that's a thing that every woman knows.'

34
William Langland, *Piers the Plowman* (c. 1390). A Description of English Society

William Langland (c. 1332–c. 1400) lived in obscure poverty. Despite a good education, he took only minor orders and, hence, never qualified for a lucrative position in the Church. He appears to have been something of a dreamer, spending much of his time writing unrhymed, alliterative poetry, a popular form of literature that had survived from the Anglo-Saxon period. *Piers the Plowman,* written and twice revised between about 1360 and 1390, is by far the best example of this type of poetry. It is a medieval allegory describing the visions of "William," presumably Langland himself. These visions, panoramas of fourteenth-century England, gradually reveal to William something of the nature of truth and righteousness.

Piers the Plowman is of importance to the social historian. The passage below describes the various social classes and reveals Langland as an astute observer. Although not a revolutionary, he was certainly a social critic, condemning in particular the failings of the higher clergy. The numerous surviving manuscripts indicate that Langland's work was highly regarded by his contemporaries, perhaps because it supported the social radicalism of the period.

Langland's poetry is also of value in studying the English language. The fourteenth century saw a renewed use of English by the

Source: William Langland, *Piers the Ploughman,* translated by J. F. Goodridge (Penguin Classics, 1966), pp. 25–28, 31.

government and in literature. Both *Piers the Plowman* and the statute of 1362 ordering the use of English in royal law courts were parts of the same movement away from French and Latin. The English used by Langland was neither the Anglo-Saxon, or Old English, of *Beowulf* and "Maldon" nor the modern English of Shakespeare. Rather, it was a "Middle English," descended from a mingling of Anglo-Saxon and French and still made up of a number of regional dialects. Langland actually used several dialects in his writings, the dominant one being that of the West Midlands.

Piers the Plowman remained popular through the turbulent fifteenth century. By the reign of Elizabeth I (1558–1603), however, English was becoming standardized, and people could no longer handle the dialects used by Langland. His work was increasingly dismissed as medieval allegory and offensive to modern tastes. No new edition of *Piers the Plowman* appeared between 1561 and 1813; only recently has Langland come to be recognized as one of the great literary talents of late medieval England.

One summer season, when the sun was warm, I rigged myself out in shaggy woollen clothes, as if I were a shepherd; and in the garb of an easy-living hermit I set out to roam far and wide through the world, hoping to hear of marvels. But on a morning in May, among the Malvern Hills, a strange thing happened to me, as though by magic. For I was tired out by my wanderings, and as I lay down to rest under a broad bank by the side of a stream, and leaned over gazing into the water, it sounded so pleasant that I fell asleep.

And I dreamt a marvellous dream: I was in a wilderness, I could not tell where, and looking Eastwards I saw a tower high up against the sun, and splendidly built on a top of a hill; and far beneath it was a great gulf, with a dungeon in it, surrounded by deep, dark pits, dreadful to see. But between the tower and the gulf I saw a smooth plain, thronged with all kinds of people, high and low together, moving busily about their worldly affairs.

Some laboured at ploughing and sowing, with no time for pleasure, sweating to produce food for the gluttons to waste. Others spent their lives in vanity, parading themselves in a show of fine clothes. But many, out of love for our Lord and in the hope of Heaven, led strict lives devoted to prayer and penance—for such are the hermits and anchorites who stay in their cells, and are not forever hankering to roam about, and pamper their bodies with sensual pleasures.

Others chose to live by trade, and were much better off—for in our worldly eyes such men seem to thrive. Then there were the professional entertainers, some of whom, I think, are harmless minstrels, making an honest living by their music; but others, babblers and vulgar jesters, are true Judas' children! They in-vent fantastic tales about themselves, and pose as half-wits, yet they show wits enough whenever it suits them, and could easily work for a living if they had to! I will not say all that St Paul says about them; it is enough to quote, "He who talks filth is a servant of the Devil."

And there were tramps and beggars hastening on their rounds, with their bellies and their packs crammed full of bread. They lived by their wits, and fought over their ale—for God knows, they go to bed glutted with food and drink, these brigands, and get up with foul language and filthy talk; and all day long, Sleep and shabby Sloth are at their heels.

And I saw pilgrims and palmers banding together to visit the shrines at Rome and Compostella. They went on their way full of clever talk, and took leave to tell fibs about it for the rest of their lives. And some I heard spinning such yarns of the shrines they had visited, you could tell by the way they talked that their tongues were more tuned to lying than telling the truth, no matter what tale they told.

Troops of hermits with their hooded staves were on their way to Walsingham, with their wenches following after. These great, long lubbers, who hated work, were got up in clerical gowns to distinguish them from laymen, and paraded as hermits for the sake of an easy life.

I saw the Friars there too—all four Orders of them—preaching to the people for what they could get. In their greed for fine clothes, they interpreted the Scriptures to suit themselves and their patrons. Many of these Doctors of Divinity can dress as handsomely as they please, for as their trade advances, so their profits increase. And now that Charity has gone into business, and become confessor-in-chief to wealthy lords, many strange things have happened in the last few years; unless the Friars and Holy Church mend their quarrel, the worst evil in the world will soon be upon us. . . .

Then there came into the field a king, guided by the knights. The powers of the Commons gave him his throne, and Common Sense provided men of learning to counsel him and to protect the people.

The king, with his nobles and counsellors, decided that the common people should provide them with resources; so the people devised different trades, and engaged ploughmen to labour and till the soil for the good of the whole community, as honest ploughmen should. Then the king and the people, helped by Common Sense, established law and order, so that every man might know his rights and duties. . . .

Besides all this, a hundred men in silk gowns stood swaying from side to side and making speeches. These were the lawyers who served at the bar, pleading their cases for as much money as they could get. Never once did they open their mouths out of love for our Lord; indeed you could sooner measure the mist on the Malvern Hills, than get a sound out of them without first producing some cash!

I saw many more in this great concourse of people, as you shall hear presently: barons, burgesses, and peasants; bakers, brewers, and butchers; linen-weavers and tailors, tinkers and toll-collectors, masons and miners and many other tradesfolk. And all kinds of labourers suddenly appeared—shoddy workmen, who would while away their hours with bawdy songs—like "Dieu vous save, Dame Emme!"—while cooks with their boys cried, "Hot pies! Hot pies! Fat pigs and geese! Come and eat!" and inn-keepers were bawling, "White wine! Red wine! Gascon and Spanish! Wash down your meat with the finest Rhenish!"—

All this I saw in my dream, and a great deal more besides.

35
The *Gest of Robyn Hode*

Robin Winks maintains that a historian's way of handling evidence is "not greatly different from the techniques employed by the detective." This is especially true when one is dealing with the facts surrounding such a murky figure as Robin Hood, who, one recent historian has argued, is to the general public "the most memorable figure in the whole history of medieval England." The first literary mention of a "Robyn Hood" is in *Piers the Plowman* in the late fourteenth century. The search for the historical figure behind this name has occupied the attention of numerous scholars over the past two centuries, but no agreement has yet been reached.

The first, and probably the most important, investigation of the historical Robin Hood was by Joseph Ritson in 1795. An admirer of the Jacobins of the French Revolution, Ritson created the popular Robin Hood—the outlawed nobleman, most likely the Earl of Huntingdon, born about 1160, who during the reign of Richard I gathered about him a band of bowmen to protect the poor from greedy barons and churchmen. Ritson's Robin Hood, similar to the character portrayed by Errol Flynn and Kevin Costner, captured the public's imagination. Ritson's interpretation was soon challenged by other scholars, who studied not only the hints in the ballads but evidence of the numerous Robin (diminutive of Robert) Hoods or Hudes (a common English surname) in government documents.

Source: R. B. Dobson and J. Taylor, eds. *Rymes of Robyn Hood: An Introduction to the English Outlaw,* London: Heinemann, 1976, pp. 79–80, 112.

Joseph Hunter in the 1850s placed Robin Hood in the household of Edward II, a thesis expanded on by J. W. Walker in the 1940s. In more recent years, J. C. Holt has persuasively argued for a Robert Hode or "Hobbehod" of Yorkshire in the 1220s.

The *Gest of Robyn Hode,* dating from the late fourteenth century, is generally acknowledged to be the oldest of the Robin Hood ballads. It was probably intended for a well-born audience, in places reading "like a manual on decorous behaviour in upper-class late medieval society." Because of the importance accorded to Sir Richard at the Lee, some scholars argue that the *Gest* was most likely commissioned by Sir John de la Lee, who had been dismissed from the household of Edward III in 1368. He may have been trying to improve his image by means of a kinsman associated, in a nonviolent way, with the already famous Robin Hood. Certainly, the *Gest* was an upper-class attempt to secure to itself the benefits of an identification with England's most popular hero. The *Gest*'s basis in fact gave "credibility for what was a piece of propaganda as much as a piece of entertainment."

No manuscript copy of the *Gest of Robyn Hode* has survived. The oldest printed edition, dating to about 1510, is in the National Library at Edinburgh.

1

Lythe and listin, gentilmen,
That be of frebore blode;
I shall you tel of a gode yeman,
His name was Robyn Hode.

2

Robyn was a prude outlaw,
Whyles he walked on grounde;
So curteyse an outlawe as he was one
Was never non founde.

3

Robyn stode in Bernesdale,
And lenyd hym to a tre;
And bi hym stode Litell John,
A gode yeman was he.

4

And alsoo dyd good Scarlok,
And Much, the myller's son;
There was non ynche of his bodi,
But it was worth a grome.

5

Than bespake Lytell Johnn
All untoo Robyn Hode:
'Maister, and ye wolde dyne betyme
It wolde doo you moche gode.'

6

Than bespake hym gode Robyn:
'To dyne have I noo lust,
Till that I have som bolde baron,
Or some *unketh* gest.

7

Till that I have som bolde baron,
That may pay for the best,
Or som knyght, or *some* squyer
That dwelleth here bi west.'

8

A gode maner than had Robyn;
In londe where that he were,
Euery day or he wold dyne
Thre messis wolde he here:

9

The one in the worship of the Fader,
And another of the Holy Ghost,
The thirde of Our dere Lady
That he loved allther moste.

10

Robyn loved Oure dere Lady;
For dout of dydly synne
Wolde he never do compani harme
That any woman was in.

11

'Maistar,' than sayde Lytil Johnn,
'And we our borde shal sprede,
Tell us wheder that we shal go
And what life that we shall lede;

12

'Where we shall take, where we shall leve,
Where we shall abide behynde,
Where we shall robbe, where we shal reve,
Where we shal bete and bynde.'

13

'Thereof no force,' than sayde Robyn;
'We shall do well inowe;
But loke ye do no husbonde harme
That *tylleth* with his ploughe.

14

'No more ye shall no gode yeman
That walketh by grene wode shawe;
Ne no knyght ne no squyer
That wol be a gode felawe.

15

'These bisshoppes and these arche-bishoppes,
Ye shall them bete and bynde;
The hye sherif of Notyingham,
Hym holde ye in your *mynde.'*

16

'This worde shalbe holde,' sayde Lytell Johnn,
  'And this lesson we shall lere;
It is fer dayes; God sende us a gest,
  That we were at oure dynere.'

17

'Take thy gode bowe in thy honde,' sayde Rob*yn,*
  'Late Much wende with the,
And so shal Willyam Scarlo*ke;*
  And no man abyde with me;

18

'And walke up to the Saylis,
  And so to Watl*in*ge Stret *e*
And wayte after some *unketh* gest;
  Up chaunce ye may them mete.

19

'Be he erle, or ani baron,
  Abbot, or ani knyght,
Bringhe hym to lodge to me;
  His dyner shall be dight.'

• • •

456

Cryst have mercy on his soule,
  That dyed on the rode!
For he was a good outlawe,
  And dyde pore men moch god.

36

Statute of Praemunire (1393). Anti-Papal Sentiment in Parliament

The long-standing rivalry between Rome and the English secular state was intensified by the conditions of the fourteenth century. The pope's transfer of residence from Rome to Avignon, adjacent to France, marked a decline in his prestige in England, especially after the outbreak of the Hundred Years' War in 1337.

Although popes had long claimed the right to make direct appointments—called provisions, the men thus appointed being called provisors—to English church offices, opposition remained slight or intermittent until this papal interference was taken up by Parliament in the mid-fourteenth century. Provisors, often foreigners and absentees, were increasingly a threat to English clerics seeking promotions and a drain on English money. The Statute of Provisors of 1351, based on the idea that the patronage of a church office was a property right protected by English courts, was designed to stop the pope's traffic in English ecclesiastical benefices. When the papacy persisted in issuing provisions and enforcing them in church courts, even with bulls of excommunication, the Statute of Praemunire of 1353 made it a crime to appeal to a foreign (meaning papal) court if an English court had jurisdiction. That these statutes were not readily heeded is indicated by the former's being renewed in stronger terms in 1390 and the latter's being renewed in 1365 and 1393. The act of 1393, reproduced below and often called the Great Statute of Praemunire, differed from earlier legislation in the breadth of its denial of papal jurisdiction in England and in the severity of its punishment.

To a great extent, the statutes were not enforced. The king generally ignored the powers the acts gave him and, instead, joined with the pope to make appointments agreeable to them both. Nevertheless, Praemunire's occasional use and its claim that the "crown of England . . . has had no earthly lord," reflects a sense of national consciousness. The Great Statute of Praemunire is important as a reminder that medieval kings did not readily bow to the papacy when their own or their kingdom's interests were at

Source: English Historical Documents, Volume IV, 1327–1485, edited by A. R. Myers, pp. 661–662.

I suppose ye should have such things of Sir John Fastolf, if ye would send to him; and also I would ye should get two or three short Poleaxes to keep with doors, and as many Jacks, and ye may.

Partrich and his fellowship are sore afraid that ye would enter again upon them, and they have made great ordnance within the house, and it is told me they have made bars to bar the doors cross wise, and they have made wickets on every quarter of the house to shoot out at, both with bows and with hand-guns; and the holes that be made for handguns they be scarce knee high from the plancher (*floor*) and of such holes be made five, there can none man shoot out at them with no handbows.

Purry fell in fellowship with William Hasard at Quarles's, and told him that he would come and drink with Partrich and with him, and he said he should be welcome, and after noon he went thither for to espy what they did and what fellowship they had with them; and when he came thither the doors were fast sparred and there were none folks with them but Mariott, and Capron and his wife, and Quarles's wife, and another man in a black, went somewhat halting, I suppose by his words that it was Norfolk of Gimmingham; and the said Purry espied all these foresaid things.

And Mariott and his fellowship had much great language that shall be told you when ye come home.

I pray you that ye will vouchsafe to do buy for me one lb. of Almonds and one lb. of sugar, that ye will do buy some frieze to make of your child his gowns, ye shall have best cheap, and best choice of Hay's wife, as it is told me. And that ye will buy a yard of broad cloth of black for one hood for me of 44*d.* or four Shillings a yard, for there is neither good cloth nor good frieze in this town. As for the child his gowns and I have them, I will do them maken (*have them made*).

The Trinity have you in his keeping, and send you good speed in all your matters.

Agnes Paston to John Paston, 12 March 1450

SON, I greet you, and send you God's blessing and mine; as for my daughter your wife she fareth well, blessed be God! as a woman in her plight may do, and all your Sons and Daughters.

And for as much as ye will send me no tidings, I send you such as be in this Country; Richard Lynsted came this day from Paston and let me weet, that on Saturday last past, Dravell, half-brother to Warren Harman, was taken with enemies, walking by the Sea side, and have him forth with them, and they took two Pilgrims, a man and a woman, and they robbed the woman and let her go, and led the man to the Sea; and when they knew he was a Pilgrim they gave him money, and set him again on the land; and they have this week taken four Vessels of Winterton, and Happisborough and Eccles.

Men be sore afraid for taking of men, for there be ten great Vessels of the Enemy's; God give grace that the sea may be better kept than it is now, or else it shall be perilous dwelling by the sea coast. . . .

Written at Norwich, the Wednesday next before Saint Gregory. . . .

John Crane to John Paston, 25 May 1455

RIGHT worshipful and entirely well beloved Sir, I recommend me unto you, desiring heartily to hear of your welfare.

Furthermore letting you weet, as for such Tidings as we have here, these three Lords be dead, the Duke of Somerset, the Earl of Northumberland, and the Lord Clifford; and as for any other men of name, I know none, save only Cotton of Cambridgeshire.

As for any other Lords, many of them be hurt, and as for Fylongley he liveth, and fareth well, as far as I can enquire, &c.

And as for any great Multitude of people that there was, as we can tell, there was at most slain six score; and as for the Lords that were with the King, they and their men were pilled and spoiled out of all their Harness and Horses; and as for what Rule we shall have yet I weet not, save only there be made new certain Officers.

My Lord of York, Constable of England; my Lord of Warwick is made Captain of Calais; my Lord Bourchier is made Treasurer of England; and as yet other Tidings have I none.

And as for Our Sovereign Lord, thanked be God, he hath no great harm.

No more to you at this time, but I pray you send this Letter to my Mistress Paston, when ye have seen it; praying you to remember my Sister Margaret against the time that she shall be made a Nun.

Written at Lamehith (*Lambeth*) on Whitsunday, &c.

By your Cousin,

own parishes, there to live as "a true man ought to do." This act was the most harsh and punitive of the poor laws passed during the Tudor period. Later acts, beginning in 1536 and finally assuming definitive form in 1598 and 1601, stipulated that the honest poor were to be assisted by a tax levied on the parish. Sturdy beggars, although still to be whipped and sent home if caught outside their own parish, were to be provided with parish-sponsored work.

Such legislation expanded the duties of the already busy justices of the peace and helped to create the parish as a subunit of county government with the primary responsibility for the oversight of the poor. Equally important, the poor laws, harsh though they might appear, marked the beginning of the attempt by the royal government to solve problems that had formerly been left to the Church and to local charity. Its attempts at providing for the commonwealth—the commonweal, or the common good—mark the beginning of the royal government's active interest in the social and economic welfare of the people.

Where in all places throughout this realm of England vagabonds and beggars have of long time increased and daily do increase in great and excessive numbers, by the occasion of idleness, mother and root of all vices, whereby hath insurged and sprung and daily insurgeth and springeth continual thefts, murders, and other heinous offences and great enormities, to the high displeasure of God, the inquietation and damage of the King's people, and to the marvellous disturbance of the common weal of this realm. . . . Be it therefore enacted . . . That the Justices of the Peace . . . shall make diligent search and enquiry of all aged, poor, and impotent persons which live or of necessity be compelled to live by alms of the charity of the people that be or shall be hereafter abiding . . . within the limits of their division, and after and upon such search made the said Justices . . . shall have power and authority by their discretions to enable to beg, within such . . . limits as they shall appoint, such of the said impotent persons which they shall find and think most convenient within the limits of their division to live of the charity and alms of the people, and to give in commandment to every such aged and impotent beggar (by them enabled) that none of them shall beg without the limits to them so appointed, and shall also register and write the names of every such impotent beggar (by them appointed) in a bill or roll indented, the one part thereof to remain with themselves and the other part by them to be certified before the Justices of Peace at the next Sessions after such search . . . there to remain under the keeping of the Custos Rotulorum; And that the said Justices of Peace . . . shall make and deliver to every such impotent person by them enabled to beg, a letter containing the name of such impotent person and witnessing that he is authorised to beg and the limits within which he is appointed to beg, the same letter to be sealed with such . . . seals as shall be engraved with the name of the limit wherein such impotent person shall be appointed to beg in, and to be subscribed with the name of one of the said Justices. . . . And if any such impotent person so authorised to beg do beg in any other place than within such limits that he shall be assigned unto, that then the Justices of Peace . . . shall by their discretions punish all such persons by imprisonment in the stocks by the space of 2 days and 2 nights, giving them but only bread and water, and after that cause every such impotent person to be sworn to return again without delay to the [*limits* . . .] where they be authorised to beg in.

III. And be it further enacted . . . That if any person or persons being whole and mighty in body and able to labour, . . . or if any man or woman being whole and mighty in body and able to labour having no land, master, nor using any lawful merchandise, craft, or mystery, whereby he might get his living . . . be vagrant and can give none reckoning how he doth lawfully get his living, that then it shall be lawful to the constables and all other the King's officers, ministers, and subjects of every town, parish, and hamlet to arrest the said vagabonds and idle persons and them to bring to any of the Justices of Peace of the same shire or liberty . . . and that every such Justice of Peace . . . shall cause every such idle person so to him brought to be had to the next market town or other place where the said Justices of Peace . . . shall think most convenient, . . . and there to be tied to the end of a cart naked and be beaten with whips throughout the same market town or other place till his body be bloody by reason of such whipping; and after such punishment and whipping had, the person so punished . . . shall be enjoined upon his oath to return forthwith without delay in the next and straight way to the place where he was born, or where he last dwelled before the same punishment by the space of 3 years, and there put himself to labour like as a true man oweth to do. . . .

IV. And be it enacted . . . That scholars of the Universities of Oxford and Cambridge that go about begging, not being authorised under the seal of the said Universities . . . and all and singular shipment pretending losses of their ships and goods of the sea going about the country begging without sufficient authority witnessing the same, shall be punished and ordered in manner and form as is above rehearsed of strong beggars . . . and all other idle persons going about in any countries or abiding in any city, borough, or town, some of them using divers and subtile crafty and unlawful games and plays, and some of them feigning themselves to have knowledge in physic, physnamy, palmistry, or other crafty sciences, whereby they bear the people in hand that they can tell their destinies, deceases, and fortunes, and such other like fantastical imaginations, to the great deceit of the King's subjects, shall upon examination had before two Justices of Peace, whereof the one shall be of the Quorum, if he by provable witness be found guilty of any such deceits, be punished by whipping at two days together after the manner above rehearsed: And if he eftsoons offend in the said offence or any like offence, then to be scourged two days and the third day to be put upon the pillory from 9 of the clock till 11 before noon of the same day, and to have one of his ears cut off; and if he offend the third time, to have like punishment with whipping, standing on the pillory, and to have his other ear cut off.

42

Reformation Statutes: Act in Restraint of Appeals (1533), Act of Supremacy (1534)

Henry VIII (1509–1547) called the Reformation Parliament in 1529, when it became apparent that his chancellor, Cardinal Wolsey, could not obtain from Rome the annulment of Henry's marriage to Catherine of Aragon. Henry's patience had run out: he wanted a legitimate male heir, and that by Anne Boleyn. He hoped that Parliament could succeed where Wolsey had failed, frightening the pope into thinking England might follow the example of Lutheran Germany. Henry, however, had to wait another three and a half years before he was free of Catherine and able to marry Anne. The Act in Restraint of Appeals, the instrument which made this possible, shows the genius of his new adviser, Thomas Cromwell. Though the act appears long and convoluted, it was, in fact, very simple. Its effect was to stop all appeals to Rome, a thoroughgoing application of the Statute of Praemunire. Thus, Henry's divorce from Catherine also began his reformation of the Church, both accomplished simply by a jurisdictional break with Rome. The following year, 1534, the Act of Supremacy recognized Henry as "Supreme Head of the Church of England." Five years later, the Act of Six Articles affirmed that the doctrine and practice of the English church should remain Catholic.

From the acts reprinted below, it is clear that Parliament still re-

Source: J. R. Tanner, *Tudor Constitutional Documents, A.D. 1485–1603, with an Historical Commentary,* Cambridge: At the University Press, 1940, pp. 41–45, 47–48. Reprinted by permission of Cambridge University Press.

tained its medieval reticence openly to legislate or to change the law, holding that the law was too sacred and eternal simply to be made. Thus, the really significant things are declared in the preambles, "that this realm of England is an empire" (i.e., a sovereign nation-state), and that "the King's Majesty justly and rightfully is . . . the supreme head of the Church of England." The strictly legislative parts of the statutes, taking for granted what was boldly stated in the preambles, proceed to work out useful consequences and to provide punishment for violations. Although Parliament's power remained limited in concept, in fact, the Reformation Parliament, sitting over a period of seven years (1529–1536), enacted more important statutes than had any previous Parliament. It gave many men legislative experience, and accustomed people to Parliament's participation in the making of important decisions. Parliament, seeming in decline since the Wars of the Roses, now began a new stage of its development, a development made more significant by the erosion of representative institutions on the continent.

AN ACT THAT THE APPEALS IN SUCH CASES AS HAVE BEEN USED TO BE PURSUED TO THE SEE OF ROME SHALL NOT BE FROM HENCEFORTH HAD NOR USED BUT WITHIN THIS REALM

Where by divers sundry old authentic histories and chronicles it is manifestly declared and expressed that this realm of England is an empire, and so hath been accepted in the world, governed by one Supreme Head and King having the dignity and royal estate of the imperial Crown of the same, unto whom a body politic, compact of all sorts and degrees of people divided in terms and by names of Spiritualty and Temporalty, be bounden and owe to bear next to God a natural and humble obedience; he being also institute and furnished by the goodness and sufferance of Almighty God with plenary, whole, and entire power, preeminence, authority, prerogative, and jurisdiction to render and yield justice and final determination to all manner of folk residents or subjects within this his realm, in all causes, matters, debates, and contentions happening to occur, insurge, or begin within the limits thereof, without restraint or provocation to any foreign princes or protentates of the world: the body spiritual whereof having power when any cause of the law divine happened to come in question or of spiritual learning, then it was declared, interpreted, and shewed by that part of the said body politic called the Spiritualty, now being usually called the English Church . . . And whereas the King his most noble progenitors, and the Nobility and Commons of this said realm, at divers and sundry Parliaments as well in the time of King Edward the First, Edward the Third, Richard the Second, Henry the Fourth, and other noble kings of this realm, made sundry ordinances, laws, statutes, and provisions for the entire and sure conservation of the prerogatives . . . to keep it from the annoyance as well of the see of Rome as from the authority of other foreign potentates attempting the diminution or violation thereof. . . . And notwithstanding the said goode statutes and ordinances made in the time of the King's most noble progenitors . . . divers and sundry inconveniences and dangers not provided for plainly by the said former acts, statutes, and ordinances have risen and sprung by reason of appeals sued out of this realm to the see of Rome . . . not only to the great inquietation, vexation, trouble, costs, and charges of the King's Highness and many of his subjects and residents in this his realm, but also to the great delay and let to the true and speedy determination of the said causes. . . . In consideration whereof the King's Highness, his Nobles and Commons . . . doth therefore by his royal assent and by the assent of the Lords spiritual and temporal and the Commons . . . enact, establish, and ordain that all causes testamentary, causes of matrimony and divorces, rights of tithes, oblations, and obventions . . . shall be from henceforth heard, examined, discussed, clearly finally and definitively adjudged and determined, within the King's jurisdiction and authority and not elsewhere, . . . any foreign inhibitions, appeals . . . or any other process or impediments of what natures, names, qualities, or conditions soever they be, from the see of Rome or any other foreign courts or potentates of the world . . . notwithstanding. . . . As also that all spiritual prelates, pastors, ministers, and curates within this realm and the dominions of the same shall and may use, minister, execute, and do, or cause to be used, ministered, executed, and done, all sacraments, sacramentals, divine services, and all other things within the said realm and dominions unto all the subjects of the same as Catholic and Christian men owe to do; Any foreign citations . . . from or to the see of Rome or any other foreign prince . . . notwithstanding. And if any of the said spiritual persons, by the occasion of the said fulminations of any of the same interdictions . . . do at any time hereafter refuse to minister or to cause to be ministered the said sacraments and sacramentals and other divine services in form as is aforesaid, shall for every such time or times that they or any of them do refuse so to do or to cause to be done, have one year's imprisonment and to make fine and ransom at the King's pleasure.

II. And it is further enacted . . . that if any person or persons . . . do attempt, move, purchase, or procure, from or to the see of Rome or from or to any other foreign court or courts out of this realm, any manner foreign process . . . or judgments, of what nature, kind, or quality soever they be, or execute any of the same process . . . that then every person or persons so doing . . . being convict of the same, for every such default shall incur and run in the same pains, penalties, and forfeitures ordained and provided by the statute of provision and praemunire made in the sixteenth year of the reign of . . . King Richard the Second.

AN ACT CONCERNING THE KING'S HIGHNESS TO BE SUPREME HEAD OF THE CHURCH OF ENGLAND AND TO HAVE AUTHORITY TO REFORM AND REDRESS ALL ERRORS, HERESIES, AND ABUSES IN THE SAME

Albeit the King's Majesty justly and rightfully is and ought to be the Supreme Head of the Church of England, and so is recognised by the clergy of this realm in their Convocations; yet nevertheless for corroboration and confirmation thereof, and for increase of virtue in Christ's religion within this realm of England, and to repress and extirp all errors, heresies, and other enormities and abuses heretofore used in the same, Be it enacted by authority of this present Parliament that the King our Sovereign Lord, his heirs and successors kings of this realm, shall be taken, accepted, and reputed the only Supreme Head in earth of the Church of England called *Anglicana Ecclesia,* and shall have and enjoy annexed and united to the imperial Crown of this realm as well the title and style thereof, as all honours, dignities, preeminences, jurisdictions, privileges, authorities, immunities, profits, and commodities, to the said dignity of Supreme Head of the same Church belonging and appertaining: And that our said Sovereign Lord, his heirs and successors kings of this realm, shall have full power and authority from time to time to visit, repress, redress, reform, order, correct, restrain, and amend all such errors, heresies, abuses, offences, contempts, and enormities, whatsoever they be, which by any manner spiritual authority or jurisdiction ought or may lawfully be reformed, repressed, ordered, redressed, corrected, restrained, or amended, most to the pleasure of Almighty God, the increase of virtue in Christ's religion, and for the conservation of the peace, unity, and tranquillity of this realm: any usage, custom, foreign laws, foreign authority, prescription, or any other thing or things to the contrary hereof notwithstanding.

43

Royal Proclamation Announcing New Coinage (1551)

A royal proclamation was an ordinance issued by the king with the advice of his council and authenticated by the Great Seal. Such proclamations dealt with many matters of concern to the government, from coinage as in that of October 30, 1551, reproduced below, to religion, monopolies, and land enclosures. More than anything else, proclamations reveal a vigorous royal administration dealing with the practical problems of government.

One of the most serious problems was the dramatic price rise. Whereas prices had remained relatively stable during the fifteenth century, then more than doubled in the first half of the sixteenth. This was due to a growing population and also to a quickening of the European economy and an influx of New World gold and silver. By mid-century, England suffered from uncontrolled inflation, hastened by Henry VIII's war spending and by successive devaluations of the English coinage. Although England's coinage was not restored to its traditional soundness until early in the reign of Elizabeth I (1558–1603), this proclamation of Edward VI (1547–1553) was an attempt to move in that direction.

The proclamation gives insight into the problem of obtaining a stable currency during a time of runaway inflation. It shows already in existence several of the English coins that remained standard throughout the next four centuries, such traditional and beloved coins as the shilling, sixpence, penny, ha'penny, and farthing. The pound sterling consisted of 20 shillings, each of 12 pence.

The King's majesty hath ordered and established to be made within his mints these several coins, as well of silver in fineness of the standard sterling, as also of gold, as hereafter ensueth:

That is to say, one piece of silver money, which shall be current for 5*s.* of the lawful moneys aforesaid; another piece, which shall be called the piece of 2*s.* 6*d.* of the lawful moneys; the third piece, which shall be called the sterling

Source: Paul L. Hughes and James F. Larkin, eds., *Tudor Royal Proclamations,* Volume I: *The Early Tudors* (*1485–1553*), New Haven and London: Yale University Press, 1964, pp. 535–536. Reprinted by permission of Yale University Press.

5s. Piece

2s. 6d. Piece

Sterling shilling

6d. Piece

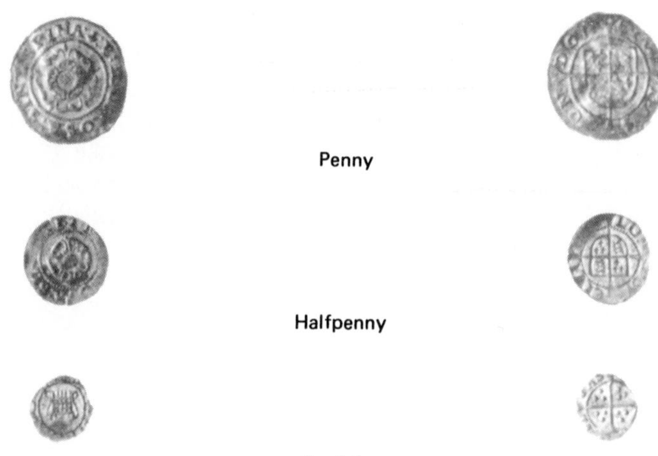

PLATE A
(By courtesy of the Trustees of the British Museum).

shilling, current for 12*d.;* the fourth piece, which shall be half of the said sterling shilling, shall be current for 6*d.* of the lawful moneys aforesaid.

And also, the King's majesty has ordered to have three pieces of small moneys made likewise current: that is to say, the first piece shall be called a penny with a double rose, and shall be current for 1*d.* of the lawful moneys aforesaid; the second piece shall be called a halfpenny with a single rose; and the third piece, a farthing with a portcullis.

And of the coins of gold, as here ensueth: that is to say, the whole sovereign of fine gold, which shall be current for 30*s.* of lawful moneys of England; another piece of fine gold, called the angel, shall be current for 10*s.;* the third piece of gold, which shall be called the angelet, half of the angel, current for 5*s.* of lawful moneys aforesaid;

And further, a whole sovereign, of crown gold, shall be current for 20*s.;* the second piece of crown gold, which shall be called the half-sovereign, shall be current for 10*s.;* and the third piece of crown gold, which shall be called a crown, current for 5*s.;* the fourth piece of crown gold, which shall be called the half-crown, which shall be current for 2*s.* 6*d.* of the lawful moneys aforesaid;

Straightly charg[ing] and command[ing] all manner of persons within his realms and dominions to receive and pay the said several pieces of moneys, as well of silver as of gold, at the several rates before rehearsed; under pain of the King's high displeasure, and to be further punished as his highness shall think convenient.

And his express commandment is that all such base moneys which his majesty did lately by his several proclamations reduce to the value of a lower rate shall pass and go current in payment in like manner and sort as his highness' last proclamation did declare, until such time as his majesty's mints may with diligence convert the same into the said new coins, which his majesty mindeth to have done with all possible expedition.

And his majesty signifieth to all his loving subjects that, if they do bring in any quantity of moneys now current into his grace's mints within the Tower of London, they shall have the same received there by tale at the value as they be now current upon bills; and they shall, in as convenient time as may, be repaid for the said moneys now current by tale in other the King's majesty's new moneys afore declared.

44

John Foxe, *Acts and Monuments* (1563). The Burning of Archbishop Cranmer, 1556

Thomas Cranmer (1489–1556) was the central figure of the English Reformation. Upon becoming Archbishop of Canterbury in 1533, he nullified Henry VIII's marriage to Catherine of Aragon. He wrote the prayer books of 1549 and 1552 by which the ceremony of the English Church became Protestant. He suffered martyrdom under Queen Mary. Yet, he was a retiring and scholarly man, little interested in politics save for his adherence to the king's position as supreme head of the Church of England. He remained faithful to Henry's Anglo-Catholicism, although his personal inclination toward Protestantism enabled him to adapt to the religious settlements of Edward VI (1547–1553).

The accession of Mary (1553–1558) placed Cranmer in a dilemma, caught between his belief in Mary's right to determine England's religion and his own adherence to Protestantism. Because of his high position in the Church and his past actions, Mary and the Catholic Church were determined to make an example of him by forcing his return to orthodoxy. Cranmer's difficulties were intensified by his having not a resolute heart but an overcareful mind, which could see the merits of both sides of a question. Perhaps this irresolution caused him to sign the six recantations

Source: John Foxe, *The Acts and Monuments of John Foxe,* edited by Stephen Reed Cattley, Vol. VIII, London: R. B. Seeley and W. Burnside, 1839, pp. 88–90.

admitting his former errors. Or was it the fires that awaited him if he refused? At the last moment, however, just as his examiners were expecting his public confession, he changed his mind again and by a seventh recantation affirmed his Protestant faith. The Catholics were dashed, and Protestants rejoiced and took strength from his glorious martyrdom.

Cranmer's death at the stake and that of almost 300 others made a vivid impression on the people of England, an impression intensified and kept alive by John Foxe's *Acts and Monuments* (1563). Better known as Foxe's *Book of Martyrs,* it recounted and by its woodcuts depicted the sufferings and heroic martyrdoms of those who died in England for their Protestant faith. Below is its account of Thomas Cranmer.

Foxe's *Book of Martyrs* became after the Bible easily the most popular and influential book in England. It justified England's ha-

PLATE A
The burning of Cranmer (by permission of the Folger Shakespeare Library).

¶ The burning of the Archbiſhop of Canturbury Doctor Thomas *Cranmer, in the Towneditch at Oxford, with his hand firſt thruſt into the* fire, wherewith he ſubſcribed before.

tred of Rome, helping to make it a permanent part of her national consciousness. Furthermore, by glorifying England's steadfastness in the face of persecution, it fostered in the English a sense of their special association with God's purpose and, in the words of John Milton, even of God's regarding them as "his Englishmen."

Cranmer. ". . . And now I come to the great thing, which so much troubleth my conscience, more than any thing that ever I did or said in my whole life, and that is the setting abroad of a writing contrary to the truth; which now here I renounce and refuse, as things written for fear of death, and to save my life if it might be; and that is, all such bills and papers which I have written or signed with my hand since my degradation; wherein I have written many things untrue. And forasmuch as my hand offended, writing contrary to my heart, my hand shall first be punished there-for; for, may I come to the fire, it shall be first burned.

"And as for the pope, I refuse him, as Christ's enemy, and antichrist, with all his false doctrine.

"And as for the sacrament, I believe as I have taught in my book against the bishop of Winchester, the which my book teacheth so true a doctrine of the sacrament, that it shall stand at the last day before the judgment of God, where the papistical doctrine contrary thereto shall be ashamed to show her face."

Here the standers-by were all astonied, marvelled, were amazed, did look one upon another, whose expectation he had so notably deceived. Some began to admonish him of his recantation, and to accuse him of falsehood. Briefly, it was a world to see the doctors beguiled of so great a hope. I think there was never cruelty more notably or better in time deluded and deceived; for it is not to be doubted but they looked for a glorious victory and a perpetual triumph by this man's retractation; who, as soon as they heard these things, began to let down their ears, to rage, fret, and fume; and so much the more, because they could not revenge their grief—for they could now no longer threaten or hurt him. For the most miserable man in the world can die but once. . . . And so, when they could do nothing else unto him, yet, lest they should say nothing, they ceased not to object unto him his falsehood and dissimulation.

Unto which accusation he answered, "Ah! my masters," quoth he, "do not you take it so. Always since I lived hitherto, I have been a hater of falsehood, and a lover of simplicity, and never before this time have I dissembled:" and in saying this, all the tears that remained in his body appeared in his eyes. And when he began to speak more of the sacrament and of the papacy, some of them began to cry out, yelp, and bawl, and specially Cole cried out upon him, "Stop the heretic's mouth, and take him away."

And then Cranmer being pulled down from the stage, was led to the fire, accompanied with those friars, vexing, troubling, and threatening him most cruelly. "What madness," say they, "hath brought thee again into this error, by which thou wilt draw innumerable souls with thee into hell?" To whom he answered nothing, but directed all his talk to the people, saving that to one troubling him in the way, he spake, and exhorted him to get him home to his study, and apply his book diligently; saying, if he did diligently call upon God, by reading more he should get knowledge.

But the other Spanish barker, raging and foaming was almost out of his wits, always having this in his mouth, "Non fecisti?" "Didst thou it not?"

But when he came to the place where the holy bishops and martyrs of God, Hugh Latimer and Nicholas Ridley, were burnt before him for the confession of the truth, kneeling down, he prayed to God; and not long tarrying in his prayers, putting off his garments to his shirt, he prepared himself to death. . . .

And when the wood was kindled, and the fire began to burn near him, stretching out his arm, he put his right hand into the flame, which he held so steadfast and immovable (saving that once with the same hand he wiped his face), that all men might see his hand burned before his body was touched. His body did so abide the burning of the flame with such constancy and steadfastness, that standing always in one place without moving his body, he seemed to move no more than the stake to which he was bound; his eyes were lifted up into heaven, and oftentimes he repeated "this unworthy right hand," so long as his voice would suffer him; and using often the words of Stephen, "Lord Jesus, receive my spirit," in the greatness of the flame he gave up the ghost. . . .

And this was the end of this learned archbishop, whom, lest by evil-subscribing he should have perished, by well-recanting God preserved; and lest he should have lived longer with shame and reproof, it pleased God rather to take him away, to the glory of his name and profit of his church. . . . But especially he had to rejoice, that dying in such a cause, he was to be numbered amongst Christ's martyrs, much more worthy the name of St. Thomas of Canterbury, than he whom the pope falsely before did canonize.

45

Sir Thomas Smith, *De Republica Anglorum* (1583). Descriptions of Parliament and Star Chamber

Sir Thomas Smith (1513–1577), a scholar and a government official, is today remembered as the author of *De Republica Anglorum: The maner of Governement or policie of the Realm of England.* Written between 1562 and 1566 while Smith was Elizabeth's ambassador to France, *De Republica Anglorum* is the best contemporary description of the form and procedures of Tudor government.

The historian can use such descriptions to learn how the English viewed their constitution at various points in its development. It is noteworthy that Smith stressed the breadth and authority of Parliament's statute-making power and the idea that in Parliament's consent "is taken to be everie mans consent." However, in Smith's description of collective sovereignty there was as yet no hint of an impending split between the two parts, that the Crown-in-Parliament of the sixteenth century would become the Crown or Parliament of the seventeenth.

Smith's great respect for the force and authority of the court of Star Chamber is indicative of Tudor, not Stuart, attitudes. Originally, the Star Chamber had been the king's council sitting in a judicial capacity, but Thomas Cromwell, by his administrative reforms of the 1530s, made it a separate body, although its basic membership remained that of the Privy Council. Its jurisdiction over riot was broadly defined to include almost any breach of the peace. Although a prerogative court, the Star Chamber was limited to administering the common law and was unable to inflict the death penalty. Its exalted membership and unfettered procedures, nevertheless, made it efficient and formidable. Not limited to formal indictments of grand juries, it could proceed on the basis of a plaintiff's bill or on information from the attorney general. Nor did it depend on trial juries or procedural technicalities that could be exploited by overmighty subjects. It is easy to see how Smith could admire the Star Chamber's prestige and usefulness and to

Source: Sir Thomas Smith, *De Republica Anglorum: A Discourse on the Commonwealth of England,* edited by L. Alston, Cambridge: At the University Press, 1906, pp. 48–49, 115–118. Reprinted by permission of Cambridge University Press.

understand why a later generation would consider it an instrument of royal oppression.

By the end of the seventeenth century, *De Republica Anglorum* had gone through eleven English editions, four in Latin translation, one in German, and a partial translation into Dutch, a testimonial to the importance accorded Smith as a constitutional analyst.

OF THE PARLIAMENT AND THE AUTHORITIE THEREOF

The most high and absolute power of the realme of Englande, consisteth in the Parliament. For as in warre where the king himselfe in person, the nobilitie, the rest of the gentilitie, and the yeomanrie are, is the force and power of Englande: so in peace and consultation where the Prince is to give life, and the last and highest commaundement, the Baronie for the nobilitie and higher, the knightes, esquiers, gentlemen and commons for the lower part of the common wealth, the bishoppes for the clergie bee present to advertise, consult and shew what is good and necessarie for the common wealth, and to consult together, and upon mature deliberation everie bill or lawe being thrise reade and disputed uppon in either house, the other two partes first each a part, and after the Prince himselfe in presence of both the parties doeth consent unto and alloweth. That is the Princes and whole realmes deede: whereupon justlie no man can complaine, but must accommodate himselfe to finde it good and obey it.

That which is doone by this consent is called firme, stable, and *sanctum,* and is taken for lawe. The Parliament abrogateth olde lawes, maketh newe, giveth orders for thinges past, and for thinges hereafter to be followed, changeth rightes, and possessions of private men, legittimateth bastards, establisheth formes of religion, altereth weightes and measures, giveth formes of succession to the crowne, defineth of doubtfull rightes, whereof is no lawe alreadie made, appointeth subsidies, tailes, taxes, and impositions, giveth most free pardons and absolutions, restoreth in bloud and name as the highest court, condemneth or absolveth them whom the Prince will put to that triall: And to be short, all that ever the people of Rome might do either in *Centuriatis comitijs* or *tributis,* the same may be doone by the parliament of Englande, which representeth and hath the power of the whole realme both the head and the bodie. For everie Englishman is entended to bee there present, either in person or by procuration and attornies, of what preheminence, state, dignitie, or qualitie soever he be, from the Prince (be he King or Queene) to the lowest person of Englande. And the consent of the Parliament is taken to be everie mans consent.

OF THE COURT OF STARRE CHAMBER

There is yet in Englande an other court, of the which that I can understand there is not the like in any other Countrie. In the Terme time every weeke once at the least, (which is commonly on Fridaies, and Wednesdaies, and the next day after that the terme doeth ende,) the Lorde Chauncellor, and the Lordes and other of the privie Counsell, so many as will, and other Lordes and Barons which be not of the Privie Counsell, and be in the towne, and the Judges of England, specially the two chiefe Judges, from ix. of the clocke till it be xi. doe sit in a place which is called the starre chamber, either because it is full of windowes, or because at the first all the roofe thereof was decked with images of starres gilted. There is plaints heard of riots. Riot is called in our English terme or speache, where any number is assembled with force to doe any thing: and it had the beginning, because that our being much accustomed either in foreine wars, in Fraunce, Scotland, or Ireland, or being overmuch exercised with civill warres within the Realme. . . . So that our nation used hereunto, and upon that more insolent at home, and not easie to be governed by Lawe and politike order, men of power beginning many fraies, and the stronger by factions and parties offering too much injurie to the weaker, were occasions of making good Lawes. First of reteiners, that no man should have above a number in his Liverie or retinue. . . . And further, because such things are not commonlie done by meane men, but such as be of power and force, and be not to be dealt withal of everie man, nor of meane Gentlemen: if the riot be found and certified to the Kings Counsell, or if otherwise it be complained of, the partie is sent for, and he must appeare in this starre chamber, where seeing (except the presence of the Prince onely) as it were the maiestie of the whole Realme before him, being never so stoute, he will be abashed: and being called to aunswere (as he must come of what degree soever he be) he shall be so charged with such gravitie, with such reason and remonstrance, and of those chiefe personages of Englande, one after an other handeling him on that sort, that what courage soever he hath, his heart will fall to the grounde, and so much the more, when if he make not his aunswere the better, as seldome he can so in open violence, he shalbe commaunded to the Fleete, where he shall be kept in prison in such sort as these Judges shall appoint him, lie there till he be wearie aswell of the restraint of his libertie, as of the great expences, which he must there sustaine, and for a time be forgotten, whiles after long suite of his friendes, he will be glad to be ordered by reason. Sometime as his deserts be, he payeth a great fine to the Prince, besides great costs and dammages to the partie, and yet the matter wherefore he attempteth this riot and violence is remitted to the common lawe. For that is the effect of this Court to bridle such stoute noble men, or Gentlemen which would offer wrong by force to any manner men, and cannot be content to demaund or defend the right by order of lawe. This court began long before, but tooke great augmentation and authoritie at that time that Cardinall *Wolsey* Archbishop of Yorke was Chauncellor of Englande, who of some was thought to have first devised the Court, because that he after some intermission by negligence of time, augmented the authoritie of it, which was at that time marvellous necessary to doe, to represse the insolencie of the noble men and gentlemen of the North partes of Englande, who being farre from the King and the seate of iustice made almost as it were an ordinarie warre among themselves, and made their force their Lawe.

ripe and ready to gather, she (without the consent of the said Joan Frynde or any other household) did gather a basket full, and filled her apron also with the said pease, and when she was ready to depart, this Joan Frynde who owned the close came, and demanded why she did gather those pease without leave, wherefore she willed her to deliver her the pease that were in her basket, and those that were in her lap she would give her.

But this ungodly woman did fling the pease down on the ground, saying, if you make so much ado for a few pease, take them all, the next year I will have enough of my own, and you shall have few enough. So she cursed the same ground and stamped on it and went her ways, and never since that time that the woman could have any pease grow in her ground or any other corn would grow in the same place.

William Frynde's wife, of the said Town of Stanmore, brought home a child to nurse from Westminster where the parents dwelt: who brought the child and showed it to her husband, but he said unless he knew the parents of the child, he would not suffer her to keep it: this witch being at her house the same time, owing her a grudge, said, what will you do with a nurse child, you will but starve it, sure I will warrant you the child shall not prosper: and the child shortly after did fall sick, and consumed to the death in most strange manner, so that in three weeks following the child died, and was consumed and parched like a green leaf that had been hanged to dry in a chimney.

She came to the house of one William Goodwin of the same town for the yeast, the servants denied that there was any in the house: notwithstanding, the stand was new filled, and the servants were loath to take of the yeast. Whereat this witch said you shall have less, and so went her ways, and the next day following, though none of the house did draw out any drink out of the same stand, yet was it found dry without drink or yeast, except a few hard dried dregs.

She came thither also another time for oat-meal, and they would give her none: and forthwith a lamb (which was kept in the same house), being in the room where the witch was, fell down and died presently. . . .

She came to one of her neighbours to borrow a horse, knowing him to have four very good indifferent geldings, the worst worth four marks: and he denied her thereof, but she said she would be even with him, and shortly after all his four geldings were dead, and died suddenly one after another.

She came to one John Frynde, of the age of twenty years, the son of Thomas Frynde being of the same town, and offered him a pair of shoes to sell, her price was ten pence, and he offered her six pence and would give her no more. Whereat she was sore vexed, because at that time she had need of money: this was in the latter end of summer, so the fellow thinking nothing, went to gathering of pears from off the tree, and upon a sudden fell down to the ground, and did hurt his cods with the said fall, so that he was constrained to keep in the house. But this witch did openly make report in the town, that he was burned with a whore, and that he came to her and desired to have his pleasure of her:

which speeches came to the fellow's ear, who a quarter of a year after he was recovered did meet this witch in the town: where he asked why she gave out such lewd speeches of him, being most unjust, demanding of her, if ever he spake to her in any such sort, but she answered that he knew best: then he charged her that he thought his harm came by her means, I, said she, I have not done with thee yet: so he went about his business and being come home, he complained of his back and his belly, saying assuredly that he thought she had bewitched him: so his pain increased more and more, and he began to grow into a consumption, and wasted away like as the child before mentioned, like a parched or withered leaf, hanged up in the smoke of a chimney, and died three months after, and before he died his side did burst, and his guts and backbone was rotted in sunder, so that his guts and bowels being rotten did issue forth of his belly: and died hereof in most pitiful and grievous manner, the said party taking it upon his death, that her witchcraft and sorcery was the cause of his death.

After whose death the townsmen made complaint of her dealing to the justice, who commanded one Master Norwood, a gentleman in the town, to go search her house: this gentleman went thither and did search her house, yet desired the justice not to apprehend her, until there were some further trial made of her. But she promised for their searching, she would requite them shortly: and forthwith, the next morning one of the gentleman's best milch kine, which was worth four mark, being well over night, was found dead. The gentleman fearing some greater injury by her, did then command his servants that they should give her nothing if she came thither to crave anything, so within two days after she came for buttermilk, but they denied her thereof: and after that they could never make cheese or butter since.

Then was she apprehended and brought before the justice, by whom she was examined, and by him committed to the gaol of Newgate, where she remained until the sessions, held for gaol delivery of London and Middlesex: And then by twelve honest substantial men for the causes aforesaid, was found guilty and worthy of death: where she had judgment and was executed accordingly.

48
Aerial Photographs

Archeologists in Britain have traditionally concentrated on the study of prehistoric and Roman Britain, periods on which there is little written evidence. More recently, the physical remains of medieval Britain have been subjected to intensive study. This new archeology has been assisted by aerial photography, a technique suggested by the air force surveys of World War II and later regularized by the surveys undertaken by Cambridge University. Because of their unique perspective and their comprehensive view, aerial photographs have proved useful in clarifying ground observations and in suggesting new areas of investigation.

The following photographs illustrate some of the uses of this new approach to the study of medieval Britain. Plate A is a Tudor diagram of the village of Toddington, showing such dominant features as the central marketplace, the church, and the moat and what remains of the medieval castle. Its similarity to Plate B, a recent photograph, shows the village's physical continuity into modern times and suggests that few radical changes occurred in the lives of its people. Some towns outgrew their medieval limits, as is shown by the photograph of the Welsh town of Caernarvon (Plate C). Sometimes villages disappeared altogether; Plate D shows the remains of Ditchford. Aerial photography can fix the sites of these deserted villages and tell the historian much about the population distribution of medieval Britain.

Finally, aerial photography can reveal the location of the open fields, divided into numerous narrow strips and shared by several families. Some of these open fields remained in cultivation until recently, as is illustrated by the 1948 photo of the Isle of Portland in Dorset (Plate E). Plate F clearly indicates the breakup of the open fields by the enclosure movement. It shows the fences built after 1795 across the fields around the village of Padbury. The ridges in these fields were the result of the strip farming of the manorial system.

Historians are constantly seeking new sources of evidence to help answer old questions. The use of aerial photography to study the landscape and the influence of human activity on it is a product of this never-ending search.

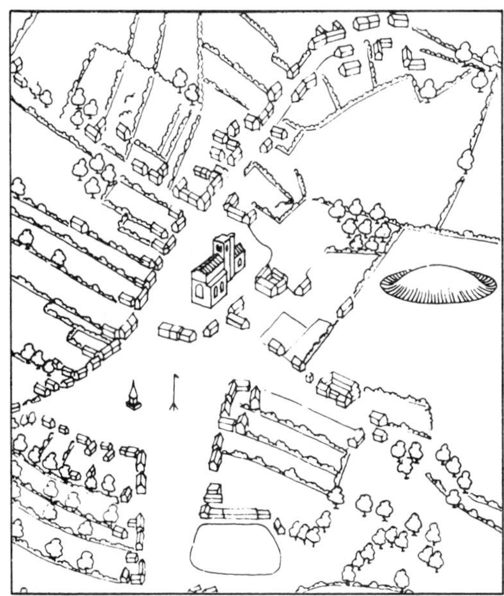

PLATE A
Toddington in 1581, after Ralph Agas (Cambridge University Collection, copyright reserved).

PLATE B
Toddington (Cambridge University Collection, copyright reserved).

PLATE C
Caernarvon (Cambridge University Collection, copyright reserved).

PLATE D
Ditchford (© British Crown copyright 1975/MOD reproduced with the permission of Her Britannic Majesty's Stationery Office).

PLATE E
Isle of Portland (© British Crown copyright 1975/MOD reproduced with the permission of Her Britannic Majesty's Stationery Office).

PLATE F
Padbury (© British Crown copyright 1975/MOD reproduced with permission of Her Britannic Majesty's Stationery Office).

49

Robert Carey, *Memoirs.* The Spanish Armada, 1588

England's defeat of the Spanish Armada was the high point of a conflict that had begun as a confrontation of two aggressive powers, which were getting more and more in each other's way. As England and Spain became respectively the champions of the Protestant and Catholic camps, their quarrel attained a cosmic level, almost a judicial duel to determine the judgment of God. The English victory in 1588 was not the end of the war, which continued until 1604, or of the Spanish navy, which better defended Spanish treasure fleets after 1588 than it had before, or of Spain's attempt to conquer England. Nevertheless, the outcome did demonstrate that England would not quickly be defeated and that Protestantism in Europe would not easily be vanquished. It fed the English myth, already alive in Foxe's *Book of Martyrs,* that England was favored by God and that the English were his chosen people.

Sir Robert Carey (c. 1560–1639) was the grandson of Mary Boleyn, the sister of Queen Elizabeth's mother. Although the youngest of ten sons, he managed to follow in his father's footsteps, as near relative and courtier to the queen. He never attained the importance of Sir Walter Ralegh, or the earl of Essex, but Elizabeth took note of his marriage and was annoyed. Late in life, probably in 1626, he wrote his memoirs, which were not published until 1759. His recollections are brief (only 2045 lines in the modern edition) and obviously written from some distance. Carey, nevertheless, presents a vivid account of the principal events in which he participated: the foiling of the Spanish Armada, reproduced below, his madcap race to be the first to inform James VI of Scotland of his accession to the English throne, and his joining Prince Charles in Madrid, whence he had gone in 1623 to woo the Spanish Infanta. Writing as an old man in the reign of Charles I, Carey gives the somber impression of one who realizes that his own youth is passed and that England's heroic age is gone as well.

Source: The Memoirs of Robert Carey, edited by F. H. Mares, pp. 9–11.

The next year (1588) the King of Spain's great Armada came upon our coast, thinking to devour us all. Upon the news sent to court from Plymouth of their certain arrival, my Lord Cumberland and myself took post horse, and rode straight to Portsmouth, where we found a frigate that carried us to sea; and having sought for the fleets a whole day, the night after we fell amongst them: where it was our fortune to light first upon the Spanish fleet; and finding ourselves in the wrong, we tacked about, and in short time got to our own fleet, which was not far from the other. At our coming aboard our admiral, we stayed there awhile; but finding the ship much pestered, and scant of cabins, we left the admiral, and went aboard Captain Reyman, where we stayed, and were very welcome, and much made of. It was on Thursday that we came to the fleet. All that day we followed close the Spanish Armada, and nothing was attempted on either side: the same course we held all Friday and Saturday, by which time the Spanish fleet cast anchor just before Calais. We likewise did the same, a very small distance behind them, and so continued till Monday morning about two of the clock; in which time our council of war had provided six old hulks, and stuffed them full of all combustible matter fit for burning, and on Monday at two in the morning they were let loose, with each of them a man in her to direct them. The tide serving, they brought them very near the Spanish fleet, so that they could not miss to come amongst the midst of them: then they set fire on them, and came off themselves, having each of them a little boat to bring him off. The ships set on fire, came so directly to the Spanish fleet, as they had no way to avoid them, but to cut all their hawsers, and so escape; and their haste was such that they left one of their four great galeasses on ground before Calais, which our men took and had the spoil of, where many of the Spaniards were slain with the governor thereof, but most of them were saved with wading ashore to Calais. They being in this disorder, we made ready to follow them, where began a cruel fight, and we had such advantage, both of wind and tide, as we had a glorious day of them; continuing fight from four o'clock in the morning, till almost five or six at night, where they lost a dozen or fourteen of their best ships, some sunk, and the rest ran ashore in divers parts to keep themselves from sinking. After God had given us this great victory, they made all the haste they could away, and we followed them Tuesday and Wednesday, by which time they were gotten as far as Flamborough Head. It was resolved on Wednesday at night, that by four o'clock on Thursday, we should have a new fight with them for a farewell; but by two in the morning, there was a flag of council hung out in our vice admiral, when it was found that in the whole fleet there was not munition sufficient to make half a fight; and therefore it was there concluded that we should let them pass, and our fleet to return to the Downs. That night we parted with them, we had a mighty storm. Our fleet cast anchor, and endured it: but the Spanish fleet, wanting their anchors, were many of them cast ashore on the west of Ireland, where they had all their throats cut by the Kerns; and some of them on Scotland, where they were no better used: and the rest (with much ado) got into Spain again. Thus did God bless us, and gave victory over this invincible navy: the sea calmed, and all our ships came to the Downs on Friday in safety.

On Saturday my Lord of Cumberland and myself came on shore, and took post horse, and found the Queen in her army at Tilbury camp, where I fell sick of a burning fever, and was carried in a litter to London. I should have been then sent ambassador to the King of Scots, but could not by reason of my sickness.

50
Richard Hakluyt, *The Principal Navigations* (1589)

Richard Hakluyt (1551–1616) was a geographer and a historian who both recorded and influenced the course of English history. He was educated at Oxford and ordained in 1578. Although he remained a clergyman of the Church of England until his death, his interest in exploration became the dominant influence in his life, as is revealed in the following selection from the "Epistle Dedicatorie" to the first edition of his *The Principal Navigations, Voyages, Traffiques, and Discoveries of the English Nation.* Hakluyt was the first to lecture at Oxford on cosmography (geography). In addition, he was an adviser to the Muscovy Company, a supporter of Sir Humphrey Gilbert's colonization plans, and a publicist for Sir Walter Ralegh. In 1584, he presented to Queen Elizabeth *A Discourse of Western Planting,* one of the first systematic treatments of the benefits to be gained by colonizing the Western Hemisphere. England would spread the true religion, relieve the problems of pauperism and overpopulation and, especially, by expanding her commerce, forestall Spain.

Hakluyt spent most of his life researching and writing his great work, *The Principal Navigations.* Although at first sight it appears to be a random collection of narratives dealing with voyages of discovery, it does have a theme—the important role of England in early exploration and the need for her to remember, glorify, and

Source: Richard Hakluyt, *The Principal Navigations, Voyages, Traffiques, & Discoveries of the English Nation,* 8 vols., London: J. M. Dent and Sons, 1907, I, 1–5. Reprinted by permission of W. & R. Holmes (Books).

continue this tradition. Throughout the 1590s, he traveled widely, interviewing survivors of early voyages, and in 1598 to 1600 he published a second and expanded edition in three large volumes.

The Principal Navigations was immediately popular. The general public found it exciting reading, and it provided valuable information to the businessman and the potential colonist. Hakluyt's reputation was such that when he died in 1616 he was honored by burial in Westminster Abbey. Today his memory is preserved by the Hakluyt Society, a scholarly organization begun in 1846, which sponsors the editing and publication of old manuscripts related to exploration.

THE EPISTLE DEDICATORIE IN THE FIRST EDITION, 1589

To the Right Honorable Sir Francis Walsingham Knight, Principall Secretarie to her Majestie, Chancellor of the Duchie of Lancaster, and one of her Majesties most honourable Privie Councell.

Right Honorable, I do remember that being a youth, and one of her Majesties scholars at Westminster that fruitfull nurserie, it was my happe to visit the chamber of M. Richard Hakluyt my cosin, a Gentleman of the Middle Temple, well knowen unto you, at a time when I found lying open upon his boord certeine bookes of Cosmographie, with an universall Mappe: he seeing me somewhat curious in the view therof, began to instruct my ignorance, by shewing me the division of the earth into three parts after the olde account, and then according to the latter, & better distribution, into more: he pointed with his wand to all the knowen Seas, Gulfs, Bayes, Straights, Capes, Rivers, Empires, Kingdomes, Dukedomes, and Territories of ech part, with declaration also of their speciall commodities, & particular wants, which by the benefit of traffike, & entercourse of merchants, are plentifully supplied. From the Mappe he brought me to the Bible, and turning to the 107 Psalme, directed mee to the 23 & 24 verses, where I read, that they which go downe to the sea in ships, and occupy by the great waters, they see the works of the Lord, and his woonders in the deepe, &c. Which words of the Prophet together with my cousins discourse (things of high and rare delight to my yong nature) tooke in me to deepe an impression, that I constantly resolved, if ever I were preferred to the University, where better time, and more convenient place might be ministred for these studies, I would by Gods assistance prosecute that knowledge and kinde of literature, the doores whereof (after a sort) were so happily opened before me.

According to which my resolution, when, not long after, I was removed to Christ-church in Oxford, my exercises of duety first performed, I fell to my intended course, and by degrees read over whatsoever printed or written discoveries and voyages I found extant either in the Greeke, Latine, Italian, Spanish,

Portugall, French, or English languages, and in my publike lectures was the first, that produced and shewed both the olde imperfectly composed, and the new lately reformed Mappes, Globes, Spheares, and other instruments of this Art for demonstration in the common schooles, to the singular pleasure, and generall contentment of my auditory. In continuance of time, and by reason principally of my insight in this study, I grew familiarly acquainted with the chiefest Captaines at sea, the greatest Merchants, and the best Mariners of our nation: by which meanes having gotten somewhat more then common knowledge, I passed at length the narrow seas into France with sir Edward Stafford, her Majesties carefull and discreet Ligier, where during my five yeeres aboad with him in his dangerous and chargeable residencie in her Highnes service, I both heard in speech, and read in books other nations miraculously extolled for their discoveries and notable enterprises by sea, but the English of all others for their sluggish security, and continuall neglect of the like attempts especially in so long and happy a time of peace, either ignominiously reported, or exceedingly condemned: . . . Thus both hearing, and reading the obloquie of our nation, and finding few or none of our owne men able to replie heerin: and further, not seeing any man to have care to recommend to the world, the industrious labors, and painefull travels of our countrey men: for stopping the mouthes of the reprochers, my selfe being the last winter returned from France with the honorable the Lady Sheffield, for her passing good behavior highly esteemed in all the French court, determined notwithstanding all difficulties, to undertake the burden of that worke wherin all others pretended either ignorance, or lacke of leasure, or want of sufficient argument, whereas (to speake truely) the huge toile, and the small profit to insue, were the chiefe causes of the refusall. I call the worke a burden, in consideration that these voyages lay so dispersed, scattered, and hidden in severall hucksters hands, that I now woonder at my selfe, to see how I was able to endure the delayes, curiosity, and backwardnesse of many from whom I was to receive my originals: . . .

To harpe no longer upon this string, & to speake a word of that just commendation which our nation doe indeed deserve: it can not be denied, but as in all former ages, they have bene men full of activity, stirrers abroad, and searchers of the remote parts of the world, so in this most famous and peerlesse government of her most excellent Majesty, her subjects through the speciall assistance, and blessing of God, in searching the most opposite corners and quarters of the world, and to speake plainly, in compassing the vaste globe of the earth more then once, have excelled all the nations and people of the earth. For, which of the kings of this land before her Majesty, had theyr banners ever seene in the Caspian sea? which of them hath ever dealt with the Emperor of Persia, as her Majesty hath done, and obteined for her merchants large & loving privileges? who ever saw before this regiment, an English Ligier in the stately porch of the Grand Signor at Constantinople? who ever found English Consuls & Agents at Tripolis in Syria, at Aleppo, at Babylon, at Balsara, and which is more, who ever

who hath given me a heart that yet never feared any foreign or home enemy. And I speak it to give God the praise, as a testimony before you, and not to attribute anything to myself. For I, oh Lord! what am I, whom practices and perils past should not fear? Or what can I do? ["These words," says our diarist, "she spake with a great emphasis"]. That I should speak for any glory, God forbid.

"This, Mr. Speaker, I pray you deliver unto the House, to whom heartily recommend me. And so I commit you all to your best fortunes and further counsels. And I pray you, Mr. Comptroller, Mr. Secretary, and you of my Council, that before these gentlemen go into their countries, you bring them all to kiss my hand."

52
William Shakespeare, *Richard II* (1595) and *Henry V* (1599). English Nationalism

William Shakespeare (1564–1616) is without question the premier figure in English literature. Although little is known of his personal life, this seems irrelevant. His work possesses a timelessness that has captivated successive generations, appealing to different people in different ways. Part of Shakespeare's attraction lies in the unprecedented range of his plays, including histories, tragedies, romances, and comedies. His powers of characterization are almost without equal, creating such enduring figures as Hamlet, Othello, Macbeth, and Falstaff. Finally, the consistent excellence of his style, be it the cleverly constructed dialogue or the philosophical soliloquy, has never been surpassed.

To his contemporaries who crowded the Globe Theatre to heckle and applaud the actors, Shakespeare had yet another quality that is today largely overlooked. He was an interpreter of the past, who during England's great war with Spain presented Britain's history in the light of a developing nationalism. In the following selections from *Richard II* (1595) and *Henry V* (1599),

Source: The Life of Henry the Fifth, ed. Robert D. French, New Haven: Yale University Press, 1918, pp. 82–84; *The Tragedy of King Richard the Second,* ed. Llewellyn M. Buell, New Haven: Yale University Press, 1921, pp. 26–28. Reprinted by permission of Yale University Press.

Shakespeare's pride in England is obvious. John of Gaunt, dismayed at the evils that have befallen England under Richard II, has, nevertheless, little doubt that England, "this blessed plot," will survive to enjoy a more glorious future. Similarly, Henry V in his speech on the eve of the battle of Agincourt contemplates the glories to be won by his army, "we band of brothers." Neither man is likely to have uttered such words, but the fact that Shakespeare places them in their mouths tells a great deal about what sentiments were acceptable to Elizabethan audiences. This distortion should alert the reader to the fact that Shakespeare was first a dramatist and only secondarily a historian. This is well illustrated in his treatment of Richard III (1483–1485). For dramatic effect, to say nothing of political expediency, Shakespeare portrayed the last Yorkist king as odious and deformed, the personification of evil. Recent scholars have attempted to present Richard III in a more favorable light, but their efforts have largely been frustrated, not least by the wider audience and dramatic appeal that Shakespeare still commands.

RICHARD II

Gaunt. Methinks I am a prophet new inspir'd,
And thus expiring do foretell of him:
His rash fierce blaze of riot cannot last,
For violent fires soon burn out themselves;
Small showers last long, but suddent storms are short;
He tires betimes that spurs too fast betimes;
With eager feeding food doth choke the feeder:
Light vanity, insatiate cormorant,
Consuming means, soon preys upon itself.
This royal throne of kings, this scepter'd isle,
This earth of majesty, this seat of Mars,
This other Eden, demi-paradise,
This fortress built by Nature for herself
Against infection and the hand of war,
This happy breed of men, this little world,
This precious stone set in the silver sea,
Which serves it in the office of a wall,
Or as a moat defensive to a house,
Against the envy of less happier lands,
This blessed plot, this earth, this realm, this England,
This nurse, this teeming womb of royal kings.

Fear'd by their breed and famous by their birth,
Renowned for their deeds as far from home,—
For Christian service and true chivalry,—
As is the sepulchre in stubborn Jewry
Of the world's ransom, blessed Mary's Son:
This land of such dear souls, this dear, dear land,
Dear for her reputation through the world,
Is now leas'd out,—I die pronouncing it,—
Like to a tenement, or pelting farm:
England, bound in with the triumphant sea,
Whose rocky shore beats back the envious siege
Of watery Neptune, is now bound in with shame,
With inky blots, and rotten parchment bonds:
That England, that was wont to conquer others,
Hath made a shameful conquest of itself.
Ah! would the scandal vanish with my life,
How happy then were my ensuing death.

HENRY V

K. Henry. What's he that wishes so?
My cousin Westmoreland? No, my fair cousin:
If we are mark'd to die, we are enow
To do our country loss; and if to live,
The fewer men, the greater share of honour.
God's will! I pray thee, wish not one man more.
By Jove, I am not covetous for gold,
Nor care I who doth feed upon my cost;
It yearns me not if men my garments wear;
Such outward things dwell not in my desires:
But if it be a sin to covet honour,
I am the most offending soul alive.
No, faith, my coz, wish not a man from England:
God's peace! I would not lose so great an honour
As one man more, methinks, would share from me,
For the best hope I have. O! do not wish one more:
Rather proclaim it, Westmoreland, through my host,
That he which hath no stomach to this fight,
Let him depart; his passport shall be made,
And crowns for convoy put into his purse:
We would not die in that man's company
That fears his fellowship to die with us.

This day is call'd the feast of Crispian:
He that outlives this day, and comes safe home,
Will stand a tip-toe when this day is nam'd,
And rouse him at the name of Crispian.
He that shall live this day, and see old age,
Will yearly on the vigil feast his neighbours,
And say, "To-morrow is Saint Crispian";
Then will he strip his sleeve and show his scars,
And say, "These wounds I had on Crispin's day."
Old men forget: yet all shall be forgot,
But he'll remember with advantages
What feats he did that day. Then shall our names,
Familiar in his mouth as household words,
Harry the king, Bedford and Exeter,
Warwick and Talbot, Salisbury and Gloucester,
Be in their flowing cups freshly remember'd.
This story shall the good man teach his son;
And Crispin Crispian shall ne'er go by,
From this day to the ending of the world,
But we in it shall be remembered;
We few, we happy few, we band of brothers;
For he to-day that sheds his blood with me
Shall be my brother; be he ne'er so vile,
This day shall gentle his condition:
And gentlemen in England, now a-bed,
Shall think themselves accurs'd they were not here,
And hold their manhoods cheap whiles any speaks
That fought with us upon Saint Crispin's day.

53
James VI and I, *A Counterblaste to Tobacco* (1604)

Christopher Columbus's discovery of or, as we now say, encounter with the New World produced profound and unexpected consequences. One of the most significant was the biological exchange, especially of plants. The Old World supplied the Americas with rice, oats, barley, and wheat; America reciprocated with maize, beans, and potatoes. America also gave Europe such drugs as coca, curare, quinine, and, of greatest immediate impact, tobacco. Tobacco was controversial from the outset, especially in England where by the 1590s smoking had become a rage. One German traveler remarked that the English were constantly puffing on their pipes and "draw[ing] the smoak into their mouths, which they puff out again through their nostrils, like funnels, along with it plenty of phlegm and defluxions from the head." It was a nasty practice a new king might well wish to discuss with his subjects.

James VI of Scotland (1567–1625) and I of England (1603–1625) was a remarkable person, in the words of a recent scholar "one of the most complicated neurotics" ever to be monarch. The only son of Mary, Queen of Scots, he became king of Scotland as an infant and spent his early life struggling, in due time successfully, to free himself from the influence of both the Presbyterian preachers and the unruly nobility. His political successes in Scotland and his later constitutional disputes with his English Parliament sometimes cause the modern observer to overlook James's considerable educational attainments and his conviction that as king—"the proper Phisician of his Politicke-body"—it was his duty to educate his subjects. Besides taking a keen interest in the translation of the Bible, he wrote treatises on such diverse topics as witchcraft, divine right monarchy, Scottish poetry, and, of course, tobacco.

In *A Counterblaste to Tobacco* (1604) James raised two objections. The first involved the impact of tobacco on the user's health. Not only were the blessings of tobacco as a cure for such diseases as "the Pockes"—syphilis—unproven, but tobacco might well

Source: James Craigie, ed., *Minor Prose Works of King James VI and I,* Edinburgh: Scottish Text Society, 1982, pp. 87–88, 96–99. With permission of the Scottish Text Society.

cause other health problems. More significant were his arguments on social grounds: tobacco was messy and offensive to others. Not content merely to instruct, James imposed a high duty on tobacco. However, both personal entreaty and legal compulsion failed. The English continued to smoke and increasingly to smuggle tobacco. The entire episode says much about the relative power of a divine-right monarch operating without public support and modern American surgeons general blessed with an understanding electorate.

A Counterblaste to Tobacco was published anonymously in London in 1604. James's authorship was confirmed in 1616 when the pamphlet was reprinted in his collected works.

That the manifolde abuses of this vile custome of *Tobacco* taking, may the better be espied, it is fit, that first you enter into consideration both of the first originall thereof, and likewise of the reasons of the first entry thereof into this Countrey. . . .

For *Tobacco* being a common herbe, which (though vnder diuers names) growes almost euery where, was first found out by some of the barbarous *Indians,* to be a Preseruative, or Antidot against the Pockes, a filthy disease, whereunto these barbarous people are (as all men know) very much subiect, what through the vncleanly and adust constitution of their bodies, and what through the intemperate heate of their Climat: so that as from them was first brought into Christendome, that most detestable disease, so from them likewise was brought this vse of *Tobacco,* as a stinking and vnsavourie Antidot, for so corrupted and execrable a Maladie, the stinking Suffumigation whereof they yet vse against that disease, making so one canker or venime to eate out another.

And now good Countrey men, let vs (I pray you) consider, what honour or policie can mooue vs to imitate the barbarous and beastly maners of the wilde, godlesse, and slauish *Indians,* especially in so vile and stinking a custome? Shall wee that disdaine to imitate the maners of our neighbour *France* (hauing the stile of the first Christian Kingdom) and that cannot endure the spirit of the Spaniards (their King being now comparable in largenes of Dominions, to the great Emperor of *Turkie*) Shall wee, I say, that haue bene so long ciuill and/wealthy in Peace, famous and inuincible in Warre, fortunate in both, we that haue bene euer able to aide any of our neighbours (but neuer deafed any of their eares with any of our supplications for assistance) shall we, I say, without blushing, abase our selues so farre, as to imitate these beastly *Indians,* slaues to the *Spaniards,* refuse to the world, and as yet aliens from the holy Couenant of God? Why doe we not as well imitate them in walking naked as they doe? in preferring glasses, feathers, and such toyes, to golde and precious stones, as they do? yea why do we not denie God and adore the Deuill, as they doe?

Now to the corrupted basenesse of the first vse of this *Tobacco,* doeth very well agree the foolish and groundlesse first entry thereof into this Kingdome. It is not so long since the first entry of this abuse amongst vs here, as this present age cannot yet very well remember, both the first Author, and the forme of the first introduction of it amongst vs. It was neither brought in by King, great Conquerour, nor learned Doctor of Phisicke. . . .

Thus hauing, as I truste, sufficiently answered the most principall arguments what are vsed in defence of this vile custome, it rests onely to informe you what sinnes and vanities you commit in the filthie abuse thereof. First, are you not guiltie of sinnefull and shamefull lust? . . .Secondly it is, as you vse or rather abuse it, a branche of the sinne of drunkennesse, which is the roote of all sinnes: for as the onely delight that drunkards take in Wine is in the strength of the taste, & the force of the fume thereof that mounts vp to the braine: for no drunkards loue any weake, or sweete drinke: so are not those (I meane the strong heate and the fume) the onely qualities that make *Tobacco* so delectable to all the louers of it? . . .Thirdly, is it not the greatest sinne of all, that you the people of all sortes of this Kingdome, who are created and ordeined by God to bestowe both your persons and goods for the maintenance both of the honour and safetie of your King and Common-wealth, should disable your selues in both? . . .

And for the vanities committed in this filthie custome, is it not both great vanitie and vncleanenesse, that at the table, a place of respect, of cleanlinesse, of modestie, men should not be ashamed, to sit tossing of *Tobacco pipes,* and puffing of the smoke of *Tobacco* one to another, making the filthy smoke and stinke thereof, to exhale athwart the dishes, and infect the aire, when very often, men that abhorre it are at their repast? Surely Smoke becomes a kitchin far better then a Dining chamber, and yet it makes a kitchin also oftentimes in the inward parts of men, soiling and infecting them, with an vnctuous and oily kinde of Soote, as hath bene found in some great *Tobacco* takers, that after their death were opened. . . .And is it not a great vanitie, that a man cannot heartily welcome his friend now, but straight they must bee in hand with *Tobacco?* No it is become in place of a cure, a point of good fellowship, and he that will refuse to take a pipe of *Tobacco* among his fellowes, (though by his owne election he would rather feele the sauour of a Sinke) is accounted peeuish and no good company, euen as they doe with tippeling in the cold Easterne Countries. Yea the Mistresse cannot in a more manerly kinde, entertaine her seruant, then by giuing him out of her faire hand a pipe of *Tobacco.* But herein is not onely a great vanitie, but a great contempt of Gods good giftes, that the sweetenesse of mans breath, being a good gift of God, should be wilfully corrupted by this stinking smoke, wherein I must confesse, it hath too strong a vertue: and so that which is an ornament of nature, and can neither by any artifice be at the first acquired, nor once lost, be recouered againe, shall be filthily corrupted with an incurable stinke, which vile qualitie is as directly contrary to that wrong/opinion which is holden of the wholesomnesse thereof, as the venime of putrifaction is contrary to the vertue Preseruatiue.

Moreouer, which is a great iniquitie, and against all humanitie, the husband shall not bee ashamed, to reduce thereby his delicate, wholesome, and cleane complexioned wife, to that extremitie, that either shee must also corrupt her sweete breathe therewith, or else resolue to liue in a perpetuall stinking torment.

Haue you not reason then to bee ashamed, and to forbeare this filthie noueltie, so basely grounded, so foolishly receiued and so grossely mistaken in the right vse thereof? In your abuse thereof sinning against God, harming your selues both in persons and goods, and raking also thereby the markes and notes of vanitie vpon you: by the custome thereof making your selues to be wondered at by all forraine ciuill Nations, and by all strangers that come among you, to be scorned and contemned. A custome lothsome to the eye, hatefull to the Nose, harmefull to the braine, daungerous to the Lungs, and in the blacke stinking fume thereof, neerest resembling the horrible Stigian smoke of the pit that is bottomelesse.

54

Sir Edward Coke, *Reports.* Defense of the Common Law, 1607

The problem of the limits of the royal prerogative, raised briefly in 1601 over monopolies, returned a few years later. This time, however, the protagonist was not Parliament but the common law, in the person of Sir Edward Coke (1552–1634), its greatest champion and the symbol of its reviving stature. The prerogative courts, especially the Star Chamber, lauded by Sir Thomas Smith, and the High Commission, had been created and sustained largely by royal prerogative. Although once viewed as a valuable supplement to the common law courts, they were now seen as an illegal and dangerous encroachment. One weapon the common law used, especially against the High Commission, was the writ of prohibition, whereby a common law court could halt any legal proceeding until it was satisfied that its own jurisdiction was not being infringed upon.

Sir Edward Coke, who in 1606 became chief justice of the court of common pleas, was avid in issuing these writs and in defending them against the arguments of Archbishop Richard Bancroft. Bancroft appealed to James I's absolute authority by divine right, but Coke based his position simply on "the law and custom of England," which not only was "a measure to try the causes of the subjects," but also "protected the king in safety and peace." When James protested that Coke's view placed him under the law, Coke repeated the often-quoted words of Henry Bracton, the great legal writer of the thirteenth century, "The king is subject not to men but to God and the law." This was, however, only the beginning of Coke's confrontations with the king. Ultimately, in 1616, James removed Coke when he would not halt court proceedings to hear James's special interests. Coke's reply was, "when that case should be, he would do what should be fit for a judge to do."

Released from the bench, Coke threw his weight and that of the common law onto the side of Parliament in its continuing struggle with the king. Coke is famous for his personal stand against the king and for his career in Parliament, but equally for his writings

Source: J. P. Kenyon, ed., *The Stuart Constitution, 1603–1688: Documents and Commentary,* Cambridge University Press, 1966, pp. 180–181. Reprinted by permission of Cambridge University Press.

on the law. His *Institutes of the Laws of England* and his *Reports* on the cases of his own day, including the discussion concerning prohibitions reproduced below, are among the most important books ever written on the English law.

Note, upon Sunday the 10th of November in this same term the King, upon complaint made to him by Bancroft, archbishop of Canterbury, concerning prohibitions, the King was informed that when the question was made of what matters the ecclesiastical judges have cognisance, either upon the exposition of the statute concerning tithes, or any other thing ecclesiastical, or upon the statute 1 Eliz. concerning the High Commission, or in any other case in which there is not express authority in law, the King himself may decide it in his royal person, and that the judges are but the delegates of the King, and that the King may take what causes he shall please to determine from the determination of the judges, and may determine them himself. And the archbishop said that this was clear in divinity, that such authority belongs to the King by the word of God in the Scripture.

To which it was answered by me, in the presence and with the clear consent of all the judges of England and barons of the exchequer, that the King in his own person cannot adjudge any case, either criminal (as treason, felony, &c.) or betwixt party and party, concerning his inheritance, chattels or goods, &c., but this ought to be determined and adjudged in some court of justice according to the law and custom of England. And always judgements are given, *ideo consideratum est per curiam,* so that the court gives the judgement; and the King hath his court, viz., in the Upper House of Parliament, in which he with his Lords is the supreme judge over all other judges; for if error be in the Common Pleas, that may be reversed in the King's Bench; and if the Court of King's Bench err, that may be reversed in the Upper House of Parliament, by the King with the assent of the Lords spiritual and temporal, without the Commons, and in this respect the King is called the Chief Justice. . . . And it appears in our books that the King may sit in the Star Chamber, but this was to consult with the justices upon certain questions proposed to them, and not *in judicio;* so in the King's Bench he may sit, but the court gives the judgement, and it is commonly said in our books that the King is always present in court in the judgement of law, and upon this he cannot be nonsuit[ed]; but the judgements are always given *per curiam* and the judges are sworn to execute justice according to law and the custom of England. . . . And the judges informed the King that no king after the Conquest assumed to himself to give any judgment in any cause whatsoever which concerned the administration of justice within this realm, but these were solely determined in the courts of justice . . . , and it was greatly marvelled that the archbishop durst inform the King that such absolute power and authority, as is aforesaid, belonged to the King by the word of God. . . .

Then the King said, that he thought the law was founded upon reason, and that he and others had reason, as well as the judges. To which it was answered by me, that true it was that God had endowed his Majesty with excellent science and great endowments of nature, but his Majesty was not learned in the laws of his realm of England, and causes which concern the life, or inheritance, or goods, or fortunes of his subjects are not to be decided by natural reason but by the artificial reason and judgement of law, which law is an act which requires long study and experience before that a man can attain to the cognisance of it, and that the law was the golden mete-wand and measure to try the causes of the subjects, and which protected his Majesty in safety and peace. With which the King was greatly offended, and said, that then he should be under the law, which [it] was treason to affirm, as he said. To which I said, that Bracton saith, *quod rex non debet esse sub homine, sed sub Deo et lege.*

55
The King James Bible (1611)

The King James Version, published in 1611, was not the first English translation of the Bible. To find that, one must go back to fragments translated into Anglo-Saxon or, for a complete translation, to the fourteenth-century efforts of the Lollards, the followers of John Wycliffe. Modern English translations began with William Tyndale's New Testament, published in 1526. Tyndale's work was completed by Miles Coverdale in 1535, and this became the basis of the Matthew Bible of 1537 and the Great Bible of 1539. The Geneva Bible, produced in 1560 by Marian exiles in Geneva, was the first English Bible to receive wide circulation and popular usage, especially among those inclined toward Puritanism. The Bishops' Bible (1568) was the official response to its popularity and Puritan inclinations. Catholic exiles in 1582 produced the Rheims New Testament and in 1609 to 1610 the Douay Old Testament. The culmination of all this work, at least of the Protestant efforts, was the King James Version of 1611.

The immediate impetus for a new translation was the suggestion of a Puritan member of the Hampton Court Conference of 1604.

Source: The Holy Bible . . . Authorized King James Version. Reprinted by permission of Eyre & Spottiswoode (Publishers), Ltd., H. M. Printers.

Although James I (1603–1625) took offense at other things said, this suggestion hit a responsive chord. He had translated parts of the Bible himself, and now gave the project not only his enthusiasm but valuable suggestions, such as the omission of the marginal comments that had encumbered the Geneva Bible. The final product, representing the collective work of 47 scholars, leaned heavily on Tyndale and was far superior to previous English versions. The tradition of calling it the "Authorized Version" is of uncertain origin and perhaps comes simply from the designation on the title page, "Appointed to be read in Churches." Its simple yet dignified style, avoiding the classical terminology and ornate flourishes that often corrupted contemporary prose, made it a literary masterpiece and suitable reading for all who were literate. The King James Version intensified the popular inclination toward Bible reading and influenced English speech and writing habits for centuries to come. Popular passages from the Psalms and Paul's First Letter to the Corinthians, reprinted below, illustrate the genius of the translators as much as the religious insight of the original authors.

"The Epistle Dedicatory," part of which is also reproduced below, is interesting and revealing. The thankfulness for the peaceful accession of James and for the safe retention of the Protestant settlement is apparent, indicative of the intensity of those concerns during the long reign of Elizabeth. And there is the recognition that the English church occupied a central position between "Popish Persons" on one hand and "selfconceited Brethren" on the other.

TO THE MOST HIGH AND MIGHTY PRINCE JAMES, BY THE GRACE OF GOD, KING OF GREAT BRITAIN, FRANCE, AND IRELAND, DEFENDER OF THE FAITH, ETC., THE TRANSLATORS OF THE BIBLE WISH GRACE, MERCY, AND PEACE, THROUGH JESUS CHRIST OUR LORD

GREAT and manifold were the blessings, most dread Sovereign, which Almighty God, the Father of all mercies, bestowed upon us the people of *England,* when first he sent Your Majesty's Royal Person to rule and reign over us. For whereas it was the expectation of many, who wished not well unto our *Sion,* that upon the setting of that bright *Occidental Star,* Queen *Elizabeth* of most happy memory, some thick and palpable clouds of darkness would so have overshadowed this Land, that men should have been in doubt which way they were to walk; and that it should hardly be known, who was to direct the unsettled State; the appearance of Your Majesty, as of the *Sun* in his strength, instantly dispelled those supposed and surmised mists, and gave unto all that were well affected exceeding cause of comfort; especially when we beheld the Government established in Your Highness, and Your hopeful Seed, by an undoubted Title, and this also accompanied with peace and tranquility at home and abroad.

But among all our joys, there was no one that more filled our hearts, than the blessed continuance of the preaching of God's sacred Word among us; which is that inestimable treasure, which excelleth all the riches of the earth; because the fruit thereof extendeth itself, not only to the time spent in this transitory world, but directeth and disposeth men unto that eternal happiness which is above in heaven.

Then not to suffer this to fall to the ground, but rather to take it up, and to continue it in that state, wherein the famous Predecessor of Your Highness did leave it: nay, to go forward with the confidence and resolution of a Man in maintaining the truth of Christ, and propagating it far and near, is that which hath so bound and firmly knit the hearts of all Your Majesty's loyal and religious people unto You, that Your very name is precious among them: their eye doth behold You with comfort, and they bless You in their hearts, as that sanctified Person, who, under God, is the immediate Author of their true happiness. . . .

There are infinite arguments of this right christian and religious affection in Your Majesty; but none is more forcible to declare it to others than the vehement and perpetuated desire of accomplishing and publishing of this work, which now with all humility we present unto Your Majesty. For when Your Highness had once out of deep judgment apprehended how convenient it was, that out of the Original Sacred Tongues, together with comparing of the labours, both in our own, and other foreign Languages, of many worthy men who went before us, there should be one more exact Translation of the holy Scriptures into the *English Tongue*. . . .

And now at last, by the mercy of God, and the continuance of our labours, it being brought unto such a conclusion, as that we have great hopes that the Church of *England* shall reap good fruit thereby; we hold it our duty to offer it to Your Majesty, not only as to our King and Sovereign, but as to the principal Mover and Author of the work: humbly craving of Your most Sacred Majesty, that since things of this quality have ever been subject to the censures of illmeaning and discontented persons, it may receive approbation and patronage from so learned and judicious a Prince as Your Highness is, whose allowance and acceptance of our labours shall more honour and encourage us, than all the calumniations and hard interpretations of other men shall dismay us. So that if, on the one side, we shall be traduced by Popish Persons at home or abroad, who therefore will malign us, because we are poor instruments to make God's holy Truth to be yet more and more known unto the people, whom they desire still to keep in ignorance and darkness; or if, on the other side, we shall be maligned by selfconceited Brethren, who run their own ways, and give liking unto nothing, but what is framed by themselves, and hammered on their anvil; we may rest secure, supported within by the truth and innocency of a good conscience, having walked the ways of simplicity and integrity, as before the Lord; and sustained without by the powerful protection of Your Majesty's grace and favour, which will ever give countenance to honest and christian endeavours against bitter censures and uncharitable imputations.

PSALM 23

A Psalm of David.

THE LORD *is* my shepherd; I shall not want.

2 He maketh me to lie down in green pastures: he leadeth me beside the still waters.

3 He restoreth my soul: he leadeth me in the paths of righteousness for his name's sake.

4 Yea, though I walk through the valley of the shadow of death, I will fear no evil: for thou *art* with me; thy rod and thy staff they comfort me.

5 Thou preparest a table before me in the presence of mine enemies: thou anointest my head with oil; my cup runneth over.

6 Surely goodness and mercy shall follow me all the days of my life: and I will dwell in the house of the Lord forever.

PAUL'S FIRST EPISTLE TO THE CORINTHIANS

CHAPTER 13

Though I speak with the tongues of men and of angels, and have not charity, I am become *as* sounding brass, or a tinkling cymbal.

2 And though I have *the gift of* prophecy, and understand all mysteries, and all knowledge; and though I have all faith, so that I could remove mountains, and have not charity, I am nothing.

3 And though I bestow all my goods to feed *the poor*, and though I give my body to be burned, and have not charity, it profiteth me nothing.

4 Charity suffereth long, *and* is kind; charity envieth not; charity vaunteth not itself, is not puffed up,

5 Doth not behave itself unseemly, seeketh not her own, is not easily provoked, thinketh no evil;

6 Rejoiceth not in iniquity, but rejoiceth in the truth;

7 Beareth all things, believeth all things, hopeth all things, endureth all things.

8 Charity never faileth: but whether *there be* prophecies, they shall fail; whether *there be* tongues, they shall cease; whether *there be* knowledge, it shall vanish away.

9 For we know in part, and we prophesy in part.

10 But when that which is perfect is come, then that which is in part shall be done away.

11 When I was a child, I spake as a child, I understood as a child, I thought as a child: but when I became a man, I put away childish things.

12 For now we see through a glass, darkly; but then face to face: now I know in part; but then shall I know even as also I am known.

13 And now abideth faith, hope, charity, these three; but the greatest of these *is* charity.

56
Sir Francis Bacon, *Novum Organum* (1620). The Scientific Method

Sir Francis Bacon (1561–1626) was one of the great men of his time. A son of Elizabeth's Lord Keeper of the Great Seal, he became a lawyer, a member of Parliament, a civil servant, and finally in 1618 Lord Chancellor. As a lawyer he championed the absolute authority of the king, in opposition to Sir Edward Coke. When the latter helped revive impeachment in 1621, Bacon was one of its first victims, admitting he had accepted money from litigants whose cases were pending before his court. Bacon was, and remains, more famous as the author of *Essays* (1597, 1625), a *History of Henry the Seventh* (1622), and several important works on philosophy and the scientific method. Even as a student at Trinity College, Cambridge, he had noted the sterility of contemporary scholarship, especially in natural science, where men still slavishly followed the logic and conclusions of Aristotle rather than emulating his example of examining things firsthand. Bacon envisioned a "Great Instauration," a great restoration or repairing, of men's approach to the investigation and exploitation of nature. In the *New Organon, or True Directions Concerning the Interpretation of Nature,* written in Latin in 1620, he emphasized the need to liberate science from the restraints of theology and from its bondage to the logic, or *Organon,* of Aristotle. What was needed was a new organon, a new method, a rigorous induction from observed fact and experiment to sound general laws and principles.

Bacon was not a great scientist or experimenter himself, although he is reputed to have died of a cold caught in a snowbank while trying to determine whether a dressed chicken could be preserved by packing it in ice. Also, he had little appreciation for the importance of mathematics or for the best scientists of his day—men such as William Gilbert, who experimented with the magnet, and Galileo, who discovered the science of mechanics. Nevertheless, by separating the study of nature from theology and by pronouncing it not only agreeable to God but useful to

Source: The Works of Francis Bacon, collected and edited by James Spedding, Robert Leslie Ellis, and Douglas Denon Heath, Vol. IV, London: Longman and Co. et al., 1860, pp. 39–42, 47–51, 115, 247–248.

mankind, Bacon became an important propagandist and an inspiration for the advancement of science. The Royal Society of London for Improving Natural Knowledge, founded in 1660, acknowledged its debt to him, as can be seen from these lines of Abraham Cowley (1618–1667):

Bacon, like Moses, led us forth at last,
The barren wilderness he past,
Did on the very border stand
Of the blest promis'd land
And from the mountain's top of his exalted wit
Saw it himself, and shew'd us it.

PREFACE

Those who have taken upon them to lay down the law of nature as a thing already searched out and understood, whether they have spoken in simple assurance or professional affectation, have therein done philosophy and the sciences great injury. . . . Those on the other hand who have taken a contrary course, and asserted that absolutely nothing can be known,—whether it were from hatred of the ancient sophists, or from uncertainty and fluctuation of mind, or even from a kind of fulness of learning, that they fell upon this opinion,—have certainly advanced reasons for it that are not to be despised; but yet they have neither started from true principles nor rested in the just conclusion, zeal and affectation having carried them much too far. . . .

Now my method, though hard to practise, is easy to explain; and it is this. I propose to establish progressive stages of certainty. The evidence of the sense, helped and guarded by a certain process of correction, I retain. But the mental operation which follows the act of sense I for the most part reject; and instead of it I open and lay out a new and certain path for the mind to proceed in, starting directly from the simple sensuous perception. . . . There remains but one course for the recovery of a sound and healthy condition,—namely, that the entire work of the understanding be commenced afresh, and the mind itself be from the very outset not left to take its own course, but guided at every step; and the business be done as if by machinery. . . .

Upon these premises two things occur to me of which, that they may not be overlooked, I would have men reminded. First it falls out fortunately as I think for the allaying of contradictions and heart-burnings, that the honour and reverence due to the ancients remains untouched and undiminished; while I may carry out my designs and at the same time reap the fruit of my modesty. For if I should profess that I, going the same road as the ancients, have something better to produce, there must needs have been some comparison or rivalry between us (not to be avoided by any art of words) in respect of excellency or ability of wit;

and though in this there would be nothing unlawful or new (for if there be anything misapprehended by them, or falsely laid down, why may not I, using a liberty common to all, take exception to it?) yet the contest, however just and allowable, would have been an unequal one perhaps, in respect of the measure of my own powers. . . . The other point of which I would have men reminded relates to the matter itself.

Be it remembered then that I am far from wishing to interfere with the philosophy which now flourishes, or with any other philosophy more correct and complete than this which has been or may hereafter be propounded. For I do not object to the use of this received philosophy, or others like it, for supplying matter for disputations or ornaments for discourse,—for the professor's lecture and for the business of life. Nay more, I declare openly that for these uses the philosophy which I bring forward will not be much available. It does not lie in the way. It cannot be caught up in passage. It does not flatter the understanding by conformity with preconceived notions. Nor will it come down to the apprehension of the vulgar except by its utility and effects.

Let there be therefore (and may it be for the benefit of both) two streams and two dispensations of knowledge; and in like manner two tribes or kindreds of students in philosophy—tribes not hostile or alien to each other, but bound together by mutual services;—let there in short be one methed for the cultivation, another for the invention, of knowledge.

APHORISMS CONCERNING THE INTERPRETATION OF NATURE AND THE KINGDOM OF MAN.

Aphorism

I.

Man, being the servant and interpreter of Nature, can do and understand so much and so much only as he has observed in fact or in thought of the course of nature: beyond this he neither knows anything nor can do anything.

XI.

As the sciences which we now have do not help us in finding out new works, so neither does the logic which we now have help us in finding out new sciences.

XII.

The logic now in use serves rather to fix and give stability to the errors which have their foundation in commonly received notions than to help the search after truth. So it does more harm than good.

XIII.

The syllogism is not applied to the first principles of sciences, and is applied in vain to intermediate axioms; being no match for the subtlety of nature. It commands assent therefore to the proposition, but does not take hold of the thing.

XIV.

The syllogism consists of propositions, propositions consist of words, words are symbols of notions. Therefore if the notions themselves (which is the root of the matter) are confused and over-hastily abstracted from the facts, there can be no firmness in the superstructure. Our only hope therefore lies in a true induction.

XIX.

There are and can be only two ways of searching into and discovering truth. The one flies from the senses and particulars to the most general axioms, and from these principles, the truth of which it takes for settled and immoveable, proceeds to judgment and to the discovery of middle axioms. And this way is now in fashion. The other derives axioms from the senses and particulars, rising by a gradual and unbroken ascent, so that it arrives at the most general axioms last of all. This is the true way, but as yet untried.

XXIV.

It cannot be that axioms established by argumentation should avail for the discovery of new works; since the subtlety of nature is greater many times over than the subtlety of argument. But axioms duly and orderly formed from particulars easily discover the way to new particulars, and thus render sciences active.

LII.

. . . There cannot but follow an improvement in man's estate, and an enlargement of his power over nature. For man by the fall fell at the same time from his state of innocency and from his dominion over creation. Both of these losses however can even in this life be in some part repaired; the former by religion and faith, the latter by arts and sciences. For creation was not by the curse made altogether and for ever a rebel, but in virtue of that charter "In the sweat of thy face shalt thou eat bread," it is now by various labours (not certainly by disputations or idle magical ceremonies, but by various labours) at length and in some measure subdued to the supplying of man with bread; that is, to the uses of human life.

57
William Bradford, *Of Plymouth Plantation, 1620–1647*. Puritanism and the New World

Puritanism, an important movement within the Church of England in the late sixteenth century, agitated for further reform. It is difficult to define these Puritans, for they were both moderate reformers, who sought to purify the established church of its Roman traditions, and separatists, like William Bradford, who left the Church of England to form separate congregations. Most Puritans, however, supported certain general principles. As Bradford points out below, they wanted a church "according to the simplicitie of the gospel," responsive to its members' interpretation of Scripture and less tied to the maintenance of "episcopall dignitie (affter the popish manner)." The Church should also be the active enforcer of personal and public morality. Critics have traditionally stressed the last aspect of Puritanism, as is indicated in these satirical lines written about 1640.

> A puritan, is he, that when he prays,
> his rowling eyes up to the heavens doth raise.
> A puritan, is he, that cannot dine,
> nor sup, without a double grace divine.
> A puritan, is he, that through the year,
> two Lords-day sermons doth either preach or hear.
> A puritan, is he, whose austere life,
> will not admit a mistress and a wife.
> That when his betters swear, doth bite the lip,
> nor will be drunken for good-fellowship.

Of Plymouth Plantation is William Bradford's story of the separatists from the village of Scrooby. Bradford describes their persecution in England, their flight to Holland in 1608 and, eventually, their voyage to America, where they hoped to preserve both their religious beliefs and their English culture. Bradford was well qualified to write such a history. A member of the Scrooby congregation and a prosperous weaver during the exile in Holland, he

Source: William Bradford, *Of Plymouth Plantation, 1620–1647,* edited by Samuel Eliot Morison, New York: Alfred A. Knopf, 1952, pp. 5–10, 23, 25, 28, 75–76.

helped in 1620 to organize the voyage of the *Mayflower,* and he later served for more than thirty years as governor of Plymouth Colony.

The history of Bradford's manuscript provides an interesting commentary on relations between old England and the new England that Bradford helped to create in America. Finished about 1646, *Of Plymouth Plantation* remained unprinted for over two centuries. During the seventeenth and early eighteenth centuries, it was used by other historians, some of whom corrected portions of it. The manuscript disappeared from the Old South Church of Boston during the American Revolution, but it reappeared mysteriously seventy years later in the library of the bishop of London. Although copied and in 1856 published, the original remained in London despite numerous private and official efforts to persuade the British to return it. Its presentation to the Commonwealth of Massachusetts in 1897 may be viewed symbolically as the end of the Anglo-American schism within the British community and the beginning of a new era of understanding and cooperation.

Mr. Foxe recordeth how that besids those worthy martires and confessors which were burned in queene Marys days and otherwise tormented, *many (both students and others) fled out of the land, to the number of* 800. *And became severall congregations.* . . . Amongst whom (but especialy those at Frankford) begane that bitter warr of contention and persecution aboute the ceremonies, and servisebooke, and other popish and antichristian stuffe, the plague of England to this day. . . .

The one side laboured to have the right worship of God and discipline of Christ established in the church, according to the simplicitie of the gospell, without the mixture of mens inventions, and to have and to be ruled by the laws of Gods word, dispensed in those offices, and by those officers of Pastors, Teachers, and Elders, etc. according to the Scripturs. The other partie, though under many colours and pretences, endevored to have the episcopall dignitie (affter the popish manner) with their large power and jurisdiction still retained; with all those courts, cannons, and ceremonies, togeather with all such livings, revenues, and subordinate officers, with other such means as formerly upheld their antichristian greatnes, and enabled them with lordly and tyranous power to persecute the poore servants of God. . . .

And this contention dyed not with queene Mary, nor was left beyonde the seas, but at her death these people returning into England under gracious queene Elizabeth, many of them being preferred to bishopricks and other promotions, according to their aimes and desires, that inveterate hatered against the holy discipline of Christ in his church hath continued to this day. . . . And many the like, to stop the mouthes of the more godly, to bring them over to yeeld to one ceremoney after another, and one corruption after another; by these wyles begyleing some and corrupting others till at length they begane to persecute all the zealous professors in the land . . . both by word and deed, if they would not submitte to their ceremonies, and became slaves to them and their popish trash, which have no ground in the word of God, but are relikes of that man of sine. . . . And to cast contempte the more upon the sincere servants of God, they opprobriously and most injuriously gave unto, and imposed upon them, that name of Puritans. . . .

But that I may come more near my intendmente; when as by the travell and diligence of some godly and zealous preachers, and Gods blessing on their labours, as in other places of the land, so in the North parts, many became inlightened by the word of God, and had their ignorance and sins discovered unto them, and begane by his grace to reforme their lives, and make conscience of their wayes, the worke of God was no sooner manifest in them, but presently they were both scoffed and scorned by the prophane multitude, and the ministers urged with the yoak of subscription, or els must be silenced; and the poore people were so vexed with apparators, and pursuants, and the comissarie courts, as truly their affliction was not smale; which, notwithstanding, they bore sundrie years with much patience, till they were occasioned (by the continuance and encrease of these troubls, and other means which the Lord raised up in those days) to see further into things by the light of the word of God. How not only these base and beggerly ceremonies were unlawfull, but also that the lordly and tiranous power of the prelats ought not to be submitted unto; which thus, contrary to the freedome of the gospell, would load and burden mens consciences, and by their compulsive power make a phophane mixture of persons and things in the worship of God. And that their offices and calings, courts and cannons, etc. were unlawfull and antichristian; being such as have no warrante in the word of God; but the same that were used in poperie, and still retained. . . .

So many therfore of these proffessors as saw the evill of these things, in thes parts, and whose harts the Lord had touched with heavenly zeale for his trueth, they shooke of this yoake of antichristian bondage, and as the Lords free people, joyned them selves (by a covenant of the Lord) into a church estate, in the felowship of the gospell, to walke in all his wayes, made known, or to be made known unto them, according to their best endeavours, whatsoever it should cost them, the Lord assisting them. And that it cost them something this ensewing historie will declare. . . .

But after these things they could not long continue in any peaceable condition, but were hunted and persecuted on every side, so as their former afflictions were but as fleabitings in comparison of these which now came upon them. For some were taken and clapt up in prison, others had their houses besett and watcht night and day, and hardly escaped their hands; and the most were faine to flie and leave their howses and habitations, and the means of their livelehood.

. . . Yet seeing them selves thus molested, and that ther was no hope of their continuance ther, by a joynte consente they resolved to goe into the Low-Countries, wher they heard was freedome of Religion for all men. . . .

AFTER . . . about some 11. or 12. years, . . . and sundrie of them were taken away by death, and many others begane to be well striken in years, the grave mistris Experience haveing taught them many things, those prudent governours with sundrie of the sagest members begane both deeply to apprehend their present dangers, and . . . to incline to this conclusion, of remoovall to some other place. . . .

The place they had thoughts on was some of those vast and unpeopled countries of America. . . .

Some (and none of the meanest) had thoughts and were ernest for Guiana, or some of those fertill places in those hott climats; others were for some parts of Virginia, wher the English had all ready made enterance, and beginning. . . .

I SHALL a litle returne backe and begine with a combination made by them before they came ashore, being the first foundation of their governmente in this place; occasioned partly by the discontented and mutinous speeches that some of the strangers amongst them had let fall from them in the ship—That when they came a shore they would use their owne libertie; for none had power to command them, the patente they had being for Virginia, and not for New-england, which belonged to an other Government, with which the Virginia Company had nothing to doe. And partly that shuch an acte by them done (this their condition considered) might be as firme as any patent, and in some respects more sure.

The forme was as followeth.

> In the name of God, Amen. We whose names are under-writen, the loyall subjects of our dread soveraigne Lord, King James, by the grace of God, of Great Britaine, Franc, and Ireland king, defender of the faith, etc., haveing undertaken, for the glorie of God, and advancemente of the Christian faith, and honour of our king and countrie, a voyage to plant the first colonie in the Northerne parts of Virginia, doe by these presents solemnly and mutualy in the presence of God, and one of another, covenant and combine our selves togeather into a civill body politick, for our better ordering and preservation and furtherance of the ends aforesaid; and by vertue hearof to enacte, constitute, and frame such just and equall lawes, ordinances, acts, constitutions, and offices, from time to time, as shall be thought most meete and convenient for the generall good of the Colonie, unto which we promise all due submission and obedience. In witness wherof we have hereunder subscribed our names at Cap-Codd the 11. of November, in the year of the raigne of our soveraigne lord, King James, of England, France, and Ireland the eighteenth, and of Scotland the fiftie fourth. An°: Dom. 1620.

After this they chose, or rather confirmed, Mr. John Carver (a man godly and well approved amongst them) their Governour for that year. And after they had provided a place for their goods, or comone store, (which were long in unlading for want of boats, foulnes of winter weather, and sicknes of diverce,) and begune some small cottages for their habitation, as time would admitte, they mette and consulted of lawes and orders, both for their civill and military Govermente, as the necessitie of their condition did require, still adding therunto as urgent occasion in severall times, and as cases did require.

58
The Petition of Right (1628)

The king's need for money was always the weakest point in the armor defending his prerogative, and Parliament's control over taxation was ever its strongest weapon. Parliament had thus through the centuries forged its privileges and defended individual rights. Such a coinciding of royal needs and parliamentary concern occurred in 1628, a result of Charles I's and the duke of Buckingham's insistence on fighting an ill-conceived war with France and Spain. The outcome was the Petition of Right, England's most important constitutional document since Magna Carta.

The document's form, a petition by which the king was asked to confirm existing rights, was due to the legal genius of Sir Edward Coke. In a statute these rights would have seemed a new creation requiring the king's approval. What Coke and the others wanted was a recognition of traditional rights. As the House of Commons had asserted in its Apology of 1604, "we most truly avouch that our privileges and liberties are our rights and due inheritance no less than our very lands and goods."

The similarity of the Petition of Right to Magna Carta was not accidental. Like Magna Carta, it listed a number of infringements of the ancient rights of Englishmen. The king's acknowledgment of such rights—not to be taxed without parliamentary consent, not to be imprisoned arbitrarily, not to have soldiers billeted in private houses without consent or compensation, not to have martial law imposed—placed them on a more solid and defensible foundation. Behind the specifics, however, was the unspoken but undoubted affirmation of the principle that the king was indeed beneath the

Source: J. P. Kenyon, ed., *The Stuart Constitution, 1603–1688: Documents and Commentary,* Cambridge University Press, 1966, pp. 82–85. Reprinted by permission of Cambridge University Press.

law. As Coke said in the debate on the Petition: "Magna Carta is such a fellow that he will have no 'sovereign.' "

The English constitution is singularly devoid of broad, theoretical statements of the people's rights. Its great documents deal with specific rights arising out of immediate problems of one time and place. It is the understanding behind them that is the real constitution of England. Being unwritten, it has been able to grow with time and circumstance, but without vigilance and effort it could as easily have been neglected and lost. Thus, again in the words of the Apology of the House of Commons: "The prerogatives of princes may easily and do daily grow; the privileges of the subject are for the most part at an everlasting stand. They may be by good providence and care preserved; but being once lost are not recovered but with much disquiet."

The Petition exhibited to his Majesty by the Lords Spiritual and Temporal and Commons in this present Parliament assembled concerning divers rights and liberties of the subject.

To the King's Most Excellent Majesty

Humbly show unto our Sovereign Lord the King the Lords Spiritual and Temporal and Commons in Parliament assembled, that whereas it is declared. . . by authority of Parliament holden in the five and twentieth year of the reign of King Edward the Third . . . and by other laws of this realm it is provided that . . . your subjects have inherited this freedom, that they should not be compelled to contribute to any tax, tallage, aid or other like charge not set by common consent in Parliament.

II. Yet, nevertheless of late . . . your people have been in divers places assembled and required to lend certain sums of money unto your Majesty, and many of them upon their refusal so to do have . . . been constrained to become bound to make appearance and give attendance before your Privy Council and in other places; and others of them have been therefore imprisoned, confined, and sundry other ways molested and disquieted. . . .

III. And where also by the statute called the Great Charter of the Liberties of England it is declared and enacted, that no freeman may be taken or imprisoned or be disseised of his freehold or liberties or his free customs or be outlawed or exiled or in any manner destroyed, but by the lawful judgement of his peers or by the law of the land.

V. Nevertheless against the tenor of the said statutes and other the good laws and statutes of your realm to that end provided, divers of your subjects have of late been imprisoned without any cause shown; and when for their deliverance they were brought before your justices by your Majesty's writ of habeas corpus there to undergo and receive as the Court should order, and their Keepers commanded to certify the causes of their detainer, no cause was certified, but that they were detained by your Majesty's special command signified by the Lords of your Privy Council, and yet were returned back to several prisons without being charged with any thing to which they might make answer according to the law.

VI. And whereas of late great companies of soldiers and mariners have been dispersed into divers counties of the realm, and the inhabitants against their will have been compelled to receive them into their houses, and there to suffer them to sojourn against the laws and customs of this realm and to the great grievance and vexation of the people.

VII. And wheras also by authority of Parliament in the five and twentieth year of the reign of King Edward the Third it is declared and enacted that no man should be forejudged of life and limb against the form of the Great Charter and the law of the land; and by the said Great Charter, and other the laws and statutes of this your realm, no man ought to be adjudged to death but by the laws established in this your realm, either by the customs of the same realm or by Act of Parliament . . . nevertheless of late time divers commissions under your Majesty's great seal have issued forth, by which certain persons have been assigned and appointed commissioners with power and authority to proceed within the land according to the justice of martial law . . . and by such summary course and order as is agreeable to martial law and as is used in armies in time of war to proceed to the trial and condemnation of such offenders, and them to cause to be executed and put to death according to the law martial. . . .

And also sundry grievous offenders by colour thereof claiming an exemption have escaped the punishments due to them by the laws and statutes of this your realm . . . upon pretence that the said offenders were punishable only by martial law. . . .

VIII. They do therefore humbly pray your most excellent Majesty that no man hereafter be compelled to make or yield any gift, loan, benevolence, tax or such like charge without common consent by Act of Parliament, and that none be called to make answer or take such oath or to give attendance or be confined or otherwise molested or disquieted concerning the same or for refusal thereof. And that no freeman in any such manner as is before mentioned be imprisoned or detained. And that your Majesty would be pleased to remove the said soldiers and mariners, and that your people may not be so burdened in time to come. And that the aforesaid commissions for proceeding by martial law may be revoked and annulled. And that hereafter no commissions of like nature may issue forth to any person or persons whatsoever to be executed as aforesaid, lest by colour of them any of your Majesty's subjects be destroyed or put to death contrary to the laws and franchises of the land.

All which they most humbly pray of your excellent Majesty as their rights and liberties according to the laws and statutes of this realm, and that your Majesty would also vouchsafe to declare that the awards, doings, and proceedings to the prejudice of your people in any of the premises shall not be drawn hereafter into consequence or example. And that your Majesty would be also graciously pleased for the further comfort and safety of your people to declare your royal will and pleasure, that in the thing aforesaid all your officers and ministers shall serve you according to the laws and statutes of this realm as they tender the honour of your Majesty and the prosperity of this kingdom.

59
John Milton, *Areopagitica* (1644). Freedom of the Press

The desire of Puritanism to reform the English church led to the belief that preachers should be allowed freely to preach, for only then could the word of God work its act of reformation. This, it turned out, was a dynamic beyond anything the Puritans envisioned. After the Star Chamber was abolished in 1641 and with it the state's control over the press, there was a flood of literature expressing all sorts of radical ideas regarding the church, state, and society. Not surprisingly, the Presbyterian majority in Parliament in 1643 ordered printing once more to be licensed and restricted. The reformation had gone far enough, and the expression of radical ideas should be halted.

John Milton (1608–1674), scholarly and independent of mind, was both a Puritan and a humanist. The poetry he had already written was the earnest of the greatness yet to come, and his polemical pamphlets denouncing bishops and justifying divorce were as perceptive as they were controversial. The budding Presbyterian settlement of 1643, which included the Solemn League and Covenant with the Scots and the new restrictions on printing, he denounced as "New Presbyter is but old Priest writ large." His motive in writing *Areopagitica* (1644) may have been to safeguard his own writings, but more likely it was to defend a principle in which he believed deeply. *Areopagitica* is in the form of a classical oration, having the same name as one Isocrates di-

Source: John Milton, *Complete Prose Works of John Milton,* gen. eds. Douglas Bush et al., Vol. II (1643–1648), New Haven: Yale University Press, 1959, pp. 492–493, 561.

rected at the Athenian *areopagus,* or assembly. The passage below remains one of the most forceful justifications of liberty.

Like the Presbyterians, Milton also reached a point beyond which he could not go. Further along in *Areopagitica,* he added, "I mean not tolerated popery, and open superstition, which as it extirpats all religions and civil supremacies, so itself should be extirpat." Milton thus raised perhaps the greatest of all questions regarding liberty: should it be extended even to those who want to destroy it?

I deny not, but that it is of greatest concernment in the Church and Commonwealth, to have a vigilant eye how Bookes demeane themselves, as well as men; and thereafter to confine, imprison, and do sharpest justice on them as malefactors: For Books are not absolutely dead things, but doe contain a potencie of life in them to be as active as that soule whose progeny they are; nay they do preserve as in a violl the purest efficacie and extraction of that living intellect that bred them. I know they are as lively, and as vigorously productive, as those fabulous Dragons teeth; and being sown up and down, may chance to spring up armed men. And yet on the other hand unlesse warinesse be us'd, as good almost kill a Man as kill a good Book; who kills a Man kills a reasonable creature, Gods Image; but hee who destroyes a good Booke, kills reason it selfe, kills the Image of God, as it were in the eye. Many a man lives a burden to the Earth; but a good Booke is the pretious life-blood of a master spirit, imbalm'd and treasur'd up on purpose to a life beyond life. 'Tis true, no age can restore a life, whereof perhaps there is no great losse; and revolutions of ages doe not oft recover the losse of a rejected truth, for the want of which whole Nations fare the worse. We should be wary therefore what persecution we raise against the living labours of publick men, how we spill that season'd life of man preserv'd and stor'd up in Books; since we see a kinde of homicide may be thus committed, sometimes a martyrdome, and if it extend to the whole impression, a kinde of massacre, whereof the execution ends not in the slaying of an elementall life, but strikes at that ethereall and fift essence, the breath of reason it selfe, slaies an immortality rather then a life. . . . And though all the windes of doctrin were let loose to play upon the earth, so Truth be in the field, we do injuriously by licencing and prohibiting to misdoubt her strength. Let her and Falshood grapple; who ever knew Truth put to the wors, in a free and open encounter.

60

The Putney Debates. Radicalism in the New Model Army, 1647

The importance of the English Revolution (1640–1660) is partly in the actions taken, culminating in 1649 in the public trial and execution of Charles I for treason, and partly in the new political ideas expressed. In both deed and thought, the Revolution remained an example for political thinkers and practitioners to contemplate and to follow or avoid.

Some of the Revolution's most serious political thought and discussion took place in the New Model Army, which had by 1647 begun to consider itself a political as well as a military body. It seized the king from Parliament and proceeded itself to negotiate with him. There were, however, in the army two points of view, that of the Independents, as represented by Lieutenant General Oliver Cromwell and his son-in-law, Commissary General Henry Ireton, and that of the more radical representatives of the regiments, such men as John Wildman and Thomas Rainborough, who can best be described as Levellers. The basic issue was the nature of England's political settlement. In the passage reproduced below, a discussion of the Levellers' "Agreement of the People," the issues were raised to the highest theoretical level. Is justice "that which is just according to the foundation of justice between man and man" or is "the justice of the thing" gauged by a higher, abstract law that can even determine "that an unjust engagement is rather to be broken than kept"? Also debated was the question of who should have a political voice in the kingdom. Was it only those with a "permanent interest," "the persons in whom the land lies, and those in corporations in whom all trading lies," or did "every man born in England" have the right to participate?

The debates achieved nothing, except to convince Cromwell that it was dangerous to allow them to continue. He and the other generals reasserted their authority, ending all participation in politics or army decisions by "Agitators" elected from the ranks. The Putney Debates are valuable for the light that they shed on the activities of the army during a period of intense and unprecedented

Source: A. S. P. Woodhouse, ed., *Puritanism and Liberty: Being the Army Debates (1647–9) from the Clarke Manuscripts,* Chicago: The University of Chicago Press, 1951, pp. 7, 24–27, 33, 53–58, 65–66. Reprinted by permission of the University of Chicago Press and J. M. Dent, Ltd.

political activity and on the difficult relationship between Puritanism and radical political thought and action.

These debates, held at Putney near London on October 28 and 29 and November 1, 1647, were recorded in shorthand by William Clarke, a clerk of the New Model Army. They were probably not written out in "a fair hand" until after the Restoration. Though these "Clarke Papers" were given to Worcester College, Oxford, by Clarke's son in 1736, they went unnoticed until they were mentioned in a catalog of manuscripts in 1852. They were edited for the Camden Society by Charles Firth in 1891. The dialogue below is taken from the edition of A. S. P. Woodhouse, who added the words in square brackets in order to make speeches and sentences intelligible.

Cromwell: Truly this paper does contain in it very great alterations of the very government of the kingdom. . . . And what the consequences of such an alteration as this would be . . . wise men and godly men ought to consider. . . . How do we know if, whilst we are disputing these things, another company of men shall [not] gather together, and put out a paper as plausible perhaps as this? . . . And not only another, and another, but many of this kind. And if so, what do you think the consequence of that would be? Would it not be confusion? Would it not be utter confusion? . . .

Wildman: And whereas it is desired that engagements may be considered, I shall desire that only the justice of the thing that is proposed may be considered. [I would know] whether the chief thing in the Agreement, the intent of it, be not this, to secure the rights of the people in their Parliaments. . . . I shall make that motion to be the thing considered: Whether the thing be just, or the people's due? And then there can be no engagement to bind from it.

Ireton: . . . when we talk of just, it is not so much of what is sinful before God . . . but . . . that which is just according to the foundation of justice between man and man. And for my part I account that the great foundation of justice . . . that we should keep covenant one with another. . . . What right hath any man to anything if you lay not [down] that principle, that we are to keep covenant? If you will resort only to the Law of Nature, by the Law of Nature you have no more right to this land, or anything else, than I have. I have as much right to take hold of anything that is for my sustenance, [to] take hold of anything that I have a desire to for my satisfaction, as you. . . .

Wildman: Our [sense] was, that an unjust engagement is rather to be broken than kept. . . . I make a question whether any engagement can be [binding] to an unjust thing. . . . I do apply this to the case in hand: that it might be considered whether it be unjust to bring in the King in such a way as he may be in a capacity to destroy the people. . . .

Rainborough: Is it not an argument, if a pilot run his ship upon a rock, or [if] a general mount his cannon against his army, he is to be resisted? I think that this [is] as clear[ly] the very case as anything in the world. . . . For really I think that the poorest he that is in England hath a life to live, as the greatest he; and therefore truly, sir, I think it's clear, that every man that is to live under a government ought first by his own consent to put himself under that government; and I do think that the poorest man in England is not at all bound in a strict sense to that government that he hath not had a voice to put himself under. . . .

Ireton: Give me leave to tell you, that if you make this the rule I think you must fly for refuge to an absolute natural right, and you must deny all civil right. . . . We talk of birthright. Truly [by] birthright there is thus much claim. Men may justly have by birthright, by their very being born in England, that we should not seclude them out of England, that we should not refuse to give them air and place and ground, and the freedom of the highways and other things, to live amongst us—not any man that is born here, though by his birth there come nothing at all (that is part of the permanent interest of this kingdom) to him. That I think is due to a man by birth. But that by a man's being born here he shall have a share in that power that shall dispose of the lands here, and of all things here, I do not think it a sufficient ground. I am sure if we look upon that which is the utmost (within [any] man's view) of what was originally the constitution of this kingdom, upon that which is most radical and fundamental, and which if you take away, there is no man hath any land, any goods, [or] any civil interest, that is this: that those that choose the representers for the making of laws by which this state and kingdom are to be governed, are the persons who, taken together, do comprehend the local interest of this kingdom; that is, the persons in whom all land lies, and those in corporations in whom all trading lies. . . .

Rainborough: Truly, sir, I am of the same opinion I was, and am resolved to keep it till I know reason why I should not. . . . I do hear nothing at all that can convince me, why any man that is born in England ought not to have his voice in election of burgesses. It is said that if a man have not a permanent interest, he can have no claim; and [that] we must be no freer than the laws will let us be, and that there is no [law in any] chronicle will let us be freer than that we [now] enjoy. . . . And therefore I say, that either it must be the Law of God or the law of man that must prohibit the meanest man in the kingdom to have this benefit as well as the greatest. I do not find anything in the Law of God, that a lord shall choose twenty burgesses, and a gentleman but two, or a poor man shall choose none: I find no such thing in the Law of Nature, nor in the Law of Nations. But I do find that all Englishmen must be subject to English laws, and I do verily believe that there is no man but will say that the foundation of all law lies in the people. . . . A man, when he hath an estate, hath an interest in making laws, [but] when he hath none, he hath no power in it; so that a man cannot lose that which he hath for the maintenance of his family but he must [also] lose that which God and nature hath given him! And therefore I do [think], and am still of the same opinion, that every man born in England cannot, ought not, neither by the Law of God nor the Law of Nature, to be exempted from the choice of those who are to make laws for him to live under, and for him, for aught I know, to lose his life under. . . .

Ireton: All the main thing that I speak for, is because I would have an eye to property. . . . let every man consider with himself that he do not go that way to take away all property. For here is the case of the most fundamental part of the constitution of the kingdom, which if you take away, you take away all by that. Here men of this and this quality are determined to be the electors of men to the Parliament, and they are all those who have any permanent interest in the kingdom, and who, taken together, do comprehend the whole [permanent, local] interest of the kingdom. . . . Now I wish we may all consider of what right you will challenge that all the people should have right to elections. Is it by the right of nature? If you will hold forth that as your ground, then I think you must deny all property too, and this is my reason. For thus: by that same right of nature (whatever it be) that you pretend, by which you can say, one man hath an equal right with another to the choosing of him that shall govern him—by the same right of nature, he hath the same [equal] right in any goods he sees—meat, drink, clothes—to take and use them for his sustenance. He hath a freedom to the land, [to take] the ground, to exercise it, till it; he hath the [same] freedom to anything that any one doth account himself to have any propriety in. . . .

Wildman: Our case is to be considered thus, that we have been under slavery. That's acknowledged by all. Our very laws were made by our conquerors; and whereas it's spoken much of chronicles, I conceive there is no credit to be given to any of them; and the reason is because those that were our lords, and made us their vassals, would suffer nothing else to be chronicled. We are now engaged for our freedom. That's the end of Parliaments: not to constitute what is already [established, but to act] according to the just rules of government. Every person in England hath as clear a right to elect his representative as the greatest person in England. I conceive that's the undeniable maxim of government: that all government is in the free consent of the people. . . . And therefore I should humbly move, that if the question be stated—which would soonest bring things to an issue—it might rather be thus: Whether any person can justly be bound by law, who doth not give his consent that such persons shall make laws for him?

61

John Rushworth, *Historical Collections*. The Trial of Charles I, 1649

Charles I (1625–1649) was a most exasperating man, as the Scots, then Parliament, and finally the New Model Army discovered following the First Civil War. His escape in November 1647 and his subsequent Engagement with the Scots inaugurated the Second Civil War and turned exasperation into complete disillusion and hatred. Parliament decided it would make no further attempts to negotiate with him, and William Goffe, at an army prayer meeting on May 1, 1648, spoke for the army when he resolved "to call Charles Stuart, that man of blood, to an account for that blood he had shed and the mischief he had done." Victory in the field was to the army proof that God favored its cause and approved its intentions. The army purged a hesitant Parliament of its 140 Presbyterian members, leaving a Rump of fifty or sixty members whose opinions matched those of the army. The Rump Parliament then appointed the court that tried the king. The court's sentence, reproduced in part below, was delivered on January 27, 1649. The king's speech was delivered on the scaffold just before his execution on January 30.

Whether Charles was in fact "a Tyrant, Traitor, and Murderer, and publick Enemy to the Commonwealth," as charged and sentenced, or "the Martyr of the People," as he claimed in his speech, each historian after much study and thought must decide. Certainly, Charles's interpretation was the one accepted by the mass of the people at the time, and Charles dead proved as troublesome to his enemies as ever he had alive. The revolutionaries, having destroyed the old government, were unable to replace it with another acceptable to the people, their more exalted view of government notwithstanding. In the end the monarchy was restored in the person of Charles II (1660–1685), and the whole interlude of civil wars and Interregnum was officially forgotten. Nevertheless, the king was alerted to the danger of exasperating his subjects, and subjects were made cautious by the certain

Source: John Rushworth, *Historical Collections*, Vol. VII, The Second Edition, London: Printed for J. Walthoe et al., 1721, pp. 1418–1419, 1429–1430.

knowledge that desperate means might well doom worthy objectives to failure.

John Rushworth (1612?–1690) held various government and army positions throughout the period of the revolution. The notes he kept and the papers he gathered were later published in eight large folio volumes (1659–1701).

Whereas the Commons of England assembled in Parliament, have by their late Act . . . Authorised and constituted us an High Court of Justice. . . .

By virtue whereof the said Charles Stuart . . . was charged, That he the said Charles Stuart, being admitted King of England, and therein trusted with a limited Power to govern by and according to the Law of the Land, and not otherwise; and by his Trust, Oath, and Office, being obliged to use the Power committed to him, for the good and benefit of the People, and for the preservation of their Rights and Liberties; yet nevertheless out of a wicked design to erect and uphold in himself an unlimited and tyrannical Power to rule according to his Will and to overthrow the Rights and Liberties of the People, and to take away and make void the foundations thereof, and of all redress and remedy of misgovernment, which by the fundamental Constitutions of this Kingdom were reserved on the Peoples behalf in the Right and Power of frequent and successive Parliaments, or national Meetings in Council; he the said Charles Stuart, for accomplishment of such his Designs, and for the Protecting of himself and his Adherents in his and their wicked Practices, to the same end, hath traitorously and maliciously levyed War against the present Parliament, and People therein represented . . . and that he hath thereby caused and procured many thousands of the free People of this Nation to be slain; and by Divisions, Parties, and Insurrections within this Land, by Invasions from foreign Parts, endeavoured and procured by him, and by many other evil ways and means, he the said Charles Stuart hath not only maintained and carried on the said War both by Sea and Land, but also hath renewed, or caused to be renewed, the said War against the Parliament and good People of this Nation to this present year 1648. . . . And that by the said cruel and unnatural War so levyed, continued and renewed, much innocent Blood of the free People of this Nation hath been spilt; many Families undone; the publick Treasure wasted; Trade obstructed, and miserably decaed; vast expence and damage to the Nation incurred, and many parts of the Land spoiled, some of them even to Desolation; and that he still continues his Commission to his said Son, and other Rebels and Revolters . . . and that all the said wicked Designs, Wars, and evil Practices of him the said Charles Stuart, were still carried on for the advancement and upholding of the personal Interest of Will, Power, and pretended Prerogative to himself and his Family, against the publick Interest, Common Right, Liberty, Justice and Peace of the People of this Nation: And that he thereby hath been and is the Occasioner, Author, and Continuer of the said unnatural, cruel and bloody Wars, and therein guilty of all the Treasons, Murders, Rapines, Burnings, Spoils, Desolations, Damage, and Mischief to this Nation, acted and committed in the said Wars, or occasioned thereby; whereupon the Proceedings and Judgments of this Court were prayed against him, as a Tyrant, Traitor, and Murderer, and publick Enemy to the Commonwealth.

Now therefore upon serious and mature Deliberation of the Premises, and Consideration had of the notoriety of the matters of fact charged upon him as aforesaid, this Court is in Judgment and Conscience satisfied that he the said Charles Stuart is guilty of levying War against the said Parliament and People, and maintaining and continuing the same; . . . and . . . that he has been and is guilty of the wicked Designs and Endeavours in the said Charge set forth. . . . For all which Treasons and Crimes this Court doth adjudg, That he the said Charles Stuart, as a Tyrant, Traitor, Murderer and a publick Enemy to the good People of this Nation, shall be put to death by severing of his Head from his Body.

The King

"I could hold my peace very well, if I did not think that holding my Peace would make some Men think that I did submit to the Guilt, as well as to the Punishment. But I think it is my Duty to God first, and to my Country, for to clear my self both as an honest Man, a good King, and a good Christian. I shall begin first with my Innocency: In troth, I think it not very needful for me to insist upon this, for all the World knows I never did begin the War with the two Houses of Parliament; and I call God to witness (to whom I must shortly make an account) that I never did intend to incroach upon their Privileges. They began upon me: It is the Militia they began upon; they confess that the Militia was mine, but they thought it fit to have it from me: . . . yet for all this God forbid that I should be so ill a Christian, as not to say that God's Judgments are just upon me; many times he does pay Justice by an unjust Sentence, that is ordinarily: I only say this, that an unjust Sentence (meaning Strafford) that I suffered to take effect, is punished now by an unjust Sentence upon me; that is, so far I have said to shew you that I am an innocent Man. . . . Now, Sirs . . . you will never do right, nor God will never prosper you, until you give him his due, the King his due (that is, my Successors) and the People their due, I am as much for them as any of you: You must give God his due, by regulating rightly his Church. . . . As for the King, the Laws of the Land will clearly instruct you for that. . . .

"For the People: And truly I desire their Liberty and Freedom, as much as any Body whomsoever; but I must tell you, That their Liberty and Freedom consists in having of Government, those Laws by which their Life and their Goods may be most their own. It is not for having share in government (Sirs) that is nothing pertaining to them. A Subject and a Sovereign are clean different things;

and therefore until they do that, I mean, That you do put the People in that Liberty as I say, certainly they will never enjoy themselves. Sirs, it was for this now that I am come here. If I would have given way to an Arbitrary Way, for to have all Laws changed according to the Power of the Sword, I needed not to have come here; and therefore I tell you (and I pray God it be not laid to your Charge) that I am the Martyr of the People."

62
Oliver Cromwell, Letter (September 17, 1649). The Capture of Drogheda

Oliver Cromwell (1599–1658) personified the English Revolution. Although he was not prominent in Parliament at the beginning, once war broke out his aptitude for organization and for military strategy and tactics soon pushed him to the fore. His cavalry regiment, the "Ironsides," was the key element in Parliament's victory at Marston Moor in 1644 and the nucleus of the New Model Army created in 1645. By 1649, Cromwell had become the dominant force not only in the army but in all of England. More than anyone else, he determined the trial and execution of Charles I, the creation of the Commonwealth, and the destruction of its enemies.

The Commonwealth's first concern was Ireland, of which England had lost control following the rebellion of 1641 and the massacre of Protestants in Ulster. Cromwell in August 1649 embarked for Ireland with a well-equipped army of 12,000 to suppress the eight-year-old rebellion and to prevent Ireland from becoming the staging ground for Prince Charles's attempt to regain the throne of his father. Cromwell's first military action, which he described in the letter below, was the brief siege and capture of the fortress town of Drogheda.

The massacres at Drogheda and at Wexford a month later may not display Cromwell's military genius, but they certainly indicate his efficiency. That his purpose was served is indicated by the royalist earl of Ormonde's assessment of his action: "It is not to be

Source: Wilbur Cortez Abbott, *The Writings and Speeches of Oliver Cromwell,* Vol. II: *The Commonwealth, 1649–1653,* Cambridge: Harvard University Press, 1939, pp. 125–128. By permission of Harvard University Press.

imagined how great the terror is that those successes and the power of the rebels have struck into this people." By tradition an army was justified in using such harshness when forced to suffer casualties in storming a fortress. Cromwell's conviction that the victory was the "righteous judgment of God upon these barbarous wretches" reflected a common English assessment of the Irish and the Puritan view of success as indicative of God's approval. Nevertheless, Cromwell's enthusiasm in attributing the success of his bloody deeds to God has always seemed excessive, something his apologists have felt they must explain and his detractors have pointed to as proof of his unbalance. The political consequences of Drogheda and its effect on Cromwell's reputation were in the long run questionable. A priest who claimed to have witnessed and escaped from the slaughter at Wexford denounced Cromwell as "that English pest of hell," a judgment the Irish have retained to this day, just as they have remembered Drogheda as England's greatest crime against them.

For the Honourable William Lenthall, Esquire, Speaker of the Parliament of England: These

SIR,

Your Army came before the town upon Monday following, where having pitched, as speedy course was taken as could be to frame our batteries, which took up the more time because divers of the battering guns were on shipboard. Upon Monday the 9th of this instant, the batteries began to play. Whereupon I sent Sir Arthur Ashton, the then Governor, a summons to deliver the town to the use of the Parliament of England. To the which I received no satisfactory answer, but proceeded that day to beat down the steeple of the church on the south side of the town, and to beat down a tower not far from the same place. . . .

Upon Tuesday the 10th of this instant, about five o'clock in the evening, we began the storm, and after some hot dispute we entered about seven or eight hundred men, the enemy disputing it very stiffly with us. And indeed, through the advantages of the place, and the courage God was pleased to give the defenders, our men were forced to retreat quite out of the breach, not without some considerable loss. . . .

Although our men that stormed the breaches were forced to recoil, as before is expressed, yet, being encouraged to recover their loss, they made a second attempt, wherein God was pleased [so] to animate them that they got ground of the enemy, and by the goodness of God, forced him to quit his entrenchments. And after a very hot dispute . . . our men became masters both of their retrenchments and the church; which . . . proved of excellent use to us. . . .

The enemy retreated, divers of them, into the Mill-Mount; a place very strong and of difficult access, being exceedingly high, having a good graft, and strongly palisadoed. The Governor, Sir Arthur Ashton, and divers considerable Officers being there, our men getting up to them, were ordered by me to put them all to the sword. And indeed, being in the heat of action, I forbade them to spare any that were in arms in the town, and, I think, that night they put to the sword about 2,000 men, divers of the officers and soldiers being fled over the Bridge into the other part of the Town, where about one hundred of them possessed St. Peter's church-steeple, some the west gate, and others a strong round tower next the gate called St. Sunday's. These being summoned to yield to mercy, refused, whereupon I ordered the steeple of St. Peter's Church to be fired, where one of them was heard to say in the midst of the flames: "God damn me, God confound me; I burn, I burn."

The next day, the other two towers were summoned, in one of which was about six or seven score; but they refused to yield themselves, and we knowing that hunger must compel them, set only good guards to secure them from running away until their stomach were come down. From one of the said towers, notwithstanding their condition, they killed and wounded some of our men. When they submitted, their officers were knocked on the head, and every tenth man of the soldiers killed, and the rest shipped for the Barbadoes. The soldiers in the other tower were all spared, as to their lives only, and shipped likewise for the Barbadoes.

I am persuaded that this is a righteous judgment of God upon these barbarous wretches, who have imbrued their hands in so much innocent blood; and that it will tend to prevent the effusion of blood for the future, which are the satisfactory grounds to such actions, which otherwise cannot but work remorse and regret. . . .

And now give me leave to say how it comes to pass that this work is wrought. It was set upon some of our hearts, That a great thing should be done, not by power or might, but by the Spirit of God. And is it not so clear? That which caused your men to storm so courageously, it was the Spirit of God, who gave your men courage, and took it away again; and gave the enemy courage, and took it away again; and gave your men courage again, and therewith this happy success. And therefore it is good that God alone have all the glory.

It is remarkable that these people, at the first, set up the mass in some places of the town that had been monasteries; but afterwards grew so insolent that, the last Lord's day before the storm, the Protestants were thrust out of the great Church called St. Peter's, and they had public mass there: and in this very place near one thousand of them were put to the sword, fleeing thither for safety. I believe all their friars were knocked on the head promiscuously but two; the one of which was Father Peter Taaff, (brother to the Lord Taaff), whom the soldiers took, the next day, and made an end of; the other was taken in the round tower, under the repute of lieutenant, and when he understood that the officers in that tower had no quarter, he confessed he was a friar; but that did not save him. . . .

63

Dorothy Osborne, Letters (1654). A Woman's View During the Interregnum

1654 was the center point in the Interregnum, midway between the execution of Charles I in 1649 and the restoration of Charles II in 1660. Oliver Cromwell was at the height of his power, having the previous year sent home the Rump of the Long Parliament, the last vestige of legitimate government, and having accepted the Instrument of Government as the written constitution for a united British Isles and the title of Lord Protector for himself. The costly and not-entirely-successful war with the Dutch came to an end, and the first Parliament of the Protectorate proved as annoying to Cromwell as had previous Parliaments been to his royal predecessors. But none of these things were as important to Dorothy Osborne and William Temple as the love letters that passed between them.

Dorothy Osborne (1627–1695) was born to an old English family noted for its education and royal service. Her father served Charles I faithfully but to his own personal loss. William Temple (1628–1699) was born to a family of comparable place and talent. His father served Charles I in Ireland and then was a member of the Long Parliament, joining the parliamentary side in the civil wars and being excluded by Pride's Purge in 1648. Dorothy and William met in 1648 on the way to France and spent several happy months at the home of Dorothy's father. They met again in 1652, rediscovered their love for one another, and began their exchange of letters, which continued until their marriage in 1655. William became one of Stuart England's most respected diplomats and authors.

Dorothy is best remembered for her love letters, which, unlike those of William, have survived. They are a valuable window through which we can see the private thoughts of people proceeding with their personal lives amidst a revolution. Men and women fell in love and found ways to communicate their affections. From these letters we learn what a bright, articulate woman of the sev-

Source: The Love Letters of Dorothy Osborne to Sir William Temple, 1652–54, edited by Edward Abbott Parry, New York: Dodd, Mead & Company, 1901, pp. 243–244, 248, 250–251, 255–256, 267–268, 295–296.

enteenth century thought about the things that were of interest to her: Should one marry for love or for money? What was the value of a royal court as a model for the opinion and conduct of the youth of the kingdom? Thomas Babington Macaulay, reviewing a memoir of the life of William Temple in 1838, was lavish in his praise of Dorothy's letters: "The mutual relations of the two sexes seem to us to be at least as important as the mutual relations of any two Governments in the world; and a series of letters written by a virtuous, amiable, and sensible girl, and intended for the eye of her lover alone, can scarcely fail to throw some light on the relations of the sexes."

Dorothy's letters were preserved first by her husband and then by successive generations of her family. A number of them were published in 1836, attracting the attention of Macaulay. This led to other, complete, editions. Most of the originals are in the British Library.

[January 28, 1654]

SIR,—Who would be kind to one that reproaches one so cruelly? Do you think, in earnest, I could be satisfied the world should think me a dissembler, full of avarice or ambition? No, you are mistaken; but I'll tell you what I could suffer, that they should say I married where I had no inclination, because my friends thought it fit, rather than that I had run wilfully to my own ruin in pursuit of a fond passion of my own. To marry for love were no reproachful thing if we did not see that of the thousand couples that do it, hardly one can be brought for an example that it may be done and not repented afterwards. Is there anything thought so indiscreet, or that makes one more contemptible? 'Tis true that I do firmly believe we should be, as you say, *toujours les mesmes;* but if (as you confess) 'tis that which hardly happens once in two ages, we are not to expect the world should discern we were not like the rest. . . .

Here is a ring: it must not be at all wider than this, which is rather too big for me than otherwise; but that is a good fault, and counted lucky by superstitious people. I am not so, though: 'tis indifferent whether there be any word in't or not; only 'tis as well without, and will make my wearing it the less observed. You must give Nan leave to cut a lock of your hair for me, too. Oh, my heart! what a sigh was there! I will not tell you how many this journey causes; nor the fear and apprehensions I have for you. No, I long to be rid of you, am afraid you will not go soon enough: do not you believe this? No, my dearest, I know you do not, whate'er you say, you cannot doubt that I am yours.

[February 4, 1654]

I shall never be ashamed to own that I have a particular value for you above any other, but 'tis not the greatest merit of person will excuse a want of fortune; in some degree I think it will, at least with the most rational part of the world, and, as far as that will read, I desire it should. I would not have the world believe I married out of interest and to please my friends; I had much rather they should know I chose the person, and took his fortune, because 'twas necessary, and that I prefer a competency with one I esteem infinitely before a vast estate in other hands. 'Tis much easier, sure, to get a good fortune than a good husband; but whosoever marries without any consideration of fortune shall never be allowed to do it, but of so reasonable an apprehension the whole world (without any reserve) shall pronounce they did it merely to satisfy their giddy humour.

Besides, though you imagine 'twere a great argument of my kindness to consider nothing but you, in earnest I believe 'twould be an injury to you. I do not see that it puts any value upon men when women marry them for love (as they term it); 'tis not their merit, but our folly that is always presumed to cause it; and would it be any advantage to you to have your wife thought an indiscreet person?

[February 11, 1654]

'Tis strange to see the folly that possesses the young people of this age, and the liberty they take to themselves. I have the charity to believe they appear very much worse than they are, and that the want of a Court to govern themselves by is in great part the cause of their ruin; though that was no perfect school of virtue, yet Vice there wore her mask, and appeared so unlike herself that she gave no scandal. Such as were really discreet as they seemed to be gave good example, and the eminency of their condition made others strive to imitate them, or at least they durst not own a contrary course. All who had good principles and inclinations were encouraged in them, and such as had neither were forced to put on a handsome disguise that they might not be out of countenance at themselves. 'Tis certain (what you say) that where divine or human laws are not positive we may be our own judges; nobody can hinder us, nor is it in itself to be blamed. But, sure, it is not safe to take all liberty that is allowed us,—there are not many that are sober enough to be trusted with the government of themselves; and because others judge us with more severity than our indulgence to ourselves will permit, it must necessarily follow that 'tis safer being ruled by their opinions than by our own. I am disputing again, though you told me my fault so plainly. . . .

'Twill be pleasinger to you, I am sure, to tell you how fond I am of your lock. Well, in earnest now, and setting aside all compliments, I never saw finer hair, nor of a better colour; but cut no more on't, I would not have it spoiled for the world. If you love me, be careful on't. I am combing, and curling, and kissing this lock all day, and dreaming on't all night. The ring, too, is very well, only a little of the biggest. Send me a tortoise one that is a little less than that I sent for a pattern. I would not have the rule so absolutely true without exception that hard hairs be ill-natured, for then I should be so. But I can allow that all soft hairs are good, and so are you, or I am deceived as much as you are if you think I do not love you enough. Tell me, my dearest, am I? You will not be if you think I am

Yours.

[May 25, 1654]

Thus much for the married people, now for those that are towards it.

There is Mr. Stanley and Mrs. Witherington; Sir H. Littleton and Mrs. Philadelphia Carey, who in earnest is a fine woman, such a one as will make an excellent wife; and some say my Lord Rich and my Lady Betty Howard, but others that pretend to know more say his court to her is but to countenance a more serious one to Mrs. Howard, her sister-in-law, he not having courage to pretend so openly (as some do) to another's wife. Oh, but your old acquaintance, poor Mr. Heningham, has no luck! He was so near (as he thought at least) marrying Mrs. Gerherd that anybody might have got his whole estate in wagers upon't that would have ventured but a reasonable proportion of their own. And now he looks more like an ass than ever he did. She has cast him off most unhandsomely, that's the truth on't, and would have tied him to such conditions as he might have been her slave withal, but could never be her husband. Is not this a great deal of news for me that never stir abroad? Nay, I had brought me to-day more than all this: that I am marrying myself! And the pleasantness on't is that it should be to my Lord St. John. Would he look on me, think you, that had pretty Mrs. Fretcheville? My comfort is, I have not seen him since he was a widower, and never spoke to him in my life. I found myself so innocent that I never blushed when they told it me. What would I give I could avoid it when people speak of you? In earnest, I do prepare myself all that is possible to hear it spoken of, yet for my life I cannot hear your name without discovering that I am more than ordinarily concerned in't. A blush is the foolishest thing that can be, and betrays one more than a red nose does a drunkard; and yet I would not so wholly have lost them as some women that I know has, as much injury as they do me.

64

Thomas Mun, *England's Treasure by Forraign Trade* (1664)

England's greatest mercantile endeavor of the seventeenth century was the East India Company, chartered by the Crown in 1600 to promote commerce with Asia. Despite its success, the company was constantly criticized by the general public. Some viewed it as just another royal monopoly restricting commerce for the benefit of a few fortunate merchants. Other critics saw the company's exchange of specie for spices as economically damaging to England. To these "bullionists," gold and silver represented wealth and power, whose shipment to India weakened England. The East India Company also had numerous defenders, the most able being Thomas Mun (1571–1641), a wealthy merchant who became a director of the company. His most famous pamphlet, *England's Treasure by Forraign Trade,* was written about 1630 but not published until 1664.

In his defense of the company, Mun presents a number of interesting ideas. In the following selection, he develops the concept of the balance of trade: England must always "sell more to strangers yearly than wee consume of theirs in value." He did not, however, believe in restricting the export of specie. The gold and silver sent to India represented seed from which you reaped a crop of greater value. He was also insistent that England's future rested largely on the shoulders of her merchants. The English must cease "besotting" themselves with "pipe and pot" and work to develop England's economic potential. Finally, it is significant that Mun as early as 1630 considered Holland, not France or Spain, as the greatest threat to England, a remarkably astute observation borne out by the great commercial wars with the Dutch in the 1650s and 1660s.

The love and service of our Country consisteth not so much in the knowledge of those duties which are to be performed by others, as in the skilful practice of that which is done by our selves; and therefore (my Son) it is now fit that I say something of the Merchant, which I hope in due time shall be thy Vocation: Yet herein are my thoughts free from all Ambition, although I rank thee in a place of

Source: Thomas Mun, *England's Treasure by Forraign Trade,* Oxford: Basil Blackwell, 1949, pp. 1, 5, 71–73, 80–82, 88. Reprinted by permission of Basil Blackwell, Ltd.

so high estimation; for the Merchant is worthily called *The Steward of the Kingdoms Stock,* by way of Commerce with other Nations; a work of no less *Reputation* than *Trust,* which ought to be performed with great skill and conscience, that so the private gain may ever accompany the publique good. . . .

Although a Kingdom may be enriched by gifts received, or by purchase taken from some other Nations, yet these are things uncertain and of small consideration when they happen. The ordinary means therefore to encrease our wealth and treasure is by *Forraign Trade,* wherein wee must ever observe this rule; to sell more to strangers yearly than wee consume of theirs in value. For suppose that when this Kingdom is plentifully served with the Cloth, Lead, Tinn, Iron, Fish and other native commodities, we doe yearly export the overplus to forraign Countries to the value of twenty two hundred thousand pounds; by which means we are enabled beyond the Seas to buy and bring in forraign wares for our use and Consumptions, to the value of twenty hundred thousand pounds; By this order duly kept in our trading, we may rest assured that the Kingdom shall be enriched yearly two hundred thousand pounds, which must be brought to us in so much Treasure; because that part of our stock which is not returned to us in wares must necessarily be brought home in treasure. . . .

If we duly consider *Englands* Largeness, Beauty, Fertility, Strength, both by Sea and Land, in multitude of warlike People, Horses, Ships, Ammunition, advantagious situation for Defence and Trade, number of Sea-ports and Harbours, which are of difficult access to Enemies, and of easie outlet to the Inhabitants wealth by excellent Fleecewools, Iron, Lead, Tynn, Saffron, Corn, Victuals, Hides, Wax, and other natural Endowments; we shall find this Kingdome capable to sit as master of a Monarchy. For what greater glory and advantage can any powerful Nation have, than to be thus richly and naturally possessed of all things needful for Food, Rayment, War, and Peace, not onely for its own plentiful use, but also to supply the wants of other Nations, in such a measure, that much money may be thereby gotten yearly, to make the happiness compleat. For experience telleth us, that notwithstanding that excessive Consumption of this Kingdome alone, to say nothing of *Scotland,* there is exported *communibus annis* of our own native commodities for the value of twenty two hundred thousand pounds *Sterling,* or somewhat more; so that if we were not too much affected to Pride, monstrous Fashions, and Riot, above all other Nations, one million and an half of pounds might plentifully supply our unnecessary wants (as I may term them) of Silks, Sugars, Spices, Fruits, and all others; so that seven hundred thousand pounds might be yearly treasur'd up in money to make the Kingdome exceeding rich and powerful in short time. But this great plenty which we enjoy, makes us a people not only *vicious* and *excessive,* wastful of the means we have, but also improvident & careless of much other wealth that shamefully we lose, which is, the Fishing in his Majesty's Seas of *England, Scotland,* and *Ireland,* being of no less consequence than all our other riches which we export and vent to Strangers, whilest in the mean time (through lewd idleness) great

66

Izaak Walton, *The Compleat Angler* (1676)

Izaak Walton (1593–1683) was born five years after the Spanish Armada and was buried in Winchester Cathedral five years before the Glorious Revolution. During his ninety years he experienced great personal loss. A devout Anglican, he wept at the execution of Archbishop Laud; a strong Royalist, he endured the beheading of his king; a dedicated family man, he buried two wives and numerous young sons and daughters. Through it all he fished, achieving both solace and fame.

Walton was an unlikely literary giant. Born the son of an innkeeper, he entered trade as a London linen draper and became wealthy. Living in the parish of St. Dunstan's, he became a friend of John Donne, the vicar and poet, and of other prominent churchmen and writers, such as Ben Jonson, Michael Drayton, and Sir Henry Wotton. His *Life of Dr. Donne* (1640) launched his career as a biographer, and his *Lives* of various seventeenth-century notables remain a standard source for the period. Walton's enduring fame resulted, however, from his book *The Compleat Angler, or, the Contemplative Man's Recreation* (1653).

The Compleat Angler is a dialogue among a fisherman (Piscator), a hunter (Venator), and a falconer (Auceps), in which each touts his sport. Piscator converts Venator to fishing and then teaches him the art of angling. The instruction is partly a discussion of the techniques of fishing and of fish habits, where one scholar argues that Walton's accuracy was a matter of "accident." It also includes moral instruction, strictures on Christian humility, and a defense of angling, including an anthology of inspirational poems and songs as well as humorous anecdotes. Walton loved his book, preparing four new editions, the last in 1676 being the basis for most of the almost 400 later editions and translations.

The Compleat Angler has an interesting history, appealing to different ages for different reasons. It was almost forgotten until 1750, when Samuel Johnson, impressed with Walton's *Lives,* recommended a new edition. Romantics such as Coleridge, Scott, and Wordsworth, who even wrote a sonnet titled "Written on a Blank Leaf of *The Compleat Angler,"* identified with Walton's love

Source: Izaak Walton, *The Compleat Angler, 1653–1676,* edited by Jonquil Bevan, Clarendon Press, 1983, pp. 173, 175–78, 241–42, 348, 370–71. By permission of Oxford University Press.

of nature. In the late nineteenth century, an urban, nostalgic England produced a "crescendo of near idolatry" for this little book. Today, Walton lives on, partly because of the environmental movement and its Izaac Walton League, partly due to the growing interest of social historians in the development of sport and recreation, and not least because of the universality of Walton's message–"Study to be quiet, I Thes. 4. II."

Pisc. You are well overtaken, Gentlemen, a good morning to you both; I have stretched my legs up *Tottenham-hill* to overtake you, hoping your business may occasion you towards *Ware* whether I am going this fine, fresh *May* morning. . . . I am (Sir) a brother of the *Angle*. . . .

Ven. And I am a lover of Hounds; I have followed many a pack of dogs many a mile, and heard many merry huntsmen make sport and scoff at Anglers.

Auc. And I profess my self a Faulkner, and have heard many grave, serious men pity them, 'tis such a heavy, contemptible, dull recreation.

Pisc. You know Gentlemen, 'tis an easie thing to scoff at any Art or Recreation; a little *wit* mixt with ill nature, confidence and *malice* will do it. . . .

If to this you add what *Solomon* says of Scoffers, that they are an abomination to mankind, let him that thinks fit scoff on, and be a Scoffer still, but I account them enemies to me, and to all that love vertue and Angling.

And for you that have heard many grave serious men pity Anglers; let me tell you Sir, there be many men that are by others taken to be serious and grave men, which we contemn and pity. Men that are taken to be grave, because Nature hath made them of a sowre complexion, money-getting-men, men that spend all their time first in getting, and next in anxious care to keep it; men that are condemned to be rich, and then always busie or discontented: for these poor-rich-men, we Anglers pity them perfectly, and stand in no need to borrow their thoughts to think our selves so happy. . . .

Venat. Sir, you have almost amazed me, for though I am no scoffer, yet I have (I pray let me speak it without offence) alwayes looked upon Anglers as more patient and more simple men, then I fear I shall find you to be.

Pisc. Sir, I hope you will not judge my earnestness to be impatience: and for my *simplicity,* if by that you mean a harmlesness, or that simplicity which was usually found in the primitive Christians, who were (as most Anglers are) quiet men, and followers of peace; men that were so simply-wise, as not to sell their Consciences to buy riches, and with them vexation and a fear to die; If you mean such simple men as lived in those times when there were fewer Lawyers; when men might have had a Lordship safely conveyed to them in a piece of Parchment no bigger than your hand, (though several sheets will not do it safely in this wiser age) I say Sir, if you take us Anglers to be such simple men as I have spoke of, then my self and those of my profession will be glad to be so understood: But if by simplicity you meant to express a general defect in those that profess and practise the excellent Art of Angling, I hope in time to disabuse you. . . .

The Anglers Song.

As inward love breeds outward talk,
The Hound *some praise, and some the* Hawk:
Some better pleas'd with private sport,
Use Tennis, *some a* Mistress *court:*
But these delights I neither wish,
Nor envy, while I freely fish.

Who Hunts, *doth oft in danger ride;*
Who Hawks, *lures oft both far and wide;*
Who uses Games, *shall often prove*
A loser; but who falls in love,
Is fettered in fond Cupids *snare:*
My Angle breeds me no such care.

Of Recreation there is none
So free as Fishing is alone:
All other pastimes do no lesse
Than mind and body both possesse:
My hand alone my work can doe,
So I can fish and study too. . . .

Pisc. These, my honest Scholar, are some observations told to you as they now come suddenly into my memory, of which you may make some use: but for the practical part, it is that, that makes an Angler: it is diligence, and observation, and practice, and an ambition to be the best in the Art that must do it. I will tell you, Scholar, I once heard one say, *I envy not him that eats better* meat *than I do, nor him that is* richer, *or that wears better* clothes *than I do. I envy no body but him, and him only, that catches more* fish *than I do.* And such a man is like to prove an Angler, and this noble emulation I wish to you and all young Anglers. . . .

Venat. I thank you for your many instructions, which (God willing) I will not forget:. . . for indeed, your company and discourse have been so useful and pleasant, that I may truly say, *I have only lived since I enjoyed them, and turned Angler, and not before.* Nevertheless, here I must part with you, here in this now sad place where I was so happy as first to meet you: But I shall long for the ninth of *May,* for then I hope again to enjoy your beloved company at the appointed time and place. . . . And my good Master, I will not forget the doctrine which you told me *Socrates* taught his Scholars, *That they should not think to be honoured so much for being* Philosophers, *as to honour* Philosophy *by their vertu-*

ous lives. . . . So when I would beget *content,* and increase confidence in the *Power,* and *Wisdom,* and *Providence* of Almighty God, I will walk the *Meadows* by some gliding stream, and there contemplate the *Lillies* that take no care, and those very many other various little living *creatures,* that are not only created but fed (man knows not how) by the goodness of the God of *Nature,* and therefore trust in him. This is my purpose: and so, *Let every thing that hath breath praise the Lord.* And let the blessing of St. *Peters* Master be with mine.

Pisc. And upon all that are lovers of *Vertue;* and dare trust in his *providence,* and be *quiet,* and go a *Angling.*

Study to be quiet, I Thes, 4. 11.

FINIS.

67
An Anonymous Account of the Popish Plot (1678)

There were undoubtedly people in 1678 who would have welcomed and encouraged England's return to Roman Catholicism. Nevertheless, the Popish Plot that came to light that year was largely the product of the fertile and unscrupulous imaginations of Titus Oates (1649–1705) and his crony, Dr. Israel Tonge (1621–1680). That the ground on which their lies and rumors fell gave them mushroom growth indicates English attitudes, still colored by John Foxe's *Book of Martyrs* and displaying a willingness to see a Catholic plot behind every national misfortune. Nearly everyone believed what Oates said or, for purposes of policy, acted as if they did. It was a case of mass hysteria, with such grave consequences as the fall of Lord Danby, the attempted exclusion of James, duke of York, from accession to the throne and, not least, the execution of 35 people, many in circumstances amounting to judicial murder.

It was more than two years before those passions were extinguished and England began to see Oates for the liar and scoundrel he was. Under James II (1685–1688), he was brought to trial for

Source: Historical Manuscripts Commission, Fourteenth Report, Appendix, Part VI, *The Manuscripts of Lord Kenyon,* London: Printed for Her Majesty's Stationery Office by Eyre and Spottiswoode, 1894, pp. 105–108.

perjury, found guilty, and sentenced to successive floggings that were surely intended to kill him. He survived, however, and was released from prison and given a government pension at the time of the Glorious Revolution. He became a member of a Baptist congregation, but in 1701 was expelled for being "a disorderly person and a hypocrite."

The extreme passions of the time and the proven unreliability of central participants make it difficult to know precisely what happened. The death of Sir Edmund Berry Godfrey has never been explained satisfactorily. The account below came to light in the nineteenth century as a result of the work of the Historical Manuscripts Commission, created in 1869 by Queen Victoria. The commission's purpose was to save from loss or destruction manuscripts and papers of general and public interest that were in the hands of private families and institutions and to make them available for scholarly use. Its numerous reports, like that describing and reproducing in part the manuscripts of Lord Kenyon of Gredington Hall, have opened up vast new sources for historical investigation.

1678, October 31.—Since my last, wherein I discovered to you the first account of this horrible plott, greate hath beene the diligence boeth of the Councell and Parliament in bringing the same to light, wherein their endeavours have beene soe happy that they are now arrived to the bottome of it, and it lies now before boeth houses in its owne monstrous shape; it being noe lesse then the murder of the King, the subversion of our religion, lawes, and properties, the introduceing of popery and a tyrannicall arbitrary government by an army, our common and statute laws to be abolished and anihilated, and a mixture of military and civil law introduced, where counsell of warr should supply this place of our courts of justice, and the racke for the jury, with many such differences too tediouse to expresse here; but I hope, by this tymely and miraculouse discovery, we may be able to distroy this cochatrice in the egge which will yet certainely devoure us if hee bee hatcht. The manner of proceedings have beene thus:—One Mr. Oates, being a minister in Sussex, by reason of some lawe suites with persons which were too powerfull for him, hee was forced to quitt his parish and, comeing into London, fell into acquaintance with Mr. Tonge, a minister who hath beene many yeares a diligent inquirer into the practices and principals of the Jesuites and had published severall bookes against them. This man findeing Oates, by reason of poverty, enclined to travell to seeke a livelyhood amongst the papists abroad, endeavoured to divert him by giveing him full information of theire wicked principles and practices. Whereupon Oates resolves to try the trueth, and promised, if hee found it to bee as Tonge informed, hee would renounce that religion and retorne againe to the Protestant Church. Oates thereupon, some yeares since, goes and enters himselfe a Noviciat in the College of the Jesuites in St. Omer's, where behaveing himselfe with great zeale, diligence, and demonstrateing his abilities, hee was soone taken notice of and thought a fitt instrument to convey the intelligence and correspondency of this hellish plott to most of the Courts in christendome. In acting whereof, by opening letters and packquetts entrusted with him and thereby gaineing some light, soe insinuated himselfe wherever hee came, that in time hee came to the depth and counsells of the designe. Whereby, about Aprill last, understanding the execution of this horrid villany to bee att hand and that comissions were signed by the Pope for all bishops and other clergy, for the officers of state and of theire armies, hee began to feare it would be executed before hee should find meanes to discover it. And being ready to lay hould of all oppertunities to come for England to doe it, it fell out that a booke called *the Jesuites' Moralls,* which Tonge had translated came to their handes, for which upon consultation it was agreed Tonge should bee killed, but a fitt person was wanting to doe it. Whereupon Oates offered to undertake it and . . . prepares for the journey . . . but in the interim, underhand resortes to Tonge and acquaints him with the whole designe, of which haveing drawne a short relation, hee desires Tonge to give it privately to the King and offer to make it good if his Majesty would conceale the thing and appoynt a counsell to sitt and heare it. . . . The matter thus settled, Tonge severall tymes presses the Treasurer, but noething done in 6 weekes; though the 2nd of September, whereon the King was to bee murdered, was past; whereon Tonge doubting some future trouble in case Oates should be killed or recant, causes Oates to draw an exact narrative containeing 15 or 16 sheetes and to sweare it before Sir Edmundbury Godfrey. . . . I say noe more, but Godfrey . . . was murdered soone after, being, as appeared plainely, strangled, and after carryed and layd in a ditch near Primrose Hill and his owne sword runne through him, noething missing but his band and pockett booke wherein were his noates concerning this affaire. His murder raised a great spiritt in the people, which could not bee outfaced by the partie and theire adherents that murdered him, though there wanted neither diligence nor impudence in that party in all places to make it appeare hee murdered himselfe. Tomorrow hee is to bee buried from the Hall of Bridewell where I believe thousands will appeare to attend his corps to St. Martins. But to retorne to the plott.

Godfrey, haveing taken the information, was forced then to bring it to counsell about the end of September 1678, where Oates appeared and made it good beyond all scruple. . . . Since the sitting of the Parliament, Oates hath beene every day examined before them, speakeing 5 or 6 hours at a tyme, giveing particuler demonstration of the whole affaire, wherein hee hath clearely proved the manner and designe of the fire of London, Southerwarke, and many other fires, with the intended massacre in the fire of London, the designe of raiseing the Blackheath Army, with the reasons and occations of the severall Dutch warrs in order to this designe, the raiseing of the present army and the generall peace to ensue for the compleateing the worke, the raiseing and maintaineing privately 20,000 men att this tyme, with the generall and all other officers, all which are now in readinesse to joyne with the army, the greatest part whereof they thought themselves sure of, and in Ireland they had likewise a generall and army ready, and Scotland the same. The manner to put it in execution was thus:—One Conyers, a Jesuite, with foure Irish ruffaines, undertooke to murder the King att Windsor, 21 September last, and thereupon a great cry was to bee made that the phanatiques had murdered the King, an alarume presently thereupon to bee given to the whole army, being then about 16,000, quartered in and neare London, whereof two regiments of 4,000 men, consisting all of Irish, Scotts and French papists, were about a month before brought out of France and quartered about Barnet, Enfeild, St. Albans, Ware, &c. were imediately to march to London to assist the proclaimeing the Duke of York, and under that pretence to fall upon and massacre and slaughter the people, under the notion of phanatiques who had murdered the King, and then to have assisted the papists all over the kingdom to doe the like. The Duke of Yorke was to take the Crowne by gift from the Pope, and least any opposition should bee made, the French were to bee ready with an army and fleete to seize upon our fleete, burne and destroy such as opposed, and take the rest, and then the whole nation to bee shared among this crew (viz) the ancient church lands amongst the clergy, the murdered protestants' lands amongst the great officers, boeth civill and military, and the plunder of citties and townes amongst the soldiers and rabble of Irish and French papists. This is the substance of what is collected from the severall informations, proofes, and papers which have beene seized and made out.

Things thus appeareing, the Commons lockt themselves up for many hours, sent for Chiefe Justice Scroggs to them, who yssued out at one tyme, 40 or 50 warrants against noblemen and others. The high constables were sent for allsoe into the House and the warrants there delivered to them, and the House kept still shutt to prevent intelligence, and that night and next day, six lords and diverse persons of lesse quality were seized and comitted to the Tower, King's Bench, Newgate Gatehouse, and other prisons. . . .

Things thus standing, some intimation was brought to the Lord Mayor and Aldermen, on Saturday last, that on Sunday in sermon tyme some attempt would bee made upon the Citty, whereupon they ordered stronge double watches to bee sett, of house keepers in person, and the lights to bee renewed att 12 aclock att night; the gates to bee shutt all Sunday, and the watches to continue till relieved att night, which was performed.

68

The Exclusion Bill (1680). The Origin of Political Parties

It is not surprising that the Popish Plot prompted Parliament to limit the political activity of Roman Catholics. Having already been excluded from holding office in the royal government by the Test Act of 1673, Catholics were forbidden in 1678 to sit in either house of Parliament, a disability not removed until 1829. Of greater importance were the exclusion bills designed to prevent James, duke of York, from succeeding to the throne on the death of his brother Charles II (1660–1685). Their interest lies not so much in their religious bias as in what they reveal of the origin of political parties.

The earl of Danby, Charles's chief minister from 1674 to 1679, had, in putting together a block of political support for the king, created the beginnings of the Tory party. Upholding the old Cavalier idea of royal prerogative and supporting the established church, it espoused the principles of nonresistance and divine-right succession to the throne. In opposition was the earl of Shaftesbury and the equally embryonic Whig party, whose principles were parliamentary supremacy and a loud "no popery." The exclusion bills, introduced and discussed between 1678 and 1681, turned these political interests into actual political parties and gave them their names. The Tories, resisting the anti-Catholic enthusiasm of the Whigs, were given the name of Irish Catholic outlaws. The Whigs, in turn, were named after roughly equivalent Scottish Presbyterians.

The exclusion bills clearly illustrate the Whig position that Parliament can alter the royal succession. The bill of 1680, reproduced below, is also interesting for the fuzziness of the last paragraph, regarding who should inherit the throne, assuming "James, duke of York, were naturally dead." Shaftesbury purposely left the way open for the accession of Charles's illegitimate son, the duke of Monmouth, who would be more pliable to Parliament and to Shaftesbury than would be the capable William of Orange, the husband of James's daughter Mary. The bill's failure in the House

Source: J. P. Kenyon, ed., *The Stuart Constitution, 1603–1688: Documents and Commentary,* Cambridge University Press, 1966, pp. 469–471. Reprinted by permission of Cambridge University Press.

69

A Medley of Nursery Rhymes

Oral evidence, usually personal interviews, is to the contemporary historian of obvious importance. In the study of the earlier periods in English history, however, such evidence is insignificant. Unlike some societies, such as those in parts of Africa, the English possessed few oral traditions that were passed from generation to generation. The existence in England of a literate class from an early date made this unnecessary. Why train someone to memorize the royal genealogy if you can simply write it down? Except perhaps for folk songs, the closest that the English have come to an oral tradition is the nursery rhyme. That this term, "nursery rhyme," was first used in the 1820s, shows that until then few of these rhymes were specifically designed for children.

Although nursery rhymes have been subjected to intense analysis, considerable debate still surrounds their origin and historical significance. Some go back to the Middle Ages. "Baa, baa, black sheep" apparently refers to a 1275 export tax on wool. Only about 25 percent of the common rhymes, however, date from before 1600, and only about 2 percent of them can be found in a written form before that date. Thus, care must be taken not to attribute antiquity to what may in reality be a product of the eighteenth or nineteenth century. Caution must also be exercised in attributing to a nursery rhyme a historical significance. Some have an obvious historical meaning: "The lion and the unicorn," refers to the struggle between England and Scotland during the Stuart period; "William and Mary, George and Anne," describes the overthrow of James II; "Over the water and over the lea," deals with Bonnie Prince Charlie; and "Little General Monk," ridicules the duke of Albermarle. Unfortunately, the historical meaning of most nursery rhymes is uncertain. For example, does "Sing a song of sixpence" refer to Henry VIII's counting of the money obtained from the dissolved monasteries or is there another, forgotten historical reference? Does "Hark, hark" suggest the general problem of beggars in Tudor England or does it refer to the Dutch "beggars" brought to England by William III? Is "Georgie Porgie" really George I? Finally, is the baby "on the tree top" James II's

Source: Iona and Peter Opie, eds., *The Oxford Dictionary of Nursery Rhymes,* Oxford: Clarendon Press, 1952, pp. 61, 88, 115–116, 152, 185, 269, 310, 394, 424. By permission of Oxford University Press.

son, who falls because the wind in 1688 blew William's fleet to England?

The first important collection of nursery rhymes, *Tommy Thumb's Pretty Song Book,* appeared in 1744. The more famous *Mother Goose's Melody* (1760) was reprinted several times and inspired numerous similar collections in the nineteenth century. Today, the best edition of nursery rhymes, complete with a discussion of their possible origins, is *The Oxford Dictionary of Nursery Rhymes.*

Baa, baa, black sheep,
Have you any wool?
Yes, sir, yes, sir,
Three bags full;
One for the master,
And one for the dame,
And one for the little boy
Who lives down the lane.

The lion and the unicorn
Were fighting for the crown;
The lion beat the unicorn
All round about the town.

Some gave them white bread,
And some gave them brown;
Some gave them plumb cake
And drummed them out of town.

William and Mary, George and Anne,
Four such children had never a man:
They put their father to flight and shame,
And called their brother a shocking bad name.

Over the water and over the lea,
And over the water to Charley.
Charley loves good ale and wine,
And Charley loves good brandy,
And Charley loves a pretty girl
As sweet as sugar candy.

Over the water and over the lea,
  And over the water to Charley.
I'll have none of your nasty beef,
  Nor I'll have none of your barley;
But I'll have some of your very best flour
  To make a white cake for my Charley.

Little General Monk
Sat upon a trunk,
Eating a crust of bread;
There fell a hot coal
And burnt in his clothes a hole,
Now little General Monk is dead.

Sing a song of sixpence,
  A pocket full of rye;
Four and twenty blackbirds,
  Baked in a pie.

When the pie was opened,
  The birds began to sing;
Was not that a dainty dish,
  To set before the king?

The king was in his counting-house,
  Counting out his money;
The queen was in the parlour,
  Eating bread and honey.

The maid was in the garden,
  Hanging out the clothes,
There came a little blackbird,
  And snapped off her nose.

  Hark, hark,
  The dogs do bark,
The beggars are coming to town;
  Some in rags,
  And some in jags,
And one in a velvet gown.

Georgie Porgie, pudding and pie,
Kissed the girls and made them cry;
When the boys came out to play,
Georgie Porgie ran away.

Hush-a-bye, baby, on the tree top,
When the wind blows the cradle will rock;
When the bough breaks the cradle will fall,
Down will come baby, cradle, and all.

70
Sir John Reresby, *Memoirs*. His Quarrels and Duels, 1660–1683

Sir John Reresby (1634–1689) was not an important figure in Stuart England. Rather, he was typical of the country gentlemen who filled the benches of the House of Commons and ran local government. He served as high sheriff of Yorkshire in 1667 and entered Parliament in 1673, where he quickly became a supporter of Charles II. For this support he was rewarded in 1682 with the governorship of York. Like many Tories, however, Reresby could not abide the follies of James II, especially his appointment of Roman Catholics to high office.

During middle age, Reresby decided to write his memoirs. For the edification of posterity he recalled the exploits of his youth. These memoirs, written in diary form largely in 1679, were first published in 1734. The Tories, then engaged in a political struggle with the Whig prime minister, Sir Robert Walpole, wanted an account of the Tory role in the Revolution of 1688 to combat the popular Whig version of Bishop Gilbert Burnet. Reresby's memoirs proved very popular, and they were consequently published in a number of editions during the eighteenth century. Most historians today regard his memoirs as valuable for portraying the life of the

Source: Memoirs of Sir John Reresby, edited by Andrew Browning, Glasgow: Jackson, Son & Co., 1936, pp. 33–34, 46, 188–189, 317–318.

country gentleman, whom one scholar has referred to as the "backbone of English society." This aspect of England was omitted from the more famous diaries of John Evelyn and Samuel Pepys, most likely because they were unfamiliar with it. The passage below, in which Reresby discussed his frequent quarrels and duels, is a vivid reminder that Restoration England, although often praised for its growing cultural and social sophistication, remained a violent age.

10 September 1660

I came into Yorkshire, and after some short stay at my own hous at Thriberge went for Yorke by the way of Selby, wher a quarrell hapning between my company and some others about first going into the boat, I was struck over the head with a cudgill, which provouked me to wound one or two with my sword. This gave soe great an alarme to the country people ther met togather upon the occasion of the markit that I was encompassed, and two gentlemen with me and our servants, and after a long defence pulled off my hors, and had certainly been knocked on the head had I not been rescued by my Moor, who gott hould of the man's arm that had me down, as he was going to give the blowe. Being gott up again, I defended myselfe till I gott into the hous of an honest man, that gave us protection till the rabble was appeased.

From Yorke I went to Mauton, a famous fair for horses, wher with other gentlemen I was invited to dinner at Sir Thomas Norclifs, who had severall hansome daughters, especially one who was to be speedily married to a yong gentleman with whom I had a quarrell about his mistriss which had near spoiled the match. We should have fought the next day, but considering better of it he submitted (though it was he that had received the affront, for I threw a glass of wine in his face), and soe we were reconcild. . . .

12 July 1663

Sir Henry Bellasis sent to invite me to dinner to the Bear at the bridge foot, wher on Mack de Mar, an Irish gentleman, was to give him a venison pasty. After dinner he provoaked me to give him some language, which he soe farr resented that he demanded satisfaction, either by my denying that I meant any injury to him by the saying of the words, and asking his pardon, or by fighting with him. I denyed the first, and soe being challenged was obliged to fight him that afternoon in Hide Parke, which I did, an Irish gentleman that he met by the way being his secound, and Sir Henry Belasis mine. At the first pass I hurt him slightly on the sword hand, and at the same time he closeing with me we both fell to the ground (he haveing hould of my sword and I of his). Sir Henry and his man were fighting at the same time close by, and Sir Henry had gott the better, wounded the other in the belly and disarmed him, and was comming in to us as we were both risen and I had gott his sword out of his hand, which I took home with me, but sent it to him the next day. The secound to Mac de Mar was in danger of death by his wound for some weeks, which made us abscond. I was with the Duke of Buckingham the best part of this time at Wallinford Hous. But at last it pleased God he recovered. . . .

22 September 1679

Was the day named to poule at Pontefract. My friends that went in with me stayed for me at Rigstone Hill a little longer than ordinary.

That day Sir John Jackson of Hickleton (the last of his family, and the fourth heir from its first being raised) came to me at Pontefract (ther haveing been some coolness between us before) and tould me I had affronted him in bringing in his tenents with me to voat for Sir John Kay, when he designed to bring them in himselfe. I answered that I writt to all (or sent to them) that I thought qualified to voat to come in, without reguarding who was their landlords, but if he took that ill in his own perticular I was a man to give him what satisfaction he required. But I found him not much inclined to fight, for after severall words he tould me that he neither desired to court my friendship nor enmity. Then I tould him we were very equall in that perticular, for I thought his friendship was very little to be valued or enmity to be feared; and soe we parted. . . .

23 October 1683

The Sunday following, being in the Minster, I found the cussin which used to be in my seat remooved into the next, wher Sir John Brook was to sitt (a person that I had thought fitt, with other deputy lieutenants, to disarm in our late search for arms). This gentleman riseing at the psalmes, I took up the cussin and replaced it in my seat. Service being ended, Sir John asked me if I had the same commission to take his cussin that I had to take his arms. I said I took it as my own, as I should always doe when I see it misplaced; and if he took his being disarmed ill from me he made choice of an ill place to quarrell in, and that hee durst not say thos things in any other.

The next day I expected to hear from him, he seeming very much disturbed with this treatment; but not sending to me for reparation, the next morning I sent the captain that then commanded a company in Yorke to tell him that I had stayed some time at home, thinkeing to hear from him, and believed the reason why I did not to be the character I bore in that citty, and did therfore now send to him to tell him that if he had any ressentment either for my takeing his cussin or arms, I was ready to give him satisfaction as a private person. He returned me this answer, that he was most concerned at my takeing away the cussin, bycaus it did prevent his giveing it to me, which he intended; but that for satisfaction he thought what had passed between us did not oblige him to aske it in his circumstances, and was willing to be quiett. Soe that the substance of this matter was this, that he foolishly owned himselfe under such circumstances as to own himselfe affronted, but not to see himselfe righted. I could have been very well content that noe occasion of such disputes had offered themselves, but when they doe I have found that the best way to prevent them for the future is not to seem too backward in seeking reparation.

71

Sir Isaac Newton, *The Mathematical Principles of Natural Philosophy* (1687). The Scientific Revolution

Sir Isaac Newton (1642–1727) was the most noted scientist of his age. This was no mean feat, since he was competing in Britain alone with Robert Boyle, Robert Hooke, and Edmund Halley. All were fellows of the Royal Society, founded in the Restoration year of 1660 to promote cooperation in understanding the workings of the natural world. Newton's preeminence was recognized by his annual election as its president from 1703 until his death in 1727. As Edmund Halley wrote of Newton:

> Then ye who now on heavenly nectar fare,
> Come celebrate with me in song the name
> Of Newton, to the Muses dear; for he
> Unlocked the hidden treasuries of Truth;
> So richly through his mind had Phoebus cast
> The radiance of his own divinity.
> Nearer the gods no mortal may approach.

Newton's *Philosophiae Naturalis Principia Mathematica,* written in Latin for the members of the Royal Society, was published in 1687 with the financial support of Halley. In it, Newton, who had played a leading role in the invention of calculus, made mathematical sense of the universe and developed the concept of gravitation. Most of his *Principia,* even in translation, is difficult for anyone but a mathematician to understand. Nevertheless, the educated public appreciated that Newton's eight definitions, three laws of motion (reproduced below), and four rules of reasoning (to say nothing of his numerous theorems, corollaries, propositions, lemmas, problems, and scholia) were important and had changed their world forever. Without Newton, the eighteenth-century "enlightenment" is difficult to imagine. Newton was not, however, a modern man. He believed in alchemy and, as his recently studied letters indicate, the millennialism of the Book of Revelations. In his conclusion to *Principia* below—the General Scholium—he ac-

Source: Sir Isaac Newton, *The Mathematical Principles of Natural Philosophy,* translated by Andrew Motte in 1729; revised by Florian Cajori (University of California Press, 1947), pp. 13–14, 544, 546–547. With permission of the Regents of the University of California and the University of California Press.

cepted the idea that though the natural world conformed to mathematical laws, this revealed nothing of "the cause of this power."

Newton began revising the *Principia* almost from the moment it was published in 1687. When it was translated into English by Andrew Motte in 1729, it was already a "classic." The next English edition did not appear until the 1770s, an indication that Newton was more revered than read.

AXIOMS, OR LAWS OF MOTION

Law I

Every body continues in its state of rest, or of uniform motion in a right line, unless it is compelled to change that state by forces impressed upon it.

PROJECTILES continue in their motions, so far as they are not retarded by the resistance of the air, or impelled downwards by the force of gravity. A top, whose parts by their cohesion are continually drawn aside from rectilinear motions, does not cease its rotation, otherwise than as it is retarded by the air. The greater bodies of the planets and comets, meeting with less resistance in freer spaces, preserve their motions both progressive and circular for a much longer time.

Law II

The change of motion is proportional to the motive force impressed; and is made in the direction of the right line in which that force is impressed. . . .

Law III

To every action there is always opposed an equal reaction: or, the mutual actions of two bodies upon each other are always equal, and directed to contrary parts.

Whatever draws or presses another is as much drawn or pressed by that other. If you press a stone with your finger, the finger is also pressed by the stone. If a horse draws a stone tied to a rope, the horse (if I may so say) will be equally drawn back towards the stone; for the distended rope, by the same endeavor to relax or unbend itself, will draw the horse as much towards the stone as it does the stone towards the horse, and will obstruct the progress of the one as much as it advances that of the other. If a body impinge upon another, and by its force change the motion of the other, that body also (because of the equality of the mutual pressure) will undergo an equal change, in its own motion, towards the contrary part. The changes made by these actions are equal, not in the velocities but in the motions of bodies; that is to say, if the bodies are not hindered by any other impediments. For, because the motions are equally changed, the changes of the velocities made towards contrary parts are inversely proportional to the bodies. . . .

GENERAL SCHOLIUM

This most beautiful system of the sun, planets, and comets, could only proceed from the counsel and dominion of an intelligent and powerful Being. And if the fixed stars are the centres of other like systems, these, being formed by the like wise counsel, must be all subject to the dominion of One; especially since the light of the fixed stars is of the same nature with the light of the sun, and from every system light passes into all the other systems: and lest the systems of the fixed stars should, by their gravity, fall on each other, he hath placed those systems at immense distances from one another.

This Being governs all things, not as the soul of the world, but as Lord over all. . . .

We know him only by his most wise and excellent contrivances of things, and final causes; we admire him for his perfections; but we reverence and adore him on account of his dominion: for we adore him as his servants; and a god without dominion, providence, and final causes, is nothing else but Fate and Nature. Blind metaphysical necessity, which is certainly the same always and everywhere, could produce no variety of things. All that diversity of natural things which we find suited to different times and places could arise from nothing but the ideas and will of a Being necessarily existing. But, by way of allegory, God is said to see, to speak, to laugh, to love, to hate, to desire, to give, to receive, to rejoice, to be angry, to fight, to frame, to work, to build; for all our notions of God are taken from the ways of mankind by a certain similitude, which, though not perfect, has some likeness, however. And thus much concerning God; to discourse of whom from the appearances of things, does certainly belong to Natural Philosophy.

Hitherto we have explained the phenomena of the heavens and of our sea by the power of gravity, but have not yet assigned the cause of this power. This is certain, that it must proceed from a cause that penetrates to the very centres of the sun and planets, without suffering the least diminution of its force; that operates not according to the quantity of the surfaces of the particles upon which it acts (as mechanical causes used to do), but according to the quantity of the solid matter which they contain, and propagates its virtue on all sides to immense distances, decreasing always as the inverse square of the distances. Gravitation towards the sun is made up out of the gravitations towards the several particles of which the body of the sun is composed; and in receding from the sun decreases accurately as the inverse square of the distances as far as the orbit of Saturn, as evidently appears from the quiescence of the aphelion of the planets; nay, and even to the remotest aphelion of the comets, if those aphelions are also quiescent. But hitherto I have not been able to discover the cause of those properties of gravity from phenomena, and I frame no hypotheses; for whatever is not deduced from the phenomena is to be called an hypothesis; and hypotheses, whether metaphysical or physical, whether of occult qualities or mechanical, have no place in experimental philosophy. In this philosophy particular propositions are inferred from the phenomena, and afterwards rendered general by induction. Thus it was that the impenetrability, the mobility, and the impulsive force of bodies, and the laws of motion and of gravitation, were discovered. And to us it is enough that gravity does really exist, and act according to the laws which we have explained, and abundantly serves to account for all the motions of the celestial bodies, and of our sea. . . .

72
The Bill of Rights (1689)

The Glorious Revolution of 1688 to 1689 was both the culmination of a century-long constitutional struggle between Crown and Parliament and the consequence of specific actions of James II (1685–1688). Seldom have subjects been so quickly and thoroughly alienated from their king. At the beginning of his reign they were favorably inclined toward him, but three years later not even the Tories and Anglicans, who believed in nonresistance and indefeasible divine right, would lift a finger to save him. Increasingly the English people saw James's active Roman Catholicism and his inclination to tyranny as related dangers. These departures from English practice justified the abandonment of their sworn allegiance to their king.

The heart of the revolutionary settlement was the Bill of Rights, Parliament's official confirmation of the original Declaration of Rights written by the Convention Parliament of February 1689 and presented to William and Mary as the terms of their invitation to become king and queen. Like Magna Carta and the Petition of Right, the Bill of Rights was a statement of specific violations of the law and the promise that in the future the law would be obeyed. This conservative pretense was, however, not always accurate. The statement on "raising or keeping a standing army" reflected more a fear than an established law or custom. Although the Revolution was accomplished by the cooperation of both political

Source: Statutes of the Realm, VI, 142–144 (1 William and Mary, Sess. 2, c. 2).

Temporall and Commons assembled at Westminster doe Resolve That William and Mary Prince and Princesse of Orange be and be declared King and Queene of England France and Ireland and the Dominions thereunto belonging to hold the Crowne and Royall Dignity of the said Kingdomes and Dominions to them the said Prince and Princesse dureing their Lives and the Life of the Survivour of them And that the sole and full Exercise of the Regall Power be onely in and executed by the said Prince of Orange in the Names of the said Prince and Princesse dureing their joynt Lives And after their Deceases the said Crowne and Royall Dignitie of the said Kingdoms and Dominions to be to the Heires of the Body of the said Princesse And for default of such Issue to the Princesse Anne of Denmarke and the Heires of her Body And for default of such Issue to the Heires of the Body of the said Prince of Orange. And the Lords Spirituall and Temporall and Commons doe pray the said Prince and Princesse to accept the same accordingly. . . . And whereas it hath beene found by Experience that it is inconsistent with the Safety and Welfare of this Protestant Kingdome to be governed by a Popish Prince or by any King or Queene marrying a Papist the said Lords Spirituall and Temporall and Commons doe further pray that it may be enacted That all and every person and persons that is are or shall be reconciled to or shall hold Communion with the See or Church of Rome or shall professe the Popish Religion or shall marry a Papist shall be excluded and be for ever uncapeable to inherit possesse or enjoy the Crowne and Government of this Realme and Ireland and the Dominions thereunto belonging or any part of the same or to have use or exercise any Regall Power Authoritie or Jurisdiction within the same [And in all and every such Case or Cases the People of these Realmes shall be and are hereby absolved of their Allegiance] And the said Crowne and Government shall from time to time descend to and be enjoyed by such person or persons being Protestants as should have inherited and enjoyed the same in case the said person or persons soe reconciled holding Communion or Professing or Marrying as aforesaid were naturally dead.

73
John Locke, *Two Treatises of Government* (1690)

The Glorious Revolution was vindicated not only by the solid facts of its immediate success and of England's ensuing prosperity, but by the common-sense arguments of England's most influential political essay. In 1690 appeared anonymously John Locke's *Two Treatises of Government: In the Former, the False Principles and Foundations of Sir Robert Filmer, And His Followers, are Detected and Overthrown. The Latter is an Essay concerning The True Original, Extent, and End of Civil-Government.* The first treatise, seldom read today, is a refutation of Filmer's Biblical justification of the patriarchal authority of absolute monarchs. In the second treatise, a passage of which is reproduced below, Locke gives his own understanding of the basis of government. It is a contract between the people and their government, the people retaining the right to recall the legislature and the executive if they violate the trust given them. All people are subject to the law of nature, which they can discern by their reason. They are understood to enter society and to set up a government—a legislature and an executive—to avoid certain inconveniences inherent in an otherwise felicitous state of nature. Their chief concern "is the preservation of property," which is understood to be not only lands and material goods but more widely "the Lives, Liberties, and Estates of the People." Despite Locke, however, it has remained a concern whether lives and liberties should take primacy over estates, or indeed whether they can be separated.

The *Two Treatises* is in reality a single work. Locke wrote in his preface, "Thou hast here the Beginning and End of a Discourse," "the Papers that should have filled up the middle, and were more than all the rest," having been lost. Although published in 1690, it was probably written between 1679 and 1681, and certainly before 1683. Thus, Locke wrote during the Exclusion Crisis, to justify what the earl of Shaftesbury, his friend and patron, was attempting, and not in 1689 and 1690, to justify what had already been accomplished. As such, Locke's ideas were potentially dangerous.

Source: John Locke, *Two Treatises of Government: A Critical Edition with an Introduction and Apparatus Criticus,* by Peter Laslett, Second Edition, Cambridge: At the University Press, 1967, pp. 430–432. Reprinted by permission of Cambridge University Press.

This helps to explain his exile from 1683 till 1689 and his extreme care in not acknowledging his authorship of the *Two Treatises* until a few days before his death.

It was Locke's genius to combine the radical ideas of the Puritan revolution and the Exclusion Crisis with tradition and common sense, making them palatable and useful, even if not always consistent and logical. In all respects, the *Two Treatises* was the intellectual counterpart of the Glorious Revolution, owing its success to the Revolution more than the Revolution owed its justification to the *Two Treatises.* Its primary importance in the long run was to put English ideas and practice in a packaged form available for export. In the eighteenth century England began to eclipse the once-mighty France, and French thinkers and politicians looked to England, and preeminently to Locke, for an alternative to absolute monarchy.

The Reason why Men enter into Society, is the preservation of their Property; and the end why they chuse and authorize a Legislative, is, that there may be Laws made, and Rules set as Guards and Fences to the Properties of all the Members of the Society, to limit the Power, and moderate the Dominion of every Part and Member of the Society. For since it can never be supposed to be the Will of the Society, that the Legislative should have a Power to destroy that, which every one designs to secure, by entering into Society, and for which the People submitted themselves to the Legislators of their own making; whenever the *Legislators endeavour to take away, and destroy the Property of the People,* or to reduce them to Slavery under Arbitrary Power, they put themselves into a state of War with the People, who are thereupon absolved from any farther Obedience, and are left to the common Refuge, which God hath provided for all Men, against Force and Violence. Whensoever therefore the *Legislative* shall transgress this fundamental Rule of Society; and either by Ambition, Fear, Folly or Corruption, *endeavour to grasp* themselves, *or put into the hands of any other an Absolute Power* over the Lives, Liberties, and Estates of the People; By this breach of Trust they *forfeit the Power,* the People had put into their hands, for quite contrary ends, and it devolves to the People, who have a Right to resume their original Liberty, and, by the Establishment of a new Legislative (such as they shall think fit) provide for their own Safety and Security, which is the end for which they are in Society. What I have said here, concerning the Legislative, in general, holds true also concerning the *supreame Executor,* who having a double trust put in him, both to have a part in the Legislative, and the supreme Execution of the Law, Acts against both, when he goes about to set up his own Arbitrary Will, as the Law of the Society. He *acts* also *contrary to his Trust,* when he either imploys the Force, Treasure, and Offices of the Society, to corrupt the *Representatives,* and gain them to his purposes: or openly pre-ingages the *Electors,* and prescribes to their choice, such, whom he has by Sollicitations, Threats, Promises, or otherwise won to his designs; and imploys them to bring in such, who have promised before-hand, what to Vote, and what to Enact. Thus to regulate Candidates and *Electors,* and new model the ways of *Election,* what is it but to cut up the Government by the Roots, and poison the very Fountain of publick Security? For the People having reserved to themselves the Choice of their *Representatives,* as the Fence to their Properties, could do it for no other end, but that they might always be freely chosen, and so chosen, freely act and advise, as the necessity of the Commonwealth, and the publick Good should, upon examination, and mature debate, be judged to require. . . . What Power they ought to have in the Society, who thus imploy it contrary to the trust went along with it in its first Institution, is easie to determine; and one cannot but see, that he, who has once attempted any such thing as this, cannot any longer be trusted.

To this perhaps it will be said, that the People being ignorant, and always discontented, to lay the Foundation of Government in the unsteady Opinion, and uncertain Humour of the People, is to expose it to certain ruine; And *no Government will be able long to subsist,* if the People may set up a new Legislative, whenever they take offence at the old one. To this, I Answer: Quite the contrary. People are not so easily got out of their old Forms, as some are apt to suggest. They are hardly to be prevailed with to amend the acknowledg'd Faults, in the Frame they have been accustom'd to. And if there be any Original defects, or adventitious ones introduced by time, or corruption; 'tis not an easie thing to get them changed, even when all the World sees there is an opportunity for it. This slowness and aversion in the People to quit their old Constitutions, has, in the many Revolutions which have been seen in this Kingdom, in this and former Ages, still kept us to, or, after some interval of fruitless attempts, still brought us back again to our old Legislative of King, Lords and Commons: And whatever provocations have made the Crown be taken from some of our Princes Heads, they never carried the People so far, as to place it in another Line.

74

The Massacre of Glenco (1703). Scotland in the Glorious Revolution, 1692

The political events of 1688–1689 came, in England, to be called the "Glorious Revolution." Unlike the Puritan Revolution of 1640–1660, it was brief, bloodless, and successful, as subsequent history was to demonstrate. In Scotland the revolution was at most half-glorious—in Ireland it was not glorious at all.

The Scots Parliament, dominated by Protestant Lowlanders, followed England's lead in 1689 and with its Claim of Right declared the abdication of James VII and the accession of William and Mary. But the Highland clans, remembering their Gaelic and Catholic traditions, inclined to Jacobitism. At Killiecrankie in July 1689, Viscount Dundee led the wild charge of half-naked Highlanders, scattering the government forces sent against them. But Dundee was killed, and, without his leadership, the clans drifted back to their glens and took up again their traditional pastimes of stealing nolt (cattle) and fighting among themselves. The government set out to subdue them piecemeal.

The passage below is taken from the report of the government commission which in 1695 investigated the massacre which took place in Glencoe in February 1692. The chief of the MacDonalds of Glencoe, a lesser but notorious branch of the great MacDonald clan, was slow to swear allegiance to William. Going to the wrong place and then being delayed by bad weather, he made his submission on January 6, almost a week after the deadline. The Scottish officials of William's govenment, having lost patience with the Highlands and with Glencoe most of all, seem already to have marked the Glencoe MacDonalds for savage retribution.

The brutality of the attack and even the death toll of some 38 killed at the time and many more killed by a winter snowstorm as they attempted to escape over the hills, were not outside the tradition of Highland violence. What made this massacre noteworthy was the meditated calculation with which it was carried out and

Source: The Massacre of Glenco. Being a True Narrative of the Barbarous Murther of the Glenco-men, in the Highlands of Scotland, by way of Military Execution, on the 13th of Feb. 1692. London: Printed, and Sold by B. Bragg, at the Blue-Ball in Ave-Mary-Lane, 1703, pp. 11–18.

the government sanction, perhaps even from William himself, which it seemed to have. It clashed with a growing European and British sense of acceptable government and human behavior. More than anything else, it intensified the Highlanders' hatred for the governments of Edinburgh and London, and it confirmed the clans in their Jacobite loyalties. Though the Scots Parliament, representing principally the Lowlands, accepted union with England in 1707, the Highlands, in the Jacobite uprisings of 1715 and 1745, had twice more to be subdued. After Bonnie Prince Charlie and his Highland forces were finally destroyed at Culloden in 1746, the repression of the clans was resolute and thoroughgoing. The Highland clearances destroyed a way of life, but they made available a hardy and enterprising people for the conquering and populating of an overseas empire.

His Majesty's Proclamation of Indemnity was publish'd in Aug. 1691, offering a free Indemnity and Pardon to all the Highlanders who had been in Arms, upon their coming in and taking the Oath of Allegiance betwixt and the first of January thereafter: And in compliance with the Proclamation, the deceas'd Glenco goes about the end of Decemb. 1691 to Col. Hill, Governor of Fort-William at Inverlochie, and desir'd the Colonel to minister to him the Oath of Allegiance, that he might have the King's Indemnity: But Col. Hill in his Deposition . . . doth farther depone, That he hasten'd him away all he could, and gave him a Letter to Ardkinlas to receive him as a lost Sheep, and the Colonel produces Ardkinlas's Answer to that Letter, dated the 9th of January 1691, bearing, that he had indeavoured to receive the great lost Sheep Glenco, and that Glenco had undertaken to bring in all his Friends and Followers as the Privy-Council should order, and Ardkinlas farther writes, that he was sending to Edinburgh that Glenco, tho' he had mistaken in coming to Colonel Hill to take the Oath of Allegiance, might yet be welcome, and that thereafter the Col. should take care that Glenco's Friends and Followers may not suffer, till the King and Councils Pleasure be known. . . .

After that Glenco had taken the Oath of Allegiance as is said, he went home to his own House, and as his own two Sons above name'd depone, He not only liv'd there for some Days quietly and securely, but call'd his People together, and told them he had taken the Oath of Allegiance, and made his Peace, and therefore desir'd and engag'd them to live peaceably under King William's Government. . . .

These things having preceeded the Slaughter, which happen'd not to be committed until the 13th of February 1692, six Weeks after the deceas'd Glenco had taken the Oath of Allegiance at Inverary. The Slaughter of the Glenco Men was in this manner, viz. John and Alexander Mac-Donald, Sons to the deceas'd

Glenco, depone, That . . . Glenlyon, a Captain of the Earl of Argyle's Regiment, with Lieutenant Lindsay and Ensign Lindsay, and six score Soldiers, return'd to Glenco about the 1st of February 1692, where, at their Entry, the elder Brother John met them with about 20 Men, and demanded the reason of their coming, and Lieutenant Lindsey shew'd him his Orders for quartering there under Colonel Hill's Hand, and gave assurance that they were only come to Quarter; whereupon they were billeted in the Country, and had free Quarters and kind Entertainment, living familiarly with the People until the 13th Day of Feb. and Alexander farther depones, That Glenlyon being his Wive's Uncle came almost every Day and took his Morning Drink at his House, and that the very Night before the Slaughter, Glenlyon did play at Cards in his own Quarters with both the Brothers, and John depones, That old Glenco his Father had invited Glenlyon, Lieutenant Lindsay, and Ensign Lindsay, to dine with him upon the very day the Slaughter happen'd. But on the 13th day of February, being Saturday, about four or five in the Morning, Lieutenant Lindsay, with a party of the foresaid Soldiers, came to old Glenco's House, where, having call'd in a Friendly manner, and got in, they shot his Father dead with several Shots as he was rising out of his Bed; and the Mother having got up and put on her Clothes, the Soldiers stripp'd her naked and drew the Rings off her Fingers with their Teeth. . . .

The said John Macdonald, eldest Son to the deceas'd Glenco depones, the same morning that his Father was kill'd there came Soldiers to his House before Day, and call'd at his Window, which gave him the Alarm, and made him go to Innerriggen, where Glenlyon was quarter'd, and that he found Glenlyon and his Men preparing their Arms, which made the Deponent ask the Cause; but Glenlyon gave him only good Words, and said they were to march against some of Glengaries Men, and if there were Ill intended, would not he have told Sandy and his Neice? meaning the Deponents Brother and his Wife; which made the Deponent go home and go again to his Bed, untill his Servant, who hindred him to sleep, rais'd him; and when he rose and went out, he perceiv'd about 20 Men coming towards his House with their Bayonets fix'd to their Muskets; whereupon he fled to the Hill, and having Auchnaion, a little Village in Glenco, in view, he heard the Shots wherewith Auchintriaten and four more were kill'd; and that he heard also the Shots at Innerriggen, where Glenlyon had caus'd to kill nine more, as shall be hereafter declar'd and this is confirm'd by the concurring Deposition of Alexander Macdonald his Brother, whom a Servant wak'd out of sleep, saying, It is no time for you to be sleeping, when they are killing your Brother at the Door; which made Alexander to flee with his Brother to the Hill, where both of them heard the foresaid Shots at Auchnaion and Innerriggin: And the said John, Alexander and Archibald Macdonald's do all depone, That the same Morning there was one Serjeant Barber and a Party at Auchnaion, and that Auchintriaten being there in his Brother's House with eight more sitting about the Fire, the Soldiers discharg'd upon them about 18 Shot, which kill'd

Auchintriaten and four more; but the other four, whereof some were wounded, falling down as dead, Serjeant Barber laid hold on Auchintriaten's Brother, one of the four, and ask'd him if he were alive? He answer'd, That he was, and that he desir'd to die without rather than within: Barber said, That for his Meat that he had eaten, he would do him the Favour to kill him without; but when the Man was brought out, and Soldiers brought up to shoot him, he having his Plaid loose flung it over their Faces and so escap'd; and the other three broke through the back of the House and escap'd: And this Account the Deponents had from the Men that escap'd. And at Innerriggin, where Glenlyon was quartered, the Soldiers took other nine Men and did bind them Hand and Foot, kill'd them one by one with Shot; and when Glenlyon inclin'd to save a young Man of about 20 Years of Age, one Captain Drummond came and ask'd how he came to be sav'd, in respect of the Orders that were given, and shot him dead; and another young Boy of about 13 Years ran to Glenlyon to be sav'd, he was likewise shot dead. . . . And another Witness of the same declares, That upon the same 13th of February, Glenlyon and Lieutenant Lindsay, and their Soldiers, did in the Morning before Day fall upon the People of Glenco when they were secure in their Beds and kill'd them, and he being at Innerriggin fled with the first, but heard Shots and had two Brothers killed there, with three Men more and a Woman, who were all buried before he came back. And all these five Witnesses concur, That the foresaid Slaughter was made by Glenlyon and his Soldiers, after they had been quarter'd, and liv'd peaceably and friendly with the Glenco-Men about 13 Days, and that the Number of those whom they knew to be slain were about 25, and that the Soldiers after the Slaughter did burn the Houses, Barns and Goods, and carried away a great Spoil of Horse, Nolt and Sheep, above a 1000. . . .